ARLOTT ON WINE

David Rayvern Allen is a full-time radio producer with the BBC. Author of *A Song for Cricket, Samuel Britcher, the hidden scorer* and *Sir Aubrey* (a biography of cricketer, actor, film star, C. Aubrey Smith) and compiler of a collection of John Arlott's broadcasts and commentaries entitled *A Word from Arlott*, he has also contributed to *Wisden Cricket Monthly* and *The Cricketeer* among other magazines. Married with two children he lives in Herfordshire.

D1346959

ARLOTT
ON WINE

Edited by
David Rayvern Allen

Fontana/Collins

First published by William Collins (Willow Books) 1986
First issued in Fontana Paperbacks 1987

Copyright © John Arlott 1986

Made and printed in Great Britain by
William Collins Sons & Co. Ltd, Glasgow

Dedicated by the author and editor
to two favourite wine men
Christopher Fielden
and
Robert Arlott

Contents

Acknowledgements

If with water you fill up your glasses,
You'll never write anything wise
But wine is the horse of Parnassus,
That carries a bard to the skies.

So wrote the Greek poet Athenaeus some eighteen hundred years ago and if the translation is somewhat slavish the spirit is not disguised. The inherent truth of those lines is, no doubt, manifested on every page that follows, now, mostly between hard covers for the first time, after initial appearances as articles for magazines, periodicals and newspapers penned over a lifetime of assiduous exploration and delighted discovery.

The old *Evening News* provided one of the first outlets; *The Adelphi* and *The Fortnightly* were tributaries along the way and though all three are long dried up, the freshness and character of the pieces therein never will.

The powerful current of John's wine writing from around the early 1970s has, of course, been through *The Guardian* and special thanks are due to that newspaper for allowing so many of his articles to reappear here. Their librarian, Ken Murphy, deserves the highest accolade for his invaluable and most intelligent assistance in sending copies of John's work that gave the widest possible choice: this book could not have been compiled without him.

Throughout the recent run of *Kitchen Choice*, John offered seasonal guidance to the readership on wine and related subjects. Nicola Hemingway and Vanessa Berridge, editors successively, both were hugely helpful in providing material and because of that some mouth-watering essays are now resurrected more permanently.

Gratitude also to *The Mail on Sunday*, *Countryside* and *Decanter* for permission to reprint single pieces, and to Davis-Poynter Ltd who kindly allowed the reproduction of a chapter each from two publications of 1976, *Krug: House of Champagne* and *Burgundy Vines and Wines*.

Christopher Fielden, co-author of the latter book, was totally supportive with ideas and convivial inspiration; Robert, John's son, who works in the wine trade, spent time, when he had little to spare, in checking important facts; former Collins editor, Tim Jollands readily gave hours to the finer points of the product; and dear John himself, who encouraged me, without so much as an arm-twist, to selflessly taste the veracity of his written word.

Salutations to them all and to any other kindly co-operator who, inadvertently, temporarily may have been forgotten at this moment of writing.

Editor's Introduction

The room was crowded, the conversation animated. On my right, an extremely liberated young woman with the unquenchable enthusiasm of one who had, at last, found her crusade; on my left, John, engaged by her equally attractive colleague in a conversation that was far less demanding. A stimulating occasion – the annual dinner of the Southampton University Wine Society to which John, who is President, had kindly given the invitation.

The food was superb and so was the wine, the service speedy – so fast, indeed, that when a nearly-full bowl of onion soup was upended over my jacket, the accident was not entirely unexpected. The stock spread generously, as did the silence, gasps of shock arrived stereophonically and the sudden tension that descended on the assembly promised to stay and probably would have done so, but for an acute observation from the President. 'Spectacular', he said.

That event, memorable, if for no other reason than it provided the necessary punctuation for the lady 'libber' to rest her tongue and fill the vacuum with an undeniable look of self-satisfaction, which seemed to imply that such a male chauvinist had received his just deserts – even if it was the first course – was a re-enactment of an almost similar happening some years earlier. Then, John had been the recipient.

The restaurant, an excellent one, was local to his Hampshire home; the evening, a time for quiet companionship and maybe gentle distraction after harrowing circumstance. The menu was select and the dishes all the better for it. John had anticipated our choice and we had decided to purchase a very acceptable white burgundy – Mâcon Prissé – to accompany the hors d'oeuvre. The main course was to be honoured with a magnificent vintage '61 Château Pétrus from his own cellar that forever would be indelibly etched on the palate. The place was peaceful – just the two of us in situ – the service solicitous.

11

The bottle of thirst quenching burgundy had been mostly consumed, the Pomerol, cru exceptionnel, uncorked, awaiting our assured appreciation. Two waitresses busied themselves at the table – napkins fluttered – an unguarded gesture – a bottle tipped – an involuntary cry – the liquid contents spilled over John's lap. A look of sheer horror passed over his face. I buried my head in my hands. Surely, not . . . A quick glance. The joy of relief. Château Pétrus remained unconquered, static as before, steady as a rock. There was, once again, life after death.

Those two incidents have another connecting door: communication. John has always struck a common chord whether he be commentating on cricket or writing about wine, for he maintains an instinctive ability to convey the spoken and written word in a manner that encapsulates a subject while offering comprehension. His approach to wine is down to earth, not for him the trade *lingua franca* encouraging mystique; the long-lasting run of 'Honest bottles' in the pages of *The Guardian* is evidence enough of that. Undoubtedly, through his writings, many a one-time non-wine bibber has been persuaded to venture into areas of the supermarket or off-licence that he or she would not have contemplated before, and the inspiration of and from his words was given deserved recognition in 1978, with the Glenfiddich Wine Writer of the Year Award, specifically for a piece on vigneron Ernest Aujas and Beaujolais that finds its way into these pages.

John's sheer enjoyment of wine is never more apparent than when he is entertaining at home. His hospitality is legendary and every guest is treated in exactly the same way whether they be casual royal caller or urgent delivery boy. A bottle appears from the well-stocked cellar below, a glass is immediately to hand and an air of contentment and conviviality surrounds the table. The wine could be a domaine Saché, Azay-le-Rideau or a standard Rioja, or indeed, another bottle from another vineyard – the distinction being only in that which would best complement the occasion and the tastes of those about to drink.

So many pictures remain in the mind of John and his association with wine, some loosely linked, others pertinent to his pen – tastings in London, fairs in Bristol, meals at various times and at different places, a peroration in French in the town hall at Briquebec to celebrate the twinning of that town with Alresford, a glass at Alderney Airport to greet Tony Lewis arriving from the mainland after being delayed by fog – but one cameo has particular radiance.

The theatre was at a new town in Essex. The event – an evening of a lecture tour round Britain a few years ago – every seat taken, an expectant audience. The house lights dimmed and a single spot centred on a bare stage. The applause for John was of an emotional intensity that surprised the audience themselves, obvious in the ensuing release of their laughter after he had seated himself on the solitary chair alongside a small table which supported an empty glass and a full bottle.

'Thank you – bless you,' he said, as he stretched forward with a smile to pour from one receptacle into the other. 'You couldn't possibly expect me to begin a talk without first taking a glass of wine . . .'

DAVID RAYVERN ALLEN
Chorleywood
April 1986

Author's Preface

Of course, a boy who grew up in a working class family in a South of England market town during the 1920s would hardly know anything about wine, would he?

Wine, what was it? It was the stuff mothers used to make, parsnip wine, elderberry, wines from various wild and garden vegetables or fruits. There was a so-called sherry made partly out of potatoes; and oh, of course, ginger wine which was not alcoholic; and grocer's port and that was wine to most ordinary people. And very contented they were with it; especially boys who did not drink any of it. Many and dedicated advocates of temperance used to sink the home-made stuff by the half-pint and still maintain they were teetotallers.

There the lads were growing up and fancying themselves as adolescent drinkers of shandy and, eventually, mild beer. Mild instead of bitter on completely economic grounds. So, why did it happen? Heaven knows why it happened.

As a personal recollection, the effective impression was made on the way back from South Africa in 1949, after the '48-'9 cricket tour, during which the election took place that threw out Smuts and put in the Nationalists and gave birth to apartheid. In South Africa, especially after the shortages of wartime England, drinking whisky seemed luxury; and often, because there was nothing to go with it, one who could not stomach neat whisky found himself drinking whisky and bottled beer. That was not too good for the constitution and anyone going back home looking like that would be most reasonably suspected of spending his time in South Africa the way he *had* spent his time in South Africa. Hence the decision to split that wonderful Speedbird journey – the most gloriously luxurious form of travel ever devised – in Sicily. Asking the girl in the Overseas Airways office 'Is it all right to stop over here?' elicited the reply 'Not for more than three months, sir.'

'No, not that long, would a week be all right?' 'Yes: do you want to stay in the staff hotel where the aircrews stay? We could get you a discount there.'

'No; thank you; but where is there to go to up into Sicily?'

'Well, Taormina now is glorious, because the spring flowers are coming up on the slopes of Etna.'

So that was it; booked into a little albergo built into the side of the theatre, with the solemn resolve not to drink – pure temperance – to go back looking so well. On the third abstention day, though, the flask of wine standing on the table – as a carafe of water might in an English boarding-house – prompted by the thought that the wine of the country could do no harm; a hand out for the bottle; a glassful poured to go with the pasta; a taste of both and it was visional enlightenment, it was delight; and a wine drinker was created: as raw, ill-informed – but as eager – a wine drinker as ever drew vinous breath; knowing nothing, but determined to find out. The owner of the taverna, amused but interested by the conversion he had observed, volunteered 'I'll take you up the mountain to my brother's vineyard.' The visit and the bottles tasted cemented the interest; and it was a confirmed enthusiast who, next morning, went down to the coast where he met two Americans on embarkation leave. 'Say, are you into this wine?'

'Well, I'm trying to learn.'

'Yeah, so are we.'

More tasting, back to the albergo, where the Americans booked in. The proprietor conducted another tour to his brother's vineyard and between them they unearthed the fact that the next day a removal van was going down to Syracuse. Five hours in the town and around its bars resulted in the consumption of a – nowadays – appalling amount of sweet white wine. Now it would mean nothing; then it taught a little more.

A few weeks later dear old John Marshall, the editor of the London *Evening News*, catching his reporter drinking cheap fizz, asked 'What's that like?'

'Well, it's drinkable.'

He said, 'Because I've got a christening party for my baby boy and I've got to ask all the bosses. Can't really afford champagne. Will this do?'

'Yes – but only just.' A nice chap who lived in the East End was shipping sparkling wine from the Languedoc. Obtained at a vastly reduced price, it passed at the christening party. Indeed, the Chairman of *The Evening News* as he left, said, 'Marshall, that was a most splendid champagne, you must give me the name of your wine merchant.' After mutual blushes the conspirators went back in and drank an awful lot of it. It was not really very good.

That was slight evidence on which to appoint a new – indeed the first – wine correspondent of the London *Evening News*. Mind, there were only rare calls on him – twice, three times a year, something like that – but that was enough to procure the invitation to join a Press tour of the Bordeaux vineyards. Talk of going there in one of the gluepot pubs that surround the BBC, was overheard by the Head of Features, Laurence Gilliam, who, a quick man about enthusiasms, said, 'Look, we're taking a BBC trip out to Bordeaux. Would you like to come on that?' 'Well, yes, I would; but I'm not going to turn this other one down.' He said, 'Well, ours starts a month after yours finishes.' Now this is the crucial point of it all. Once out there: the resolution to take a holiday, the whole year's entitlement of a month between those two tours. The guide on the first tour was the great wine man, Daniel Querre of Château Monbousquet, on the edge of St-Emilion, Chairman of the CIVB – Conseil Interprofessionel du Vin de Bordeaux. 'You want to stay on? Then come and stay with me.'

That month was, minute by minute, education, learning what wine was about; what eating was about, watching Madame Querre with her little girls from the village who worked in the kitchen, and the wonderful sizzling – the burning of the vine roots and branches on which they roasted and grilled and devilled – was education. The cooking was fantastic, the drinking was glorious and at the end old Daniel used to pull out a great shaggy bottle of eau de vie de marc, that gross, brandy-like spirit and, waving his hand coolly, say 'Not for boys' and then he shared it out between himself and his mates.

Not until he died did it emerge that he was five years the younger. He was, though, dead right: so far as eau de vie de marc was concerned his visitor was a boy all right: and never able to drink it.

The right things that he wanted absorbed were mostly absorbed. He was the great salesman of Bordeaux after the War, a man of immense ebullience, humour, generosity, argument; a joy to live with, and all the time – whether he knew it or not – he was teaching his guest more about wine than anybody else in the world has ever done or ever could do. Above all, he was teaching how to enjoy it, to drink it, to savour it. Without being, or pretending to be, the world's greatest connoisseur of wine, his pupil became, and remains, well up in the front rank among those who enjoy it.

Now, the fact is that, if you grow up in France or Spain or Italy or Portugal, Greece or Yugoslavia or the wine regions of Germany – and they are not all white wine either – Hungary, or anywhere where wine is native, you grow up as a wine drinker. Wine is as natural as beer is to Englishmen; it is the automatic quaff with something to eat. There is a picture in mind of being on a very high-falutin' wine tour in Italy and looking out of the place from where the experts were tasting, across some farmland opposite; and there, an Italian labourer at his midday meal time picking the shelter of about the only tree within half a mile. Under the boughs he sat down with a great sausage sandwich and a bottle of wine. What a fool to wonder what the label was. Of course, there was no label. That was his wine, he made it – or his brother or his uncle, father or grandfather: they drank wine automatically. Then the understanding, ever since that day, that a man must drink and ensure his friends, and family and children, drink wine naturally and easily.

It is true that you must drink the wine you like. It may be that you have been a sweet white wine drinker; maybe you have grown up a deep red wine drinker, but you know what you like and what goes with what *for you*. One of the lessons you learn is that if somebody – and you may be shocked the first time anybody says it to you – if somebody wants to take hock with a peppered steak, that is right for that person.

It is natural to drink wine: be sure of that. Perhaps less natural in Britain, but the vineyards in Britain are coming back, the vineyards where they used to grow vines years ago, where the Roman legions stationed here made their wine. Those vineyards are springing up again. Down at the bottom of the garden there are over a hundred vines: bought as white wine grapes from a man in the Midlands, they have produced red grapes infallibly ever since. To tell the truth, their wine is not the greatest: it explodes – about once a fortnight a bottle blows up and hits the ceiling of the rather inadequate cellar. Inadequate? That is unfair. It holds enough to keep a family drinking.

Asking Daniel Querre, once, 'Daniel, which to you suppose would be the worse fate – to run out of wine or to die and leave all your best wines to your heirs and executors?' He grinned broadly and said, 'The first one will never happen to me. I hope the second does.'

That is what we may all hope. Always to have enough to drink and that, when we go, there will be enough for our children to drink for a time and to share with our friends and their friends. Because – it is the most civilized tipple in the world. Not only has it many, many names, it has many flavours, many subtleties, many succulences; and it is the greatest drinking delight in the world.

JOHN ARLOTT
Alderney
April 1986

1
First Thoughts

Back to the Vine Roots

July 1973. It is healthy as well as salutary for the habitual wine drinkers and certainly for the wine writer – sometimes to go back to the beginning of the alphabet. While the percentage of wine drinkers has increased more in Britain than in any other European country in the past decade, we are still not a nation of wine drinkers; and many who do drink it are sceptical about it.

Few of us grew up in households where wine was generally taken with meals; and there is lingering mistrust of a habit which was only lately the prerogative of the well-to-do minority. There is doubt about the dogma as to which wine goes with what food. The suspicion that wine snobs create a mumbo jumbo about particular vineyards and vintages is reflected in the inverted snobbery of 'plonk is good enough for me'.

Recognition of a few elementary facts should break down these barriers. Wine – simple fermented grape juice – is a natural beverage. For many unsophisticated people, like the peasants of France, Italy, Spain, Portugal, Greece, Hungary, Rumania, Algeria, Morocco, it is a staple diet. Indeed, in Italy, the law grants convicts a daily ration of wine.

These are theoretical arguments. On the other hand, anyone may try the practical experiments which prove that wine makes the simplest meal – sausage and mash, or bread and cheese – vastly more satisfying. It can, too, be demonstrated that at a blind tasting the most unambitious drinker can generally rank three or four wines in order of merit – and find the most expensive with murderous accuracy.

Wine may be an acquired taste, but many an eventual pint-swigger first drinks beer as a pleasureless 'manly' pose. St Paul's 'take a little wine for thy stomach's sake' is not a recommendation for dyspepsia but a piece of human wisdom. The justification for drinking wine is pleasure.

This factor refutes the 'which with what' theories. Anyone who enjoys drinking a sweet wine – a Sauternes or one of the more sugary hocks – with a steak should do so. Palates change: the young and the old tend to sugarhunger: in between, their taste is generally for savoury food and dry drink. 'White with fish, red with meat' is a counsel of safety, not a rule. Although fish can make red wine taste metallic, some deeply versed wine drinkers would advocate claret with salmon, an Alsace riesling with pork, or a moselle with veal; a big white burgundy will stand up with most meat dishes. The division is as non-existent as that; and virtually any wine is shown off to advantage by cheese.

The term 'plonk' was coined for the cruder, souped-up wines used simply as vehicles for alcohol. It has latterly been extended to include ordinaires, which is an injustice to the daily beverage of the lifelong drinkers in the countries that produce them. The determined, self-styled British plonk drinker ought at least to establish which kind of plonk he or she finds most pleasant – that is a matter well worth experiment. *The Guardian*

2
Vintage Personalities

André Simon

October 1977. André Simon who, surely, had a happier effect on English social life than any other Frenchman, was born a hundred years ago. Christie's have marked the centenary with a small but nostalgic exhibition of Simoniana.

When he died in 1971, he had long written clear expressive English; and spoke it lucidly, with the most beguilingly French accent. For many years he expressed his affection for this country by acting as its gentle mentor in eating and wine drinking. Born in Paris, he was the son of one unremarkable painter and, through his mother, the grandson of another. At 17 he came to Southampton with 200 francs (at 25 to the £) to learn English. There he fell in love with Edith Symons, England, and English literature; and, by his own earnings, stayed on in the town until he returned urgently to Paris on his father's death in 1895.

He decided then to do his three years of military service; often, though, contriving when freed on Saturday afternoons, to travel – on third class wooden train seats and by steamer – to England, arriving in time for Sunday breakfast with the Symons family and returning that night to be at the Ecole Militaire on Monday morning.

By chance the Marquis de Polignac, who had known his father, offered him a post with Pommery champagne. He accepted and, a year later, married his Edith and brought her back to Rheims. He worked so ably that, in 1902, he was asked to represent the firm in Britain ('I

21

dared not tell the Marquis that my wife, although English, had married me to live in France, which she loved. And I accepted what was a very good offer indeed.')

He became a considerable figure – the personification of Pommery champagne – in the trade here. He also began to write scholarly books of wine history never before attempted in England. The first was *The History of the Champagne Trade in England*; the next, the still authoritative three volume, *History of the Wine Trade in England*. *Star Chamber Dinner Accounts, The Supply, Sale and Care of Wine, Wine in Shakespeare's Day and Shakespeare's Plays*, were other early books; and he lectured illuminatingly to the Wine Trade Club, which he helped to found.

When the First World War broke out, he left his wife and five children in Sussex, and caught the first possible train to report to his artillery unit in France ('Of all the many foolish things I did in haste in the course of my long life, one of the most foolish'). His blue train ticket for that journey to Paris Nord is in the exhibition. He won the Medaille Militaire – awarded only for service under fire – and, at the 1918 Armistice, returned to England and his post with Pommery.

He flourished, made many friends, and became a figure althogether more important than the representative of a champagne firm. Amazingly, in 1933 when he was 55, the new owner of Pommery sacked him: he was staggered but not bitter; indeed, he refused offers to join other champagne houses. Instead, he entered on the most important phase of his life when he founded the Wine and Food Society and became – and remained for 30 years – editor of its Journal.

As writer, editor and, above all, as lecturer in that splendid voice, he preached a fresh standard of gastronomy for everyone in England – careful cooking of wholesome but not necessarily costly food, and the appreciative drinking of sound wine. Most of all, he sought to introduce the appreciation of wine to what had hitherto in this country been regarded as the non-wine drinking class. He never ceased to teach that inherently French lesson by speech, writing and zestful example.

When his eyesight failed, in his eighties, he taught himself to type. His ninetieth birthday was marked by a series of celebratory lunches and dinners at which his gusto, good nature, and stamina were gloriously impressive. His centenary is being celebrated by the society which has contributed some interesting items to the exhibition. There are rare, early wine books from the remarkable collection on which he based his definitive *Bibliotheca Bacchica*, a bibliography of books about wine published up to 1600.

His membership of the Legion d'Honneur and the CBE are followed by virtually every decoration wine bodies could bestow, including the unusual Honorary Freedom of the Vintners Company. There is the well known portrait in oils by James Gunn, and the even more evocative pencil study by Youngman Carter; a bust made when he was a young man; a bronze bas relief and a profile medal for the Wine and Food Society; and a splendidly caught photograph, taken in his old age, with his grand-daughter Marie-Madeleine. There is, too, one charming idea, a masterly still life by Tristram Hillier – exhibited at the Academy in 1959 – of the memorable bottles drunk at George Rainbird's party given to honour André's eightieth birthday.

Illuminated guest lists indicate his immense standing within the wine trade; and printed versions, the admiration for this early wine trade lecturer. A handsome bronze of Bacchus came from his own collection. Poignantly, though, there lingers in the memory the pen with which he wrote most of his books, and scores of letters in that ebulliently sweeping handwriting; it is vast, thick as a man's thumb, with a generously large gold nib, lettered on its heavy gold band, Mont Blanc-Meister Stock. *The Guardian*

Baron Philippe de Rothschild
Cadet Tour de Force

November 1982. Mouton Cadet, claimed to be 'the best selling claret in the world', is a blend; and blended wines are generally accorded little respect by connoisseurs. It also costs more than it is strictly worth; yet it sells. It sells largely because, picked off even the most unambitious restaurant wine list, it is authentic claret; reliable, not exciting, but honest – safe. It is also the creation of a most considerable person.

Some writers have devoted their main attention to Baron Philippe de Rothschild's large scale, unconventional personality: the mobile, sensitive, mischievous face, the dry humour, the jackets he designs for himself; his habit of deciding day by day where his meals shall be served, the dining table moved to suit his decision; and his capacity for carrying off any situation.

This can mean that the scale of his achievements is sometimes overlooked. It is generally well known that he performed the virtual miracle of procuring the only change ever made in that vinous law of the Medes and Persians – the 1855 classification of the wines of the Médoc – by which his Château Mouton-Rothschild was elevated from the second class to join the original, exclusive, four in the top premiers crus class.

Sixty years ago, in October 1922, Philippe de Rothschild took over the vineyards his great-grandfather, Nathaniel, had bought in 1853. The residence was a sound but undistinguished farmhouse. Under his direction it has become an harmonious, imaginative series of buildings, constantly reshaped and extended and improved by his resident architects (still established there).

He extended and landscaped the estate, buying up the two neighbouring fifth-growth châteaux of d'Armailhacq, now known in pious memory as Mouton-Baron-Philippe and Clerc-Milon. The entire vignoble has been redesigned and, quite unique in vineyards, the massive circular garage is surrounded by a series of concentric rings of vines.

Over many years he enthusiastically and knowledgeably drove his maîtres de chai to perfect his blackcurrant-tasting, cabernet-sauvignon-preponderated Mouton-Rothschild wine. Made from 75 hectares of vines, a substantial proportion of such age as gives it quality rather than quantity, it reached such a peak of intensely flavoured, full-bodied excellence that elevation to premier cru could hardly be denied.

In 1934, after a series of tragic vintages in Bordeaux had created a demand for sound ordinary claret, he marketed the red Mouton Cadet (he is the 'cadet' or younger son of the family). Its commercial success was such that he followed it with Mouton Cadet white.

Thanks largely to his lately deceased, and much missed, second wife, the Baroness Pauline, the Mouton estate houses the finest private museum of wine artifacts and wine-related art in the world.

Generous, priceless, superbly presented, it is quite awe-inspiring in the quality and variety of the artistic works, which stretch back about 3400 years. In a non-tourist area it draws 100,000 visitors a year.

Below, in the magnificently arranged and genuinely ancient cellars, is a vast 'library' of over 100,000 bottles of the finest and rarest clarets in the world, many of them not represented at the châteaux which produced them. Every year since 1945, too, he has had the Mouton-Rothschild labels designed by famous artists: Jean Cocteau, Braque, Dali, Chagall, Kandinsky, and Henry Moore, among others.

As an apéritif, he serves his own marque champagne of Henriot with whom he is associated: at meals, from decanters he himself designed, wines of many vineyards, brought up by his cellarman and friend of 50 years, Raoul Blondin: afterwards, his own brandy, prunelle and creme de cassis.

His achievements have not been only in the field of wine. He has published five books of poems, an autobiography, subtitled *From the Frankfurt Ghetto to Mouton Rothschild*, fairy stories and translations of Elizabethan poetry, six plays of Christopher Fry, Christopher Marlowe's *Faust*, and *Tamburlaine*.

He created and directs the Theatre Pigalle; drove a Bugatti in the le Mans 24-hour race of 1924; and was awarded the Croix de Guerre and an OBE for his spectacular escape from the German concentration camp where his first wife died, and for his service with the Free French forces and liaison with the British.

With support from his explosive and amusing actress daughter – Philippine – and her son, heir to the estate, christened – what else but? – Philippe, the Baron remains at the age of 83, a splendid host, hospitable, diverting, infinitely refreshing and of the same frame of mind as for many years. 'I love life, good wine and good company.'

The Guardian

Daniel Querre

The Enthusiast

We waited for Daniel Querre in the courtyard of the Hôtel de Plaisance in the Gironde wine town of St Emilion. The usual visitors to St Emilion are vintners, concerned with the surrounding wine-growing châteaux rather than with the town itself: but there are others, outriders from the main touring army – the church-fancier, the rubber of brasses, the connoisseur of rood-screens or the student of ecclesiastical history. These, since they belong by nature to the fabric of such a place, leave it uninvaded, and the full caravan of tourism does not enter St Emilion. The town could not contain it. At such threat of commerce, there would be panic in the little house-shops which religiously display the original macarons, yet do so, it seems, more out of respect for tradition than from hope of real profit. The tread of so many strange feet would choke the thousand-year-old monastery town with the dust of its dead prelates, and the pulse of the impatient touring motorcar stream through the narrow streets and tiny squares would burst those age-hardened arteries. Thus, there is in St Emilion no alien noise – which is only really disturbing form of noise. Its sounds are the native sounds, which are part of the pattern of quietness.

We waited for Daniel Querre when even the usual church-front loungers were away at the grape harvest, leaving the Place to a stillness in which waiting became intransitive, a state of grace. Above us, the bell of St Emilion simultaneously marked and mocked the passage of time. Out of compassion for centuries of those who sleep late before mass, it strikes the hour a full two minutes ahead of the hands of the clock: but, with equal compassion for clockmakers, strikes it again, punctually upon the hour.

At a table there, the contents of a glass are as enjoyably contemplated as drunk. Behind, the firm, grey ecclesiastical walls promise eternal rest. The bell tower climbs from our side eighty feet into the air, and its far more ancient monolithic chapel is directly beneath your feet. So the floor is a roof, this green wooden cafe-table a lookout tower. Beyond the low courtyard wall, the V of the immediate houses carves a sharp gulf, and the vineyards which run as far as the horizon are, even at their nearest, more dimly distant than their distance. The light is solicitous to protect the eye from the search for detail: even at full sunshine the lines of the houses are smudged to a crayon softness. Though it is early afternoon, and no mist rises, there is an impression of haze over this stretch of the Gironde, where every mile has named a bottle.

I believe that Daniel Querre's sense of the contemplation induced by the Plaisance courtyard prompts him to appoint his meetings there. A man who is always late for appointments must be either shameless, or thus imaginative in his choice of a meeting place. It has one further advantage as a rendezvous for the latecomer; those waiting for him are conscious of his approach – and so cease to account him late – a full ten minutes before his arrival. The imperious horn of Daniel Querre's long, French car is to be heard several kilometres away. He refuses to recognize travelling time between one activity and the next, but he is indignantly intolerant of any check. He drives with a characteristically French estimate of safe speeds and margins of clearance, but with a due consideration for children, women, animals and men, in that order. Level-crossings, on the other hand, rouse him to an ecstasy of anger. Let him find the gates closed against him and he begins his address to the crossing keeper as he applies the brake and continues it, from the middle of the road with contemptuous gestures at the passing train, until the gates open again – when he immediately gives precedence to a hobbling farm-cart.

His car cries in top gear up the one-cart-width hill of St Emilion and swings into the Place with a glorious disregard of centrifugal force. Then, he is with you – even as he leaves his car, twenty yards away, to walk to your table. Although one leg drags a little from some old foot injury, he seems to swallow walking distances in a movement. He is heavily square in build but, in the flick of the small dark eyes in his wine-and-weather red face and the uprush of his short black hair, there is a quick, eager note. A spread of his hands conveys an embrace to everyone. A look, a containing sweep of the arms, admits an entire concourse to his affection. No need to call for the waitress; she, hitherto elusive, is at his side, waiting for his order. Now, an apéritif. Next, lunch: the meal ordered for an hour ago has, at this moment, been completed: the rich, dark dish of lampreys is smoking on the table. The wine is from our host's own cellar, for this is an occasion. To Daniel Querre, every meal is an occasion, bringing food and wine and people and conversation; lacking one of these ingredients, it would not be a meal – *not* an occasion. Above all, the occasion of his finest setting is dinner at his own château: he will take lunch anywhere within a hundred miles, but his dinner is only properly to be taken at home.

To the normal French regard of the home as the centre of the life of the family, the châtelain of the wine-growing districts adds another and almost equally strong tie – that of the life of the vigneron. This is a concept difficult for any Englishman, even an English farmer, completely to comprehend. Because Daniel Querre has lived his entire life in two châteaux in the greatest wine-growing district in the world, his attitude to his home and wine is fundamental and, in his case, a form of mysticism.

He was the eldest of the three sons of the proprietor of Château Mazeyres, at Pomerol. I write, even now, with the taste of Château Mazeyres on my palate, from the bottle I shared at dinner. It has that typically gentle yet rich and mature flavour which, unremarkable among the average clarets, is unique among all the other wines of the world. With this wine as his daily table beverage, Daniel Querre grew up – as his own son is growing up now – in the care and teaching of a father whose life had been spent in vines and wines. He passed his boyhood and adolescence watching and tending the vine, helping to make and cellar the wine, tasting and comparing wines identical to less skilful palates. As the eldest son, he took his share of the inheritance early and set up a wine cellar in the nearby town of Libourne. But, even when he married, he did not leave the château where he had been born. His business flourished, until, in 1946, he achieved the purpose of his existence. He was able to buy Château Monbousquet, a vineyard once famous for its wines but then, after a hundred and fifty years of absentee landlords, producing a pedestrian drink from tired grapes.

As he has suggested, the life of the châtelain of the Bordeaux wine area is not quite parallelled in any other pastoral community in the world. Although their châteaux themselves are spacious and of a dignity and handsomeness sufficient for an English manor house, their estates are small. Many of the great vineyards are scarcely half a mile across – and often separated from the next château by no more than a low wall or a footpath. That boundary may confine – on one side – a wine whose labels has borne its château's likeness as a familiar device before the eyes of the drinking world. Meanwhile, the wine on the other side may not be sufficiently remarkable to be saved from sale under the bare name of the district.

An English farmer may survey his fields stretching as far as the weather allows the eye to see: he may pick up the soil of his land and crumble it between his fingers with pride at its richness; or he may contemplate – and invite the rest of the world to do so – the huge majesty of his beeves or the magnitude of his crops. With the wine grower it is different. The land of his narrow domain is only suitable for grapes by virtue of its stony or sandy poverty. His wine, be he never so careful a husbandman, must be content with greatness in a single year of the average decade. Then, if he is to balance his accounts, its price must be such that few can afford to taste its greatness and admire. On the other hand, within his own château, he may serve to his guests his own wine, and he himself will drink it daily in a domestic and culinary setting automatically sympathetic.

At the strong square table of his own château, Daniel Querre is, unmistakably, a great lord, the grower, maker and giver of wine. When he bought Château Monbousquet with almost all his money, he dedicated the latter half of his life to raising its wine again to the high peak which is eminence among the great clarets. It is a long, slow process, this digging up of meagre vines, then ten fallow years of long-planted ground, the slow, fifteen-year coming of new vines to maturity. There are summers – all too frequent – when a single ill-timed frost, a single week of rain, will reduce a great vintage – for all that any man may do – to a mediocre one. After the pressing of the wine and the maturing years in barrel before bottling, there are years – no one can foretell how many – before it comes to its greatest in bottle. These anxieties Daniel Querre embraced with the zeal of one entering a life of devotion.

In 1946, Monbousquet had vines which would produce wine for some years to come – but not a great wine. All but the finest of the vines must be grubbed up and fresh ones – of the best – must be planted. Then arose the still present problem of young grapes, for vines do not produce wine fit to bear the name of a man's home until they are ten years old. Normally, there is only a small percentage of young grapes on a single estate and their wine is drunk by the family in the château. But here, at Monbousquet, stood row upon row of young grapes, gallon upon gallon of young wine, young wine enough for all the châteaux of St Emilion. Wine grower, wine historian and businessman met in the châtelain's brain. There was, once, a wine of the young grapes. Make a wine now of the young grapes. It was made. Wine takes three years in barrel to ferment. This wine was made and had finished fermentation in five days. Market it. Call it 'Clairet'. Take it to Paris. Set up barrels of it in the Tuileries for all Paris to drink it free. Take the red-robed Jurade from St Emilion to Paris. Stand before the barrels and make a great speech to all Paris. Clairet is thought of, invented, made, marketed, known, in a few weeks. It is fresh, light, young: it is a drink worth its price. Its price means peace, consolidation, to produce, from the vines worthy to be saved, a Château Monbousquet which, even in three years, could promise to satisfy its owner's pride.

The man who crams his hours so full does not rise early. Although, at ten each night, bed follows immediately upon dinner, the house barely stirs before eight in the morning, and the propriétaire rarely takes his coffee before nine. Then, outside, to see the foreman, the maître de chai, the vineyards, the cow. Next, the car and the office: the journey is fast, but not so fast but that three or four points along the road are impressed upon the passenger's memory by a history, old or modern, but always living. The cellars, the vats, the bottles, the books at the office of the wine merchant receive the attention of two bursting hours. Decisions are made. The telephone is challenged to contain words explosive in their urgency. Then the market quiet of Libourne descends upon the establishment as the black car drives out of the gate.

If the next matter of the day is one of business, it will be conducted smilingly: it is between friends: there is no argument, each party knows the ground too thoroughly, each knows that the other knows. If it is a civic function, if there is a speech to be made, then, with head upthrown, he pours out words like trumpet notes. The lilt of his orations is the lilt of folk poetry, the extravagance is the extravagance of one who knows that, upon the subject of wine, there is no extravagance except failure to drink. There is lunch: let it be here: let there be wine: let the rest of our world stop, not even entering our thoughts, as we eat and drink.

Now . . . with the coffee he may make plans. 'The Château of St Michel de Montaigne?' 'Oh but yes, no more than sixty kilometres away – we shall go.' But why not – it is nothing. 'See, this is it.' He has an air of ownership: but greater is his tact. Of wine there can be no two opinions. Of art, it is different. Here, see the greatness of the man: here is sympathy, but it is unspoken: the wrong word is never said: nor the word too many.

Shall we return for dinner? But yes – there will be two guests – four guests – six guests – eight guests. There is no telephone at Monbousquet. As we drive along the gravel road and under the arch, the car is not going anywhere, it is coming home, quietly. The Jersey cream wall of the château runs its shutter-windowed length beside the drive, looking down on the lake where the bullfrogs grunt. Madame Querre is at the door: there is accustomed and easy affection between husband and wife at seeing one another. 'How many guests?' 'Dinner will not be long.' Room gives on room: there are apéritifs, armchairs: a friend painted those pictures which capture the attention. There is a family to meet, a family interested in itself and in its guests. The château ceases to be merely an architectural delight: it is a family. The head of the family sits down to the dinner table with his wife, his two sons – both bright, dark eyed and quick in response as their father – with the daughter of the brother whom the Gestapo treated characteristically and tragically, the son of a distant cousin studying the vine as an agriculturist, and with his friends. He eats with a catholic and critical enjoyment and drinks with a round, uncomplicated delight founded on knowledge and a palate which he does not allow tobacco to dull. The wines of the other châteaux of Bordeaux come to him with the automatic courtesy of one wine-grower to another, and he tastes them with critical gratitude. He takes his holidays and other periodical visits in Burgundy so that, on those two – the greatest – wine districts, he is an authority.

Always the formula with a glass of a wine is the same; in an Englishman it can hardly but appear affected, but with the Frenchman of wine it is a reflex. Holding the wine glass by the foot, he surveys the wine reflectively against the light. Then, quietly, he brings the glass towards his nose, rotating it by the foot until the wine rises in a racing wave to precisely the height of rim. Then, having thus washed the air in wine, he savours the bouquet. Then drinking becomes the third, and the greatest of the taster's pleasures. Asked his opinion of the wine, such a man rarely uses terms of 'good' or 'bad'. For him it is sufficient to agree with the label – say, a Château Latour 1939. That is sufficient. It means that the wine has all the normal attributes of a Château Latour wine – and they are practically invariable – blended with the characteristic of the year – 1939 – whose weather, with that of every other year, every French wine expert knows automatically.

Turn the talk to the identification of wine when the serious and non-conversational business of eating is over, and your host will follow and sympathize with your conversation and then you may hear the story of an evening in Paris. Memory does not recall even the language in which the story is told, for its gestures, the pointed tenseness of the words, dispel the need for effort of translation.

Monsieur Querre was in Paris. It was, you will understand, a matter of business and goodwill. He had – with a wry sadness – been drinking 'à l'Américaine'. He and his party returned to their hotel. It is a good hotel – and, at this juncture, you may, in some versions of the story, receive the address of the hotel and of some good restaurants in the district. But . . . the hotelier welcomed his returning guests and, after preliminary refreshment had been taken, he made a proposal. If M. Querre could identify the wines which should be poured for him out of two magnums from the hotel cellar, then those bottles should be drunk by the party at the hotelier's expense. The honour of all French viticulture was at stake. You may still feel the silence which falls as the first bottle comes in, carefully wrapped in a napkin: a flick of the teller's hand shows the sharpness of the creases in the laundered linen. You understand it is not possible to obtain a glimpse of cork or label. The magnum is tilted over Daniel Querre's glass.

He lifts the glass at arm's length and surveys it against the light.

'Bordeaux' . . .

'Médoc' . . .

A nod to his own memory – 'Grand Médoc'.

He brings the glass slowly to his nose: his eyes are alight with the recollection.

'1925.'

He tastes it, and, eyes closed, rolls it round his tongue.

'Margaux.'

'Château Margaux.'

'Château Margaux, 1925.'

A disclamatory slicing of the right hand indicates that no confirmation was needed.

The hotelier provides the magnum.

The second wine appears, also carefully obscured under a napkin: it is poured.

Again it is held to the light: it is regarded.

'Not of my district – Burgundy.'

'1915.'

The glass is brought under the nose, slowly rotated: eyes close in concentration upon the bouquet.

'No – too young – not '15 . . . '23.'

'Yes, '23.'

Now he tastes it – ah! – yes . . .

'Chambertin.'

'Chambertin' slowly, with relish, triumph, delight, '1923'.

The hotelier bows: even at second hand, his respect is apparent in the bow: he presents also the second bottle.

Daniel Querre reaches under his chair. The wine bottles are there. This bottle bears his own label – Château Monbousquet. The picture on the label is of the house in which we sit: in the centre of the picture is the window of the room where we are dining. Of courtesy, the châtelain takes the first taste, a little in his glass to ascertain and to demonstrate that it is fit hospitality for his guests. If it were not for business, he says, he would never leave this château, never drink any wine but his own Monbousquet. The enthusiast looks at his enthusiasm against the light. Gravely, almost sternly, he ascertains that the scent is as he would have it. He tastes it and his pride is confirmed. Across his own table, he pours his own wine for his guests.

The Adelphi, 1959

Ernest Aujas

October 1978. You are on the north road out of Juliénas when you pass the Coq d'Or and Chez la Rose, next door to each other on your left. Tiny as they are, they are two of the dozen best restaurants in the entire Beaujolais. The road, like any other in Beaujolais, never continues straight for more than a few metres; but soon it runs like a shelf let into the hillside of south-east facing vineyards. After perhaps a kilometre, a stream, less than a yard wide, comes sparkling down the hillside on your right. It crosses the road through a shallow conduit and then leaps into the wall of a grey stone house, of which only a single – windowless – storey shows at road level.

This is the home, presshouse, cellar, and bottling shed of the vigneron, Ernest Aujas. There is no footpath; the wide wooden doors at the end of the building give directly on to the narrow road and, when they are opened, the ancient, hand wine press can be filled directly from trucks standing in the roadway.

At the other end, the path just wide enough for the family truck, turns, hairpin, quickly down to bottom floor level of the house, while the hill tumbles on steeply away, so steeply indeed that the plough is drawn up the vineyard slope by a winch. The cellar yard is cut deeply into the hill and on the bank rest the carcasses of a couple of cars, a dozen or so worn out tractor tyres, a heap of gnarled, grubbed-up vine roots, and an orderly mountain of empty, green burgundy bottles waiting to be filled.

The ground floor of the house, its windows looking out across its own hill to others, and the cellar, are one solid, stone-built unit, running far back into the earth. The stream bursts from its under-floor tunnel, across the yard and gushes on, between the rabbit hutches and the dog kennels, through the garden patch and the olive trees, and down the hill.

Ernest Aujas is strongly built, six feet tall, sixty years old; his face weather-beaten to a brick red; a sun bleached beret partly covers his white hair; the frilly stub of a hand-rolled cigarette clings to his lower lip. No spendthrift of words, he answers questions with the quiet certainty of a man who has worked out his problems.

He shares the labour of a six hectare (14.4 acres) vineyard with his son. They split the proceeds 3½/2½: the son will inherit. Roughly speaking, the son cultivates the vineyard, the father maintains the cellar, vinifies, bottles and packs. This, though, is a harsh workload possible only with family help from wives, cousins, even grandparents, at busy times; a team of as many as two dozen Portuguese – mainly students – in the ten- to fifteen-day vendage.

The cellar is gravity fed from the press at road level; five vast and four smaller, but still mighty, barrels hold the wine. In March 1978, the 1976, big and tannic, was still unbottled. M. Aujas, content that he had a fine vintage, did not propose to hurry it. It was safe in his cellar, where the temperature is safely static, and he takes regular samples of all his wines – and allows them to his visitors – in the traditional tastevin which hangs, worn and gleaming, from a tape about his neck. He never fines nor filters; his is a natural wine that throws a natural deposit.

He bottles it himself – as many as 20,000 bottles in a good year – in his primitive one-man bottling machine. His 1976 was still a big tannic wine last spring. As always, he refused to bottle except when the wind was in the north and the moon on the wane.

Now some of that wine has arrived in England, ready to drink; but it will be better yet. Substantially bigger than a normal Beaujolais, almost of the stature of a fine burgundy, is has the usual Juliénas bouquet of summer fields; and, while the taste is fresh, clean and young in the classic Beaujolais fashion, on the palate it is full and round with a perfumed quality which is by no means usual. It is as if it were the essence of Beaujolais.

It is not cheap; inclusive of transport and VAT, it costs £46.35 per dozen case. Not long ago that would have seemed an impossible figure for Beaujolais, but every year fresh factors inflate the price. The ultimate Beaujolais enthusiast and specialist, Roger Harris, has shipped it. His address is Loke Farm, Weston Longville, Norfolk, NR9 5LG; neither he nor the phlegmatic Monsieur Aujas has any difficulty in selling it. Their problem is to replace it; and, so fine is it, that they may never do that. It is a Beaujolais experience to have tasted it.

The Guardian

Libero Raspa and Giorgio Lungarotti

November 1978. Libero Raspa was christened in the atmosphere of dawning liberty in the Italy of a century ago. He lived in Brufa di Torgiano, in central Umbria, where he owned a small vineyard. He was seen working in it, efficiently if not strenuously, when he was a hundred years old. He did at 101; and when he was buried, one Saturday afternoon last September, all the shops in Brufa closed.

A procession of villagers followed his coffin to the church and swarmed in through the doors behind it, barely parting for the coffin bearers, who, silent, burly, black-suited, purposeful, pushed their way out through them for all the world like some grim bodyguard which, of course, in their way, they were.

Afterwards in the cottage that had at last descended to his elderly grandson, wine was dispensed in jugs once used for the vino bono, which used to be served to women in childbirth to give them strength. A grave discussion estimated that, in his worthy and happy lifetime, Libero had drunk at least 100,000 litres of the wines of the district. From the window, the rich Umbrian landscape stretched away exactly as the painters of five centuries have recorded it.

The fertile vineyards and olive groves lie, perched aslant, on hills, capped here by cypresses, there by oaks, and, most strikingly, nearer at hand, by a clump of pines oddly pollarded like umbrellas; otherwise the countryside is punctuated only by church towers; the flat-roofed, sun-accustomed, houses; and a few, freshly-ploughed brown fields.

The country is dominated by the three cathedral cities. Perugia, the hilltop fortress; Orvieto on its great, tunnelled volcanic rock; Assisi, one vast aspiring shrine. It is, too, wine country, which for more than a thousand years has produced the straw-coloured Orvieto. Pinturicchio's contract for his frescoes in Orvieto cathedral included an unlimited supply of its Trebbiano wine. Fragrant, delicate, described as abbocato – slighty sweet – it is traditionally bottled in a straw-flask even shorter and fatter – and holding less – than the Chianti fiasco. The Trebbiano grape preponderates; with Malvasia for sweetness; Verdelho and Grechetto for the gentle bouquet; and all allowed to ripen towards rot – though noble rot, of course – between picking and pressing.

The elder Raspa, though, lived to see the twentieth-century palate demand, and get, a drier Orvieto, made with more Trebbiano, and by vinifying immediately after picking. Now, more than half the annual seven million bottles are dry. Orvieto is consistently of surprisingly high standard and ages extremely well – for a wine from grapes largely grown in *coltura promiscua*. This is the mixed agriculture, in which vines are trained over growing trees, against orchard walls, or with vegetables or tomatoes. Both sweet and dry have DOC status. Those from the Orvieto cellars of the Florentine house of Marchesi Antinori are as good as any.

Vin Santo – wine of Holy Week – is made all over Italy but only in relatively small quantities and, until lately, largely for the household use of the growers themselves; though now some is beginning to come on to a wider market. It is a dessert white, made in Umbria, from Trebbiano and Malvasia grapes hung in lofts to dry for some six months after the picking, until two thirds of their juice has dried out.

Then they are pressed, the rich juice is run into small barrels left only three-quarters full, for some four years – usually in a roof – to suffer a wide range of temperatures, particularly heat. That would be sheer destruction for any ordinary wine, which would become undrinkably maderized. The vin santo, however, is a freak; although it varies in quality and sweetness, it is always a rounded, powerful wine – about 16° of alcohol – and, at best, full and rich on the palate, with a dry aftertaste like a fino sherry.

Restaurants and cafés in Assisi invariably have the local Bastia, an ordinary but refreshing dry white; and two stronger, fuller reds, called Scacciadiavoli and Sagrantino. In Perugia you will find, as well as Orvieto, red and white Fontesgale, and the Colli Perugini from its own hills. None of these, though, is particularly distinguished.

The newest Umbrian DOC is the Colli del Trasimeno from the slopes above the vast, but shallow, Lake Trasimene whose shores are being developed as a holiday area. There is red and white; dry, light (the white 10.5°, the red 11°); the white, with a hint of sweetness, is best drunk young. The red, bright garnet in colour, is dry, generally with good tannin; and ages well.

The most interesting vineyard area of Umbria, though, is Torgiano, also known as Torre di Giano (tower of Janus, the two headed Roman god of doors), which forms a map-triangle with Perugia and Assisi, near the Tiber valley. The vineyards there have been known for centuries; but their present reputation was virtually created by one man, in an anticipatory microcosm of the modern development of Italian viticulture.

The marriage of Giorgio Lungarotti's parents united the two major landowning families of the district. Most of their farms, althogether about 440 hectares, were leased to tenants who produced grapes, olives, tobacco, corn, and alfalfa on a peasant-domestic basis.

In 1935, the young Lungarotti took a doctorate in agriculture, specializing in oenology, at Perugia. Observation of his father's and uncle's estate management convinced him that this small mixed farming was damaging the land, those who owned it, and those who worked it. Meanwhile, experiments with grape types satisfied him that known cepages, suited to the soil, would produce a wine in the traditional local character but of consistently higher quality than previous haphazard methods allowed.

When he assumed control of the two estates, in 1953, he began a steady process of taking over the farms from the tenants and concentrating all resources on the production of meat-cattle and wine. 'The other three directors are my wife and two sisters so there are no arguments,' he says. In 1959 and 1960 he embarked on an ambitious programme of replanting established vineyards, and creating others, where most of the former tenants are employed in greater security than before. There the latest vinicultural processes and safeguards are used for a yield controlled in size to ensure high quality.

At the same time he replaced the former six press houses with one modern, sophisticated and hygienic plant where a stable wine is made, stored, matured and bottled under a single roof. So, when the Italian government introduced its DOC – Denominazione di Origine Controllata – legislation in 1973, Dr Lungarotti had anticipated its demands; and his white Torre di Giano and red Rubesco were among the first wines in the country to be accredited.

The white is made from grapes roughly similar to those of Orvieto, but is distinctly drier; a clear strong wine, sharp when young, it improves with age. Like Chianti, Rubesco is made mainly from the Sangiovese but, unlike Chianti, it incorporates ciliegiolo, but no white grapes or colorino.

The result is a firm wine, with a delicate nose and a full, biscuit-dry flavour. It improves with ageing and is probably at its best at eight years. It goes perfectly with the Umbrian mezzafegatti – fried salted pig livers, flavoured with pepper and coriander; and any un-blinkered claret drinker will relish both its taste and its price.

So far the Riserva – four years in cask before bottling – has been consumed within a decade of making. Already the 1973 is in short supply, even in Italy; for white substantially outweighs red in an annual output of barely 400,000 bottles.

His are the only wines to have gained the Torgiano DOC, but Dr Lungarotti, a tall, spare, scholarly, quiet man, philosophically claims no omniscience: 'I hoped my ideas would come to fruition, but I did not know. Now, though, I have faith to go further and I am planting new vineyards.'

The Lungarotti cantina also produces a vin santo (from the Grechetto) and a rosé called Castel Grifone. Most surprisingly in Italy, though, they use an artificial sherry to make a well balanced dry apéritif called Solleone which is much nearer a fino sherry than many bottles which assume that name.

Dr Lungarotti has not been content merely to create and establish the wines of Torgiano: he has sought to invest the small town itself with importance. It is inescapably overshadowed architecturally, historically, and artistically by both Perugia and Assisi no more than ten kilometres away. Dr Lungarotti, though, has set out to make it a place of wine pilgrimage. He has established a wine museum remarkably well endowed with glasses, artefacts, and decorated from his own collection of engravings.

Nearby he has reopened, enlarged and completely renovated an old hotel which he calls 'Le Tre Vaselle' which serves the best vintages of his wines, with well prepared Umbrian dishes. It has all modern conveniences; plus an ancient, but hygienically scoured, secret tunnel, and if some of the prices are surprising, the service is thoughtful. His package for the national tourist organization is completed by a visit to his press house and cellars for a guided tour, a tasting and a buffet of local food. The coachloads from Rome come almost every Sunday; and Torgiano remains a significant port of call for any student of Italy and its vineyards. *The Guardian*

Freddie Whitting

October 1980. The wine trade has lost one of its independent thinkers; wine students one of their most enthusiastic fellows; and collectors of unusual wines one of their outstanding suppliers. In short, that alert, bubbling, friend-making man, Freddie Whitting, is dead. He had delivered one of his favourite wines, Poggia Romita (he was right in calling its 1969 Riserva superb) to a customer. On the way back he fell asleep at the wheel, slewed off the road, hit a tree and was killed instantly. As he would have wished, it was final and uncomplicated; involving no one else.

Any British student of Italian wines who did not buy from him had an incomplete file. He was 62 when he died; but he had the enthusiasm of youth for his subject; perhaps because unlike most wine merchants who make a personal impact, he came late to the trade.

Originally he was, like his father, a professional soldier; a gunner, but completely unlike the general view of the career soldier. Original, unconventional, witty, regarded by his fellows with affection; always much concerned to improve the quality of the soldier's life.

He went to France with his RA battery, in 1939; came out through Dunkirk; went out to North Africa, made the Anzio landing, followed up through Italy, past Florence, to the hills beyond Fiesoli. There, his battery was supporting the Hertfordshires; he was observing the German dispositions with their Colonel and radioing instructions back to his battery when they came under fire, and he lost his right eye. 'Actually,' he used to say, 'because I was not wearing a tin hat.' The surviving eye observed and twinkled brightly enough for two.

Service in Haifa, Egypt, as instructor in the Tactics Wing of the School of Artillery; and command of an independent battery in Germany followed. Peace-time soldiering, though, did not satisfy him. Doffing his forage cap, he joined the grocery group, Allied Suppliers. Taking the immense change in eager strides, he became a prime mover in the firm's development of supermarkets and, specializing in wine and spirits, their negotiator for licensing – no task for an amateur of business – with marked success.

Here a longstanding interest in wine became a matter of serious study. In 1972, at the age of 54, Freddie Whitting stepped into the most rewarding of the three phases of his life.

After a few months of intensive study of the subject, he founded Stonehaven Wines with his wife Elaine, son Peter – and very limited capital. The business premises were, improbably enough, the spare room and garage of an inter-war house on a lesser Hampshire country road. Such a situation should, surely, have killed any kind of commercial enterprise.

Amazingly, it succeeded. That is explicable only in terms of Freddie's fierce and communicable enthusiasm. At first a general wine dealer, he soon became absorbed by the Italian. He arranged and conducted tours to their vineyard areas – at extremely little profit – and used them to increase his own knowledge.

If he heard of a fine wine in short supply, or, especially, not available, in Britain – Sassicaia, Tignanello, Carmignano Villa Capezzana, Draceno, Regaleali, John Dunkley's Riecene Chianti Classico, Badia a Coltibuono – he would track it down and, however small the stocks, however reluctant the producer (it does happen), win some to bring back for his collector customers.

It was a magnificent occasion – now a sadly momentous one – to have been a guest at Freddie Whitting's last tasting lunch only a few days before his death. Stonehaven has not stopped: Elaine and Peter, with Carol Shave (Freddie's right hand – and sometimes his right eye as well) continue it: that laughing man would have been angry if they had not. *The Guardian*

Harry Waugh

Million Dollar Palate

March 1982. Until recently – in fact, until Harry Waugh – wine tasters were not people of particular importance. Like the samplers of tea, cheese, ale – and, perhaps more importantly, whisky – they were employed to try, grade, value, and price the commodity in which they worked. When they were successful, the wine merchant took the credit; when not, the wine merchant sacked them.

Harry Waugh changed all that. He entered the wine trade in 1934

41

and after the war joined Harveys as their fine wine taster. He was 62 and created no great stir when he left them to become a wine consultant. In fact, he was beginning a second life of a success he can never have contemplated.

In the process of gaining an international reputation as an adviser, judge, and lecturer on wine, he entered his seventies by fathering twins, becoming a director of Château Latour and founder-president of the English branch of the les Compagnons du Beaulojais. The essay about him in a recent issue of the American *Wine Magazine* was titled 'The Million Dollar Palate'.

Volume nine – the latest – of *Harry Waugh's Wine Diary* (Christie's Wine Publications) shows the width and depth of his operations. In 1979, at 75, he made yet another tour of America. On 29 May, after he had completed a tasting in California, and tempted by the thought of visiting Alaska, he flew the 2000 miles to Anchorage where he conducted a tasting of Californian wines that night. Next morning he went to the local newspaper office for an interview and visited the Alaskan museum and local branches of Jug Wine Inc. Lunch was washed down with 1969 Bollinger R.D., Meursault Clos du Comin 1976, Château Latour 1959, 1961 and 1973; Château d'Yquem 1967 and, by way of comparison, a 1977 Château St-Jean Johannisberg Riesling Late Harvest.

That evening his lecture on the vintages of Châteaux Léoville-Lascases and Langoa Barton went on until ten o'clock. Dinner – main course king salmon – occupied him until one in the morning, and four and a half hours later he was up ('What one does in the cause of wine') to catch the first of his planes to Oklahoma City. He arrived there at 10 pm local time and, next day, guided a tasting of 1974 clarets.

Two samples – 'I stayed with Arthur Halle who has over 70 vintages of Château Latour in his cellar.' Or Memphis Tennessee – 'Apéritif; Steinberger Kabinett or Guy Beauregard Champagne, Epernay; fresh bisque or crayfish followed by paupiette de sole, sauce Albert, both of which were first rate. With these two courses we drank Corton Charlemagne 1973, domaine bottled Duchet, lighter than Louis Latour but nice all the same. The delicious sweetbreads Lucullus were covered with chopped truffles and that was all I could manage, so had to pass the main course of veal Nesselrode.'

The depth of his wine knowledge and his wine palate are as prodigious as his vitality and capacity for enjoyment. His journal – penetrating about wines, generous to people – can be vicariously tiring as well as titillating to the palate; and unflagging, informative, and unique. *The Guardian*

Fritz Hallgarten

A Nose Ahead

June 1973. The opinion that Fritz Hallgarten has 'the best nose in the wine business' does not refer to its shape, though it does fit neatly and quizzically into the top of a wine glass.

Those who smell the bouquet of a wine for pleasure can only be amazed at one who, after a look and a couple of inhalations, emerges with 'Yes, 11 degrees Oeschle' (the measure of sweetness; 10 degrees to one gramme per thousand of acidity is the ideal): or 'Amerikanisch' (the flavour of the American root stock is apparent through the European graft); or 'this has had a malo' (secondary fermentation).

He is a wine man who came from wine, left it, returned to it through what seemed mischance, and created a business – the House of Hallgarten – whose catalogues alone are collectors' items. His wine merchant ancestors, driven out of Spain by the Inquisition, settled on the Rhine, built themselves a Spanish style house at Winkel in the Rheingau wine country and went into the wine trade there.

Fritz Hallgarten grew up among those vineyards with the children of wine makers and merchants; he already had an appreciative palate for wine in his schooldays.

Although his father was an established shipper of Rhine wines, he decided to branch out on his own. He qualified as a lawyer at Heidelberg and practised successfully until 1932 when the new law banned him, and all his Jewish race, from the profession.

In post-war years the knowledge, absorbed in childhood, of the great German wines virtually obliged him to deal in them – and to do so successfully. He opened a branch office – managed by his brother – in his native town of Winkel.

Fritz is the ultimate winetaster. He will drive to a vineyard to taste half a dozen – perhaps a dozen – wines; on, with controlled motor-fury, to another, the same process; perhaps eight times in a day. Every wine is something to be explored, studied and savoured. The considered pencilled tick on his list means he will buy it. The purist tasters smell, savour and spit out. Fritz Hallgarten likes to swallow a little; the entire mouthful of a wine he favours.

Yet, oddly, he normally drinks little; the excitement and potential surprise of a tasting is lacking in a mealtime bottle. He insists anywhere on drinking not only the wine of the country but, if possible, the wine of the village: only a little, though! He is also an expert on mineral waters. In England his taste is completely catholic. He will come out from a tasting of fine German wines to take a hearty swig of some huge red Rhône wine – on which his son Peter is the leading British expert – with thirsty relish.

He is, he says, now '99 per cent out of the House of Hallgarten' – but he is still their consultant on German and Alsatian wines. Meanwhile, he has been visiting the vineyards of America and France: is writing another book on Rhine wines; and has now accepted the post of advisor to a large French wine group. At 71 he still has as sharp a palate as ever – and an even longer palate memory – and his interest remains intense: 'I shall never retire.'   *The Guardian*

Peter Sichel
The Sichel Report

June 1979. Peter Sichel is that rare creature, a wide-ranging wine expert. Most of the truly knowledgeable in that field are vignerons, insular, even parochial; born, growing up and staying in a single viticultural area. The Sichels, however, have a determinedly international outlook. Their early background is that of the Rhine vineyards; they came to England where Allan – author of *The Penguin Book of Wines* and his son Peter (who revised the latest edition) were educated and worked in the family business in The Adelphi. Peter then went to France, where he lives in, and runs, a wine château in Bordeaux; ships from Burgundy and the Rhône; buys in the other French regions.

Thus his annual report, continuing a family tradition, is as authoritative as any in the world. He can begin with Bordeaux's happy ending to its 1978 summer of anxiety which threatened the claret vintage with ruin. 'Not swollen by excessive rain, nor cooked by excessive sun, the grapes came in entirely healthy with a good sugar content and an acidity perhaps marginally higher than ideal. The fine weather of the late summer saved a situation that had been precarious to the end. With only 5.5 millimetres of rain during the whole month, that October was the driest for over 20 years and enabled picking, which started for red wines around 9 October, to take place under ideal conditions.'

Few judgements are more difficult than tasting clarets immediately after they are made and assessing their likely quality when they are ready to drink, a decade or more into the future. Peter Sichel, though, does this with the assurance of one who has been so consistently right that no one questions his opinion. Indeed, many regarded as experts in their own right regularly await his judgement before they commit themselves in the market.

'The (1978) red wines have a magnificent colour, are round and with a length of flavour which sets Bordeaux apart. Summers which climatically most closely resembled that of 1978 are 1962, 1966 and 1970 and certainly at this early stage the wines are reminiscent of those excellent years, though with an impression of more length and elegance than 1970.'

On prices, as on quality, he is coolly objective and, here, alarming. 'Compared with twelve months ago, prices of Bordeaux are now 16 per cent up, St-Emilion 20 per cent, Médoc 30 per cent. This is not outrageous but compared with two years ago, Bordeaux and Médoc have increased 80 per cent, and St-Emilion is up 120 per cent. If part of the increase over 1977 can be justified by the exceptional quality of the vintage it would be difficult to justify such an increase over the 1976 vintage on this or any other grounds.'

Peter Sichel is, though, at his best, and wise with the knowledge of long experience, when he interprets the mind of the market. 'It would be satisfying to report that the market had decided to continue in its new path of economic wisdom, with a pricing policy that continued to balance demand to supply. Until mid-January this seemed to be the case. Prices had remained sensibly stable until the late summer and if they did increase with a burst in August it seemed mainly due to some negociants, expecting prices to ease earlier in the year, not having covered their requirements for the year and finding themselves having to deal with growers who, worried by the risks of a late vintage, were in no mood to release any of their stock without a premium.

'It was at this stage that the CIVB, inspired perhaps by Cocteau's remark, *"Puisque ces mystères nous depassent, feignons d'en être les organisateurs"* (As these mysteries are beyond us, let us pretend that we have organized them), and, using sand to block the hole blown in their price policy, subsidized those negociants who had speculated on prices falling and those growers who, by retaining wine from the market, were speculating on prices rising. A strange decision, made with the best intentions but which only proved once again that, in a free market economy, no inducement will prevent transactions from taking place if a willing buyer and willing seller are agreed on the terms of a sale.

'The first classed growths have come out at prices some 50 per cent above those of 1977 (which had opened at much the same level as 1975 and 1976), have been brought up immediately; and again the howls of protest against the increase in price are only drowned by the screams for more.'   *The Guardian*

3
Family Firms

Monsieur Koenig's
Alsatian Kosher Wines

May 1973. Goxwiller is a rather Germanic village in the Alsatian wine region. It is a worthy, dusty place of solid work: the houses of its main street seem to have too few windows, and the tourist-planned 'Route du Vin' avoids it.

Two years ago Ramon Koenig retired from wine making and left to his 34-year-old son Emil his vineyard, cellars and house in the middle of Goxwiller. The cellars are sparklingly clean conversions from sixteenth-century farm buildings. The house on the street front is 1900; the dining room is also used for ironing, as the office, and for the baby; the sitting room, with its tiled stove, for discussions and tastings.

The vineyard, not small by Alsatian standards, covers 12½ acres, and it is maintained, quite immaculately, by the minimal labour of Emil, his wife – who also does the housekeeping and looks after their two small children – and a woman from the village, with help from his father in times of high pressure. Emil's son Phillipe is only six, but he is already involved in the atmosphere of wine. The Koenigs are wine makers by tradition and inclination; but without elaboration. The grapes are pressed; there is no fining, only filtering and sulphurizing; and the wine is bottled within six months. This is the exact pattern of the domaine vineyard as it was a century ago.

Although the Koenigs produce largely Edelzwicker, Pinot Blanc, and Gewürztraminer, they can offer a potential buyer eight different wines of two or three years.

The work is heavy but it satisfies Emil. Pressed as to why he does not go in for more sophisticated methods, he answers that to make wine in the same simple fashion as his father satisfies him, keeps the family, and honours their established business obligations.

The chief of these – fifty per cent of their 10,000 case production in most years since 1946 – is the making of Kosher wine. The Koenigs are not, in fact, Jewish – Emil is a Lutheran, his wife a Roman Catholic – but during his French military service between the two world wars, the elder Koenig became friendly with another conscript – a Jewish paté maker from Strasbourg – who, when his Rabbi asked him if he knew a reliable winemaker, recommended his former army friend.

Kosher wine is not inherently different from any other; but its making is strictly controlled. Emil Koenig grows the grapes: he and his helpers gather them and take them to the cellar door: but there they must surrender them. From that point until the wine is bottled only strict Shabbat-observing Jews may take any part in the process. In fact the making is generally undertaken by the Rabbi from Strasbourg with the assistance of a couple of Jewish religious students. The press, tubes, filters, funnels, and barrels are never used for any other wine and, while Emil Koenig may stand at the cellar door and advise, 'I am not allowed to touch anything – not even if the barrel is overflowing.' How well is it made? 'Oh, very well indeed, the Rabbi has become extremely skilful.'

The wine is allowed its half year in the barrel before the Rabbi and his assistants return to carry out the bottling. Only then do they relinquish their control over the wine.

There is a considerable demand for this wine – and not only from the Jewish community. Fritz Hallgarten, who ships a considerable quantity of Kosher wine, recalls being visited by some general traders who had Jewish customers and asked to taste some of his then slow-selling Alsatian Kosher. They pronounced it excellent, demanded that the Hebrew label be changed and took 80 per cent of the remaining stock.

Emil Koenig's problem arises when the Jewish New Year coincides with the Vendange, so that the Rabbi's duties prevent him from making the wine. Then he presses all his own grapes, sells that wine to non-Jewish sources and falls back on his cellared stocks to meet the demands for Kosher. It is difficult to find the Koenig house in Goxwiller: they need no bush.   *The Guardian*

Through Hostilities and Vagaries
A Remarkable Anglo-German Connection

October 1985. The London wine house of Deinhard has lately celebrated its hundred and fiftieth anniversary, and marked it with the issue of a volume of history (*A Wine Day's Work* by George Bruce). In fact the firm's very existence in 1985 is both celebration and history. That a firm of dual British-German axis, specializing in German wines, should come through two world wars, various other hostilities, the vagaries – sometimes amounting almost to perversions – of British customs charges, constant political damage to overseas markets, and changes of national palates, is quite remarkable. So remarkable, indeed, that we must search for an explanation. Mr Bruce's history would argue that the firm has always been an ambitious survivor, which is not so paradoxical as it may sound. It has aimed at high quality and the top market – which is not the puff it may seem – while never forgetting the wider market, which is an explanation rather than a contradiction.

Their basic attitude was crystallized in the very early days by Anton Jordan who, at only 20, became their first British representative. In an 1828 report back to Koblenz he wrote: 'There are two factions of wine drinkers here, one favours the artificial or doctored wines, the other the natural wines. This latter faction grows steadily. We must therefore base our business on the sale of natural wines, in particular the outstanding Moselle wines, the main pillar of our business.' The merchant in him, though, could not completely ignore the doctored wines: 'I think it would be useful to have a small stock of these wines so as not to miss any opportunities of extending our business.'

The original House was set up in Koblenz, in a small way, by

Johann Friedrich Deinhard in 1794 after vibrations of the French Revolution caused the 'freeing' of some of the great German vineyards from ecclesiastical and feudal hands.

He had little capital. His sons were too young to enter the business and he needed the services of Jordan who spoke good English and, importantly, was keen, industrious and loyal. Jordan's wares matched his ambitions. In 1826 he offered his British customers 1794 Marcobrunn, 1811 and 1819 Rudesheim, 1783 Johannisberg, 1819 Hochheim, and the then fashionable Moselle, Dusemond (now known as Brauneberg) of 1822. It had to be a winning hand. In face of such problems as the death of Johann Friedrich (at 55), the awkwardly early accession of his son, Carl Deinhard, and then the deaths of two senior partners, Jordan kept the firm going.

In 1834 he married Louise Deinhard, became a partner of Deinhard & Jordan, and settled in Koblenz, while Carl Deinhard took over in London. The next year saw the firm establishment in London of not merely an offshoot of Deinhard of Koblenz, but a house eventually to become wholly independent. Hence 1985 as the hundred and fiftieth anniversary.

The British – especially English – taste for Rhenish wines grew. Cyrus Redding wrote in *Modern Wines* (1833): 'The Germans are a distinct class in character from all other wines.' Deinhard's London ledgers read like a page from Debrett, and they issued some of the best vintage reports Britain had seen. The 1840s and 1850s proved their richest period. First they established their sparkling Moselle in public taste and popularity. Then, in 1845 when Queen Victoria and Prince Albert went to stay at Schloss Stolzenfels, near Koblenz, as guests of King Friedrich Wilhelm of Prussia, the court commanded Deinhard & Jordan, of all the German merchants, to provide the Royal visitors with 1200 litres of finest Rheingau wine.

The Royal Household was the biggest single consumer of wine in Britain and Deinhard now supplied it with fine wines of all kinds. Their sales ledger for 1856 records six dozen cases of three dozen bottles each of Steinberg Cabinet invoiced to Victoria Regina, not through a merchant, but direct to the Comptroller of the Royal Household. When the new Deinhard cellars were opened at Koblenz in 1875, the ceremony was performed by Queen Victoria's daughter, the Empress Augusta of Germany.

One triumph followed another. The London house began to export, especially its sparkling wines, to India, Canada, Africa, Australia, North and South America, and eventually, whisky to China. An officer in the British Expeditionary Force to Afghanistan wrote home to say they were taking 'two camel-loads of Manilla cigars and Sparkling Moselle'.

The latter half of the nineteenth century was full of events which must be crammed into little space for the firm of Deinhard. In 1857 two young men, Jakob (James) Hasslacher and Julius Wegeler were engaged for the London Office. In 1864, August Deinhard split with Anton Jordan who set up in opposition to him in Koblenz and London. Next year, August died and the two surprised young men took over, Wegeler in Koblenz and Hasslacher, who became a British citizen, in London. Their former rivalry had warmed into friendship and in 1868 the widowed Hasslacher married Wegeler's sister, Emilie, as his second wife.

Although there was no longer a Deinhard in the firm it maintained the established name, and flourished. Then, in 1890, Anton Jordan died at the age of 86, leaving a fund of money to help poor artisans. But, amazingly, bequeathing his own breakaway firm, with its wine and bank balances, entirely to Deinhard & Company. His reason may be pondered. Was it an act of conscience, or restitution? He left no indication.

Deinhard now rode a high tide indeed. Julius Wegeler entertained the composer Brahms at Koblenz, handing him a glass with the words 'This, Johannes, is among wines what you are among composers.' 'Then away with it,' exploded Brahms, 'and bring me a glass of Johann Sebastian Bach.'

For Cecil Rhodes, the empire builder's secretary wrote, assuming that 'since he sees very clearly that he must adopt your wine for his future consumption you would not mind taking the trouble to send him ten cases of the rarest old hock you possess'. Order or command?

Deinhard had long been acquiring fine Rhine vineyards. In 1900 however, they achieved the triumph of buying an appreciable proportion of the great Moselle Doktor vineyard at Bernkastel for the highest price that had ever been paid for Rhine wine territory.

Ahead lay many major problems. In the 1914 war, Charles's eldest son, James, was killed in action. The family was split between Britain

51

and Germany. The firm felt obliged to buy back wines it had sold to restaurants and hotels who now found it embarrassing to offer German wines for sale. Prohibition in the United States and bureaucratic obstacles elsewhere, were eventually overcome. The Second World War found the House of Deinhard better prepared; they had long stocks. They subsequently diversified widely into whisky (The Famous Grouse), Lustau sherries, Prosper Maufoux burgundies, Château de Blomac Minervois, Maillac armagnacs, Taylor Fladgate ports and Vinhos Barbeito madeiras.

After that war the two houses of Deinhard, London and Koblenz, agreed to sever their link, which had brought anxieties as well as benefits. The British section may doubt the advantages of that move. There remains an old sentimental bond, but Deinhard London is the Hasslachers'.

They are long-lived, the Hasslachers. James, 1835-1906, Charles, 1865-1961, Alexander, 1876-1953, Alfred, 1898-1981, and Austin, 1909-1981, while Heinz, born in 1914, retired in 1978. Charles, the father figure of the family, joined the company in 1883 and made token visits to the firm, walking from Monument tube station to the office almost until his death at 93. In 1958 the Ambassador of the Federal Republic of Germany presented him with the Order of Merit, first class, in recognition of a life's work for Anglo-German understanding.

André Simon, in an obituary in *The Times*, described him as 'the last of a generation of great wine shippers, whose sensitive palates, retentive wine memories and unchallenged integrity raised the wine trade in England from the commercial to the professional level'.

The present three Hasslacher directors, Peter, Michael and Robin, have much to live up to. *Decanter*

Whitwhams and Turnbull's

They Are Enthusiastically Knowledgeable about their Wares

September 1971. The off-licence chains controlled by the big brewing and distilling interests sell most of the wine drunk in England. This means that many of the rapidly increasing number of wine drinkers in the country hardly ever buy from a private wine merchant; indeed, many of them regard him as in the same remote class as the bespoke tailor. It also means that, since the days when wine-buying was smaller, the emphasis has changed from individuality towards the acceptance of a Brand X uniformity.

There is no typical wine merchant. Their numbers shrink yearly as more are bought up by the chains: the survivors have varying merits. In truth their enemy is less the multiple wine store than the supermarket which, with the repeal of retail price maintenance, seized much of the wine merchant's rapid turnover trade in spirits and apéritifs. The quick return on sales of whisky, gin, brandy, sherry, and vermouth enabled the single-shop business to buy and keep slow-selling wine in cellar until it was mature.

The undercutting of those prices enforced the closure or takeover of many independent vintners, some of whom, especially in the provinces, had sold the best wines obtainable in their districts. Those who remain have a tenacity of purpose reflected in a combination of expertise, understanding of local demand, and an individuality the chains cannot provide. There is no typical independent wine merchant, but two of contrasting character are Whitwhams, in the Old Market Place at Altrincham, on the Chester side of Manchester, and Turnbull's, of Church Road, at Hove, on the Hampshire side of Brighton.

Whitwhams is timbered black and white. It was a chandler's shop as long ago as the seventeenth century and is still part of an individualistic grocery store. Tony Littler inherited it from his father, and his son works in it. The eldest, as well as running the business, was a writer and photographer who shortened his name, Arthur Littler, for a pen-name to 'Arlit'. His son has used that title for the wine society through which he meets wine drinkers, airs ideas about wine and, ultimately, sells his wares. The society's annual banquet offers unusual fine wines.

Last month the stock, in the warren of cellars under his shop, in bond and stored overseas, ran to 17,844 bottles of wine – excluding spirits and beers. Whitwhams flourishes because Tony Littler encourages, informs and creates wine enthusiasts, and goes to considerable pains to meet their needs. While he cannot match chain prices, he stocks reliable cheaper lines and keeps a generous choice of the classic growths of Bordeaux, Burgundy, and Germany as well as the best ports and sherries. Thus he stocks Lebegue's French Country Wine range at 69p; Spanish red, and sweet or dry white at 60p; Mâcon Supérieur at 70p; Bordeaux Blanc, 70p; and a Médoc at 73p. Château-bottled Pichon-Longueville Baron 1961 is £2.75; Lafite-Rothschild 1957, £6; Brane-Cantenac 1962, £2; English bottled la Tour Figeac 1966; £1.40; and Langoa Barton 1962, £1.35.

His additional strength stems from his study of wine and the fact that by buying much of his stock in a group of 14 other independent merchants he can keep some costs low. Among his unusual items are a white Châteauneuf; the Gaulin Americano, and Chambéry. He is an advocate of Alsatian wine, which he considers neglected: his Riesling Seigneur d'Alsace is £1.15p; his Gewürztraminer Aulese, Reserve Exceptionelle, Jean Hugel 1964, £2.30; and the Gewürztraminer Beerenauslese Reserve Exceptionelle, Jean Hugel 1959, £4. His association with the similarly placed vintners is reflected in his Château Cantegrive (Margaux) 1964 at £1.10 and Château Romonet 1967 at £1.05, two acceptable bourgeois clarets of which the group bought almost the entire output.

Albert – 'Tommy' of course – Atkins became Mr F. J. Turnbull's office boy in 1925; after his employer died in 1937 he was made manager and, now a director, he still runs the family-owned business at Hove. Within a short saunter of his shop there are 20 establishments, from supermarkets to off-licences, who undercut him on quick-selling lines. He remains in competition for three main reasons. His stock is immensely wide; while he does not disdain cheap drink, he considers the enthusiast; and he never passes on a rise in tax or production cost to his customers so long as he has stock bought before the increase.

His stocklist – a hand-written book available to the interested on request – is impressive. Under the heading 'Red Wine' it lists 42 clarets, 37 burgundies, 6 Rhône, 11 other French, 11 Italian, five Spanish, three Portuguese, three Yugoslav, two German, two Austrian, and one each from Hungary, Switzerland, Rumania, Bulgaria, Greece, and Chile. The 133 liqueurs include seven different cherry brandies and seven Curaçaos. There are 29 minerals, 16 lagers, 69 sherries, 136 white wines. He is the only wine merchant around who stocks two kinds of Chinese brandy ('the Chinese restaurants buy it'):

sake and green tea liqueur are commonplace sales for him. In the temperature-graded cellar there are ones and twos of other exotic liqueurs and venerable sherries, stocks too small for the list. There too, is Chambéryzette, the rare Alpine-strawberry flavoured vermouth.

Last year's stocktaking credited Turnbull's with almost £25,000 worth of drink, much of it unusual enough for most wine merchants to call it unobtainable. He supplies rarities and oddities to the trade in the area and, while he is no man to utter slogans, he will admit, 'If we haven't got it they will have to go to London for it.' He and his shop assistant, Mrs Darling, are enthusiastically knowledgeable about their wares: only they know where to locate the odd, dusty bottles of German fruit brandy and such. And they are not averse to an impromptu tasting.

Mr Atkins has been scrupulously honest about his refusal to add increased costs he did not incur. The concession does not last long in the case of the spirits and cheaper wines ('most of the people who buy wine here every week buy cheap wine: we have been selling a lot of Moroccan lately'). On middle bracket wines, such as château bottled Montrose 1961, £2, Château Siran and Château Musset, both 1959, at £1 and 94 p, it is still apparent. Has this attitude made him fresh customers? 'I'm not sure; the public are very fickle; but when we had done it often enough to show it was genuine, some casual buyers became regulars.' He is inclined to think that willingness to deliver – his one van and vanman are busy all day – is a more important asset in these days of urban cash-and-carry.   *The Guardian*

Augustus Barnett

September 1977. One of the most remarkable phenomenons in the growth of British wine drinking during the past two decades has been the emergence of the firm of Augustus Barnett. Augustus, the father, has given his name to the operation conducted by his son, Brian, who shocked the traditional wine trade by coming up, as it were, out of the ground within the stockade.

Brian Barnett followed the pattern of the supermarkets in paring the selling price of spirits to the bone. Thus he contributed to the dilemma of the wine establishment which could only store and mature its stocks of fine wines on the profits from spirits sold well above modern cut price levels.

Having captured his customers with named gin and whisky at the lowest possible price, he offered them cheap wines at the bottom prices and a wide range of vintage bottles at what they would fetch.

The trade forecast his ruin weekly; but every such rumour was capped by the opening of another two, three, or six branches. The typical Barnett shop is in a suburban district with ample unrestricted parking space. It stays open during the normal lunch hour, generally until eight in the evening, and on most local early closing days. Presentation means opening the cartons and showing the bottles with a price ticket. There are no discounts; no delivery; no credit. You go to the shop, see what you want, pay for it, and take it away with you. The shop manager can order any special item you wish, including fine wines from the 'Big List' which contains bottles as remarkable as Château Haut-Brion 1929 (£55 a bottle), Château Mouton-Rothschild 1934 (£50), Château Latour 1945 (£54) and Château Lafite 1945 (£70).

Essentially, though, Augustus Barnett is established in the minds of most wine drinkers as the place where acceptable wines are cheapest. There may not be complete agreement as to what is acceptable. Certainly some of the Barnett bottles have not pleased everyone. On the other hand, their spotting and estimating have been shrewd and, often through relatively small parcels, they have made a narrow but not negligible profit and, at the same time, won customers.

These tight margins, attractive prices and quick turnover are fundamentally the outcome of skilful, if sometimes hair's breadth, financial decisions; when to buy, when to borrow, when to hold, when to sell. In years of insecurity, recession, inflation, fluctuating interest, increased taxation, the late explosion in the French wine market, and the Italian invasion, it was little short of a miracle for a new firm to keep afloat, leave alone flourish. Yet it expanded; there are now 145 Augustus Barnett branches, mostly in and about London or the home counties, but an increasing number further afield, increasingly in the Midlands and the North.

A few weeks ago the firm was taken over by Rumasa, the Spanish conglomerate created and controlled by Don Jose Maria Ruiz-Mateos Y Jiminez de Tejada. Brian Barnett remains chairman and Leslie Clarke managing director; and Rumasa say there will be no change in policy. Certainly Brian Barnett's temperament would not be satisfied by a figurehead post; he thrives on competition.

Rumasa, based on banking, is involved in wine (including major sherry firms and two large montilla producers), hotels, property, insurance, agriculture, finance, construction, shipping, and publicity: over 260 companies. Augustus Barnett will provide a wider outlet for the firm's wines, especially the sherries – Don Zoilo, the former Williams and Humbert range including Dry Sack, Palomino, Marqués de Misa, Bertola, Bodegas Varela; and the most famous of all Spanish table wines: the Rioja of Paternina.

To cope with such sales the number of Barnett branches is to be quickly increased to 250. They are already responsible for some 10 per cent of all sherry sales in Britain; the new expansion will lift the proportion to 15 per cent; and Rumasa's holdings are put at a third of Spain's sherry stocks.

At the moment Augustus Barnett span an extensive variety of sherries; in future they are likely to concentrate on the Rumasa range, but that will still allow their customers a wide choice. Presumably, too, they will make much of the Paternina Rioja which has a considerable reputation for quality but may have problems in producing the quantity to justify the expense of the Rumasa promotion.

It will take time for all the changes to work through: but the latest Barnett announcement offers Montilla – dry, medium, and cream – at 99p a bottle. Montilla, of course, is the wine from Andalusia which used often to be blended with, or sold as, sherry. Recently, though, the sherry shippers brought an action which, after many years, deprived the Montilla producers of the right to use the terms amontillado – which was originally derived from Montilla – oloroso or fino. The Rumasa Montillas will find a ready outlet.

Meanwhile Barnett offer as good value as is to be found in the wine trade of this country at the moment in 'double bottle magnums' of the Italian red Bardolino and Valpolicella and the white Soave at £1.89. A rate of 90p a bottle is most unusual nowadays. These three, though, are Italian bottled and carry the DOC imprimatur of authenticity. In several shops, a week's delivery has been cleared on the day it arrived. Already, too, the lower-taxed sherries in the range of fino, amontillado, and cream are coming through at £1.20.

The Merlot Isola Augusta – an Italian red – is 99p a bottle; the Sunset Golden, made in Marsala, as cheap as 79p.   *The Guardian*

Rumasa

Bottled History

September 1982. When most of us grew up, wine businesses were controlled by wine men; publishing by book men; garages by motor men. All that, though, has been shattered. The actuaries have taken over. Cartels, the multi-nationals, the supra-nationals are now in charge.

Odd, therefore, to find a wine man creating and ruling a financial empire. Jose Maria Ruiz-Mateos first set up his company in 1961, as a small sherry-broking business. Now called Rumasa, it owns the sherry houses of Williams Humbert and Harveys; the Rioja Bodegas Paternina, Bodegas Franco Espanolas; two major Spanish sparkling wines; has extensive holdings in Montilla, La Mancha and Spanish brandy; the 300 Augustus Barnett wineshops in Britain; and the Skjold Burne chain in Denmark.

Senor Mateos has moved out far beyond wine, though. Rumasa – still a family business, completely owned by Jose Maria, his four brothers and a sister – now controls more than 350 different companies.

Outside their commercial activities they have also acquired – reportedly for £100,000 – the Chicote Museum, the remarkable collection of wines, liqueurs and liquors built by the famous Madrid barman, Pedro 'Perico' Chicote. Rumasa have added 500 to the 10,000 bottles of their original purchase; but it was already unique. There are bottles of vodka from the private cellar of Nicholas II, the last Czar of Russia, Chinese chrysanthemum liqueur, wines in crystal and porcelain bottles.

No one knows what is in the two splendidly decorated Ming dynasty wine jars, for it was Chicote's firm purpose never to open a bottle. He is reported to have paid a nun to smuggle the bottle of Pius XII's favourite wine – the Spanish Diamante – from the Papal quarters. There is a decanter made for him by Picasso, and a 1788 cognac from the cellars of the Tour d'Argent restaurant in Paris. The American astronaut, Neil Armstrong, contributed a plastic cup of moon coffee from a space flight; and there is a brown medicine bottle of some presumably highly potent 'cough remedy' retailed in the United States during prohibition.

Bottles from Chiang Kai Shek, Luis Miguel Dominguin, Ava Gardner and Haile Selassie are outdone by two from China, labelled Ha Jie H Jiu and Hai Kai Chiew, of a clear liquid fierce enough to pickle the couple of lizards they contain. Chicote wanted his museum to remain in Madrid, and Rumasa have honoured his wish and have called it Patronato Museo Chicote. *The Guardian*

Family Houses of le Beaujolais

June 1978. The problem of the Beaujolais is that all the clichés about it are true. From the time the leaves unfold until they fall, it *is* a green sea of vines; the villages do stand up among the vineyards like islands; the vines do lap up to the very feet of the houses; and it is a place dedicated to wine. Nowhere is the French attitude to land – especially vine-growing land – more apparent. Particularly in the Haut-Beaujolais, even the cemeteries are strictly confined; year by year the gravestones seem ever closer to one another within their strict walls; the vines run up to them, too.

Perhaps it is for this reason that the villages of the area are all so small and closely built. The Beaujolais Villages, known by name wherever wine is drunk with knowledge as well as pleasure, are minute. The population of Juliénas is 649; of Chénas, 406; St-Amour, 538; Vaux-en-Beaujolais, the original of Clochemerle, 606; though Fleurie, where visitors are directed to cash cheques, has 1416 and Romanèche-Thorins has 1915 inhabitants, known specifically as Romanèchois.

Beaujeu, the old capital of the Beaujolais, certainly has as many as 2372 people but, faded, and not in the best vineyard land, it is the anachronism all former capitals become. Whether the railway and the Route Nationale 6 avoided the vineyards, or clung to the valley of the Saône, they and that river form the eastern boundary, plus a narrow buffer zone, of suitable vineyard land: the commercial centres of Villefranche-sur-Saône, Belleville, and Pontanevaux lie out on those traffic routes; and even Romanèche-Thorins stands in lesser vine country on the railway.

These – especially Villefranche – are the places where the trading is done. It would be an intrusion to join two men talking on the pavement edge outside the Café des Promenears on the Avenue Liberation in Villefranche on a Monday morning. They are negociant and vigneron striking a deal with the pièce (a Beaujolais barrel which holds 47 gallons) on one side, francs on the other: for this is the traditional, though unofficial, wine market of the region. These wines are known as Beaujolais; some as Beaujolais Villages; others again for their separate villages of Brouilly, St-Amour, Juliénas, Chénas, Moulin-à-Vent, Fleurie, Chiroubles, Morgon or Côte de Brouilly, rather than of specific vineyards. Thus the names of the negociants or, in some cases, of co-operatives, are important to buyers. An outstanding co-operative is that of Fleurie, whose president is the formidable, convivial and highly informed Mademoiselle Marguerite Chabert, daughter of the founder and, like him, also owner of the local charcuterie; and herself the pre-eminent Beaujolaise. Her wine is joyously drinkable, floral indeed, scented, light, fresh and full of flavour.

Pontanevaux, strung along the main road, is a village of shippers. Prominent among them is the house of Loron, pre-eminently concerned 'to preserve the flavour of the Gamay' (grape). Long established, and distinguished by the high quality of its shipments to this country, like so many of these firms, it is a family owned company. Members of the family may own vineyards separately, the company can buy from them or any other growers. There is no boasting about size; but Loron, standing modestly beside the road, not even displaying the name, with a storage capacity of 80,000 hectolitres (10,640,000 bottles), are probably the biggest shippers in the region. Thorin, also of Pontanevaux, have a reputation for single vineyard crus.

The family of Pasquier-Desvignes has been at the Domaine du

Marquisat, on the eastern side of the Brouilly vineyards, since 1420. Their courtyard is admirably planted with lime trees, ideally sited to wreck the bumpers of backing cars. Marc Pasquier-Desvignes is the president of the Beaujolais-Mâconnais Wine Syndicate; a Beaujolais purist, and enthusiast for the crus of the villages and the export trade; he sent his son to the University of Wisconsin. This is another house of impeccable quality.

The firm of Mommessin at La Grange Saint-Pierre, on the edge of Mâcon, are also Beaujolais specialists; Jean Mommessin is one of the wise men of the region, a considerable thinker about wine, its history and politics.

Most of these are long established family houses based originally on vineyard holdings. Georges Duboeuf of Romanèche-Thorins, however, is a newcomer among them; involved in production only through a share, with his brother, in a white wine vineyard in the Mâconnais. An original; dressed in the fashion of the 1970s; lean, alert, quick-thinking and fast-moving, he has tasted professionally since he was 16. He will go through a cellar awarding marks – for bouquet, flavour, alcohol, acidity, body – to each cask, buying those of his choice and ranking them in the hierarchy of his cellars. He maintains that he has never bought or sold a cask without tasting it personally. *The Guardian*

4
Palace, Museum and Auction Room

A Plea for the Gin Palace

May 1951. More than 2300 English inns have now been scheduled as of such historical or architectural importance that they are to be preserved against destruction or vital alteration. This could be taken to mean that the English pub is preserved for ever.

Unfortunately that is not the case. These inns – like the other protected buildings – were practically all built before 1830. That is well enough for the Regency, Georgian or Tudor houses, although the interiors of some of them have suffered changes of staggering proportions and lack of taste. What, however, of the Victorian pub? Look, for instance, at The Salisbury, in St Martin's Lane. Could anyone devise a better pub than that with its glowing mahogany and its mirror-magnified space?

It is easy to condemn Victorian architecture and much of it was indeed monstrous. But the pub of that period is an exception. It was not built to stun the beholder: it was meant to look homely. So 'gin palace' architecture merged much of Georgian mellowness – notice for instance the pediment that carries the sign of The Half Moon in Holloway – with Victorian elaboration. If, in that prosperous age, it also looked prosperous the Victorians were not likely to object. So, in the last century, the pub – that is the tavern as distinct from the hotel or coaching house – ceased to be a small and furtive place and became large and solid.

The tavern of earlier days had been a house – even a cottage – revolving round the kitchen: a series of rooms linked by their common use.

The Victorian 'gin palace' was different. It was one huge room with a central bar, but divided by partitions into separate drinking compartments for the different social levels or aspirations of its customers.

There were intimate alcoves, like those at The Edinburgh Castle whose magnificently bracketed, wrought-iron lamp hangs out into Mornington Crescent. There were little glazed louvres set round the bar at face level so that a customer might converse confidentially with the landlord, or make himself a nine-inch cubicle in which to sip his drink privately. You may see them still in the Fitzroy Tavern, in Windmill Street, where they have been carefully preserved, with the gilt-lettered mirrors, the carved arch, the overmantel-type shelves and the iron grille.

In place of the former smallness and relative darkness now came huge windows and high ceilings. Even the partitions between the bars were light – mahogany panelling or glass. In glass the Victorian architect or furnisher was superbly served; he could still command the work of vast numbers of first-class glass engravers.

Look – for all its dully modernized exterior – at the house sign engraved in colour on the mirrors in The Eagle, by Camden Road Station; the advertisements for penny soup and halfpenny bread-and-cheese cut on the glass panels of the pillars in Whitelock's in Leeds; the head of the Iron Duke on the windows of The Wellington at Turnpike Lane. Above all, if you would see acid-etched and cut-glass at its richest go to The Assembly House in Kentish Town, at the moment being so intelligently redecorated. Acres of glass sparkle floral designs across it and back from the mirrors and, at the bottom of one front window, the creator of it all has signed his work – 'JAMES, KENTISH TOWN'.

The huge over-all ceilings, too – like the one in The Crown and Sceptre in Great Titchfield Street, or, again, The Assembly House – were glorious opportunities for vast revels in elaborate plasterwork or anaglypta paper.

The handles of beer engines became little triumphs of the potter's craft. The huge core of bottle racks, towering to the ceiling in rolls and curlicues of carefully worked mahogany, invited the display of brightly glazed pottery barrels or – and most of them have gone now – rows of brass railings: you may see them still in The Black Horse in Rathbone Place. There were gay tiles like those at The Porcupine whose plaster-gilt sign nestles heraldically above its door round a corner of Charing Cross Road.

Gaslight from elaborate chandeliers reflected back from the depths of the profoundly polished mahogany and made cut-glass wink like a nest of diamonds. Low-wattage or overshaded electric lights are but pinchbeck substitutes for those many mantled lights.

The solid exteriors discourage alteration; the unique interiors are more vulnerable to 'jazzing up'. The Nag's Head at Holloway, like, alas, many another Victorian interior, has been modernized; it is now done out in lighter wood; it is new, very hygienic – and utterly without character.

Let us beware the tendency to condemn the entire Victorian pub as 'out of date', to tear out its insides and substitute for them plastics, synthetics and veneers which do not compare in workmanship or durability with the fittings they replace. Even some of those I have quoted have flawed the general effect by destroying other period-pieces as pleasant as those they have retained.

There is a sense of permanence in the Victorian 'gin palace', to which its successors may aspire in vain.

Let us hope that, by the time the 'gin palaces' are old enough for the planners to recognize them as worth preserving, there will still be some left to preserve.   *The Evening News*

Of Rare Vintage

May 1980. Once the earnest imbiber accepts that wine museums contain no wine, the only barrier is removed. The collection at Château Mouton-Rothschild, created with exquisite taste and prodigal finance, contains many items that transcend the bounds of the subject. It should be seen by everyone, interested in wine or not, who visits

the Bordeaux area. At Beaune there is an althogether different concept; nearer the vineyard earth than the Baron's, but none the worse
for that.

The British wine museum has been created, not surprisingly, by
Harveys, best known as the sherry people but, in fact, all round wine
merchants. In the past they have brought out some imaginative illustrated and sensitively produced lists and literature. The museum,
called The History of Wine Collection, is, to borrow Harry Lauder's
phrase, 'a splendacious affair'. It has two versions. One is permanent, in the twelfth century cellars at the mercantile centre of Bristol, under what was Gaunt's House for four hundred years until it
was destroyed in the bombing of November 1940. The other is a
travelling exhibition constantly on tour throughout Britain.

Happily, when they moved their main operation to Whitchurch,
on the outskirts of the city, Harveys retained the old site where they
had been since 1796. They established the museum in the cellar, and
accommodated its overflow in a restaurant, the best in Bristol, above
it.

The museum was based on the E. J. Pratt collection – probably
the finest of its kind – of more than 500 silver wine labels (or bottle
tickets) which Harveys bought in 1960. Recognizing the opportunity
that offered, they have not only added to it but extended its range,
buying up other collections to create a visual history of wine.

The main gallery, dominated by a solera system constructed from
a series of vast sherry butts, contains the pictorial display, dealing
with the methods and characteristics of wines of the main producing
countries and types.

In the Clifton cellar is a collection of old and modern wine merchants' artefacts; along one wall, sheets of popular wine songs of the
nineteenth century (like George Leybourne's *Champagne Charlie* and
Cool Burgundy Ben), on another, caricatures and prints, mainly
eighteenth century; there are corkscrews of every kind, many of
amazing ingenuity; while the Jack Harvey library contains some extremely enviable rarities. Beyond it is The Unicorn, a reconstruction
of a medieval English inn.

The peaks of the museum, though, lie in the silver and glass. Although the earliest decanter labels were made of parchment, bone,
wood or ivory, by the mid-eighteenth century those in wealthy

British households were often the work of highly skilled silversmiths. The labels varied widely in shape and lettering; and some were attractively enamelled. This collection ranges from early and scarce types of 1734 to 1769, to the latter half of the last century.

The tastevins go back even further, to 1667 (a two-handed model from Paris), many of them from the Grants of St James collection. There are, too, an impressive pair of silver-gilt coaster wagons made for the Earl of Hastings by the famous silversmith, Ben Smith, in 1828.

The glass was brought together by Peter Lazarus in a historic exhibition beginning with bottle-making (the oldest example a mid-seventeenth-century earthenware jug, labelled Sack) based on the Pemberton Collection, and a progression of decanters of great elegance. The wine glasses are a selection of the highest quality. Most striking is one engraved by David Wolff, the great eighteenth-century Dutch stipple engraver, a minor miracle of creative delicacy.

It progresses, though, through all the major developments in European glass-making from the early, immediately post-Ravenscroft period of lead glass, 1690 to 1725; through air, opaque and colour-twist stems, engraved, facet cut, Newcastle, painted and coloured glasses.

The permanent exhibition may be visited in Denmark Street, Bristol; there is nothing else like it in this country and, if it is historically informative and educational on its subject, it also contains many outstanding examples of the art of the silversmith and, above all, of the glassmaker. *The Guardian*

Château Latour

June 1977. Next Thursday evening Christie's will devote an entire auction in their 'Great Rooms' at 8 King Street, St James's, to the wines of Château Latour.

No such sale has ever been held before. The 'Grand Vin de Latour' is arguably the finest of all clarets; perhaps, indeed, of all red wines; for that matter, of all wines. Its vines are still replaced by the jardinage method in which, instead of the vineyard being replanted in sections, each vine is allowed to reach maximum age and is then replaced as a single operation. So the average age of the vines is high; and the result is a low yield of a full, alcoholic wine of immense body.

When it is young, a Latour is often hard; with age – perhaps from a great vintage, like 1945, as much as 16 years – it becomes huge, always essentially masculine, a rich, noble liquor of incomparable quality. Perhaps the outstanding attribute of the château is its capacity to produce fine wines in a bad year, as it has done so often that it can virtually be said there is no such thing as a bad Latour.

The château has changed. In 1948 it was a place of ancient character and memories; dim and slightly dusty but generous in the manner of an earlier age. Its owner, the Marquis de Beaumont, in tweeds and cycling breeches, peered amiably through pince-nez at his visitors. Pierre Brugière, his régisseur, already 69 – he was 84 when he retired in 1963 – contributed to the atmosphere of a place where the clocks had stopped in the nineteenth century. Dinner, served in little more than half light, was modestly perfect French country cooking; the wines – apart from a white Domaine de Chevalier with the fish – were of the château.

Latour was first named in 1378; its vines in the seventeenth century, when it was bought by the Marquis de Ségur whose descendants owned it until 1963. A hundred years later it was known for its 'Qualité Anglaise'. Fourteen years ago a controlling interest was sold to the English Pearson Group of Lord Cowdray, with Harveys of Bristol and the former family owners as the other shareholders.

Now it is an extremely up-to-date establishment; the first of the premier cru vineyards to install stainless steel vats; everything bright, clean, modern and efficient. Only the wine has not changed. With David Pollock as chairman and two Bordelais, Henry Martin and Jean-Paul Gardère, as managers, tradition has been maintained in modern trading conditions.

When the Pearson group took over, they discovered a unique collection of early documents and archives of the château, preserved by the previous owners, which have been incorporated in a vast, two-volume history of Latour unparalleled in the literature of wine. The family had also maintained a prodigious library of their bottles, and a cross-section of that collection now forms the widest range of vintages of a single château ever offered for sale.

The auctioneers assert that this is not an unloading and observe 'The Bordeaux market has regained confidence; the market is buoyant. Latour is neither overstocked nor short of cash. You can take it from us that this sale is transparently a virtuoso display: a "just see what we are, and what we can do" type of operation.'

Eighty-two vintages are listed, including the 1863 which has never been sold before, a number of pre-phylloxera bottles, and some from every vintage between 1916 and 1974. Every bottle comes straight from the cellars of Château Latour itself; undisturbed since it was bottled except for timely and expert recorking when needed. Estimated prices per dozen bottles, per six magnums or per lot (sometimes of mixed years for collectors), range between £15 (a bottle of the generally poor year of 1910) and £800 for a dozen of the great vintage of 1945.

The catalogue has a short history of Latour by Harry Waugh, a 'founder director' of the new company; quite erudite tasting notes from Michael Broadbent's vast records; and details of the 314 lots. The first evening wine sale Christie's have ever held is on Thursday, 16 June at 8.30 pm – 'convenient for those returning from the Gold Cup meeting at Ascot'.   *The Guardian*

5
Artefacts and Other Things

Slipping Out for a Drink

October 1982. The corkscrew remains one of the few mixed blessings bestowed upon the human race. No one knows who invented it. That was recognized in an anonymous poem as long ago as 1732, only 60 years after the first reference to 'A Steel Worme used for drawing Corks out of Bottles', then known as a bottle screw.

> *Oh shame. The Bottle Scrue remains*
> *The bottle screw whose worth, whose use,*
> *All men confess that love the juice:*
> *Forgotten fleets that Man to whom*
> *We owe th' invention in his tomb.*
> *No public honours grace his name*
> *No pious bard records his fame;*
> *Elate with pride and joy I see*
> *That deathless task reserved for me.*

The first truly effective way of stoppering fluids – cork – had generally replaced the old wooden plugs and oil or clay-soaked rag stoppers by the seventeenth century.

Humorous writers had for so long recited the problems and disasters of those opening bottles by more primitive means that the invention was hailed as a Godsend. In his will (1740) Dean Swift bequeathed to Prebendary Grattan of St Audeon's 'my gold bottle screw which he gave me'.

Nowadays those who bottle liquids increasingly avoid the use of cork for reasons of cost. Plastic stoppers, the 'crown' cork or cap, tear-off steel strips, the rubberised caps of the bag-in-box operation, have all been used. Nothing, however, performs the task of keeping fine – and less than fine – wine in good condition so well as cork. That is especially true of champagne and other sparkling wine. Simply enough, cork presents an impermeable surface to most liquid. 'Corked' or ullaged wine – which might be attributed to faulty corks – is rare.

Its use has given rise to two quite blameless but, for some, irresistible activities: the invention and collection of corkscrews. There has been a surprising number of variations on the theme of the 'simple' corkscrew – between 1795 and 1908, 300 odd patents for corkscrews were registered at the British Patent Office. Many were ingenious, if long-winded in operation. Others were opulently extravagant, such as the American 'lady lou' consisting of 'bottle stopper, cap lifter and corkscrews (inside stopper), the top containing five ivory poker dice'.

Collectors have paid up to £400 in the auction room for Victorian contraptions which not long ago were left unsold in the penny trays at jumble sales.

Many modern corkscrews, especially those designed as souvenirs, are ineffective; more likely to pull out the middle of the cork than the cork itself. Ideally the helix should be strong and even, wide (most important) and at least two and three quarter inches long with the point set off centre.

Ultimately the answer was bound to be simple: it is also ingenious. Bernard Watney and Homer Babbidge end their scholarly *Corkscrews for Collectors* (1981) with 'We now await the ultimate in corkscrew design from Herbert Allen of Texas . . . employing modern technical knowhow from space research and oil rig design.' That is the Screwpull; 'the infallible corkscrew'.

Mr Allen, who 'has some 300 patents in oil-field equipment to his credit', is reported as saying 'with a chuckle' from his home in Houston: 'I'm a country boy from East Texas: I never had any trouble getting a cork out, but I noticed that many of my friends did.'

To the established formula Mr Allen has added an anti-friction coating material to the helix and fitted a guide-sleeve. The Screwpull, which made a tentative appearance here a couple of years ago, is not cheap at £6.95, but it hardly falls short of its description as 'the infallible corkscrew'.

The Guardian

On the Stocks

March 1974. How shall I store my wine? is the most frequent question in any wine correspondent's post. There is no simple answer because so much depends on what kind of wine is involved, the type of building it is to be kept in, the quantity to be stored and, above all, the time it is to be held.

The average family turnover for two or three months will come to no harm on the larder floor, or anywhere else in the house – preferably out of the sun and away from the heating system, but not in the refrigerator. Many people keep their current supply in the cupboard under the stairs, in a cold fireplace or the sideboard and it comes to no harm over a few months. It is best stored on its side to keep the cork sealed – spirits should be kept upright because they attack cork.

Wine is tougher than is sometimes thought. In 1954 there was a bottle of Château Latour 1947 standing beside the powerful striplighting in the tropically humid bar at Jakarta Airport. Although it was covered with long-settled grime, and no one could remember when it had first been put there, it seemed a reasonable gamble at 30*s* to drink with our cold meat. When it transpired that, in addition to the normal sales tax, it had to carry a further 100 per cent 'because it is for pleasure' it appeared a less attractive bargain. In the event, though rather over-chambré, it was something more than drinkable; its quality was unmistakable. Less distinguished wines could not survive such conditions for long.

Everyone must decide for himself where hand to mouth supplies end and where the activities which need an adequate cellar – collecting, storing, and maturing – begin. The average cellar, so long as it does not house a heating plant, needs only to be shielded from draughts to serve. The basement flat-dweller has the facility inbuilt, and might easily locate the original bin-recesses. Wartime, outdoor, concrete-bedded air-raid shelters can be suitably cool – in the range between 10°C and 15°C. Some people simply use the cavity under ground level floorboards, but this is generally dusty and – for the wine – dangerously draughty.

A hall cupboard on a cool side of the house or in an unheated passage will do well, particularly if it is insulated – though not on the wall side – with Polystyrene.

Eventually the would-be wine collector must decide – or take advice on – whether his accommodation is adequate for longterm storage. This is no matter for taking risks. Fine wine is too expensive to be put in jeopardy; there is no money back if it turns to vinegar because it is kept in too hot an atmosphere. For those who want to keep a stock but cannot do so at home, most wine merchants provide facilities for their customers' purchases, though the increased buying – especially for investment – in recent years has meant that some of them have no storage capacity left.

Racking can be as simple as taking the space between two walls of a room (perhaps at the back of the pantry) and simply laying bottles, one row on top of another – with laths at intervals – up to the ceiling. This method is generally used for a considerable quantity of the same wine since bottles can only be taken from the top.

The original cartons, turned on their sides, will serve – to a depth of two or three – provided the top layer is emptied first. Wooden beer crates can be useful.

The best known racks in this country are those produced in square, single-bottle openings of metal secured on wooden corner pieces. They are strong and secure and can be slanted or staggered to fit under the stairs or in any asymmetric recess in the house.

In America many serious wine collectors use insulated and thermostatically controlled, above-ground wooden 'cellars' which can be of considerable size. No doubt they will soon be available in this country – at a high price which could still compare favourably with that of excavating a cellar.

Those who plan to expand their storage may be interested in the Rutherford rack. Made of a tough, virtually unbreakable, black plastic, the basic model – 16½in. × 14in. × 8½in. – will take a dozen bottles separately cradled, or two dozen halves. The racks can be extended, attached or detached vertically or laterally, in four-bottle units, by their preformed and inbuilt couplings, as easily as it sounds.

In simplest terms, keeping wine in the British climate is no problem over months: over years, it becomes the different – and possibly expensive – problem of preserving valuable property.

The Guardian

Laying it Down

September 1976. The wine collector is largely a British or American phenomenon, indulging a mild, amusing hobby. If a Frenchman of the wine-producing areas collects wine that is a much rarer, and quite different, matter. When the remarkable Dr Barolet of Beaune – where he lived on the Faubourg Saint Nicholas – died in 1968, he left a cellar of more than 100,000 bottles of fine burgundies.

As well as those from his own vineyards and some bought from others, he would buy grapes from different vineyards and vinify them in the traditional fashion for himself. Many items of his collection, including some legendary cuvées, are still in circulation and may be bought.

The doctor, however, collected only burgundies; the smaller British collector has a wider range, though no comparable depth. He will scour wine merchants' shops, though that is not so simple nor so rewarding as it once was since so many became parts of chains, disseminating standardized bulk purchases.

Increasingly he must turn to the one-shop business that keeps going by shunning the high street and maintaining a mail order trade in cases of a dozen – preferably, for the collector, mixed dozens.

Collectors in the Manchester area can still go to Whitwhams, who have now moved back to their former half-timbered establishment in the Old Market Place at Altrincham. There anyone who can afford it – and is prepared to take the risk with such age – can buy the great pre-phylloxera rarities: Château Lafite 1864, a fair but not great year, will cost £260 a bottle; Latour 1878, an erratic vintage, £185. Before everyone is frightened out of sight, a Château Cos d'Estournel 1955 is £8.30; a 1959 Château Lagrange £5.90, or Palmer £12.50.

These are single occasion wines. It is possible to buy unusual, but mildly priced, wines to keep; to drink when the subject comes up, or merely to raise it in conversation. One of the collectors' wine merchants is Duchy Vintners of Truro. They are, clearly, enthusiasts. Their list, which is splendid catalogue shopping, is also partly a travelogue; and they now issue a newsletter. They tend to emphasize Alsatian, burgundy and the great Italians; and while they sell genuinely cheap carafe wines, they incline towards the good bottle, prices between £2 and £3.

There are 14 Alsatians of nine different kinds – Sylvaner, Pinot Blanc, Riesling, Muscat, Tokay, Edelzwicker, Pinot Noir, Gewürztraminer and sparkling – from £1.78 (four below £2) to £6 a bottle; a mixed dozen of four different types is £22.

A dozen different Beaujolais are priced between £1.85 for the Cave Ragot de Malvozaux, and £2.43 for the Moulin à Vent 1973, and Quinson 1973; the Beaujolais Blanc is £2.20.

Among the notable and fine Italians, Barbera d'Alba 1973 is £2.06; Carema 1967 or 1969, from the highest vineyards in the world on the Val d'Aosta, £2.33; and Ghemme, once said to cure 'all physical and moral ailments', the 1970 version, £2.98.

All these are fine robust Italian reds. The greatest red wine of Italy, though, is probably the Brunello di Montalcino, matured four years in wood before it is bottled. Big and dry and tannic, it should be opened at least 12 hours before drinking, and will not hurt for 24. The 1968 costs £6.64. Their vermouth is Gaudin Chambéry (£2.04), the best of them; and there is the wild strawberry-flavoured Chambéryzette for the same price.

For the hard-up mind-drinker, as well as prospective purchasers, the list is free from Duchy Vintners, 9 New Bridge Street, Truro, Cornwall. *The Guardian*

Investing in Wine

Should you invest in wine? Twenty years ago most people who knew the wine trade would have said 'No'. Since then, though, many things have happened on so many different levels, that many wine investors have made money. On the other hand, some of those who plunged late into the vintages of the 1960s had their fingers badly burnt – in some cases, burnt off. So, for fear of scaring anyone off, or driving anyone too far in, we must look at all the pieces which make up the wine world jigsaw as it affects Britain in 1985.

Until lately wine drinkers were in a minority here. Some people drank sweet sherries, cheap port – even port-and-lemonade. Primarily, though, we were a nation of beer drinkers. Serious wine drinking was a class matter, confined to the upper and middle classes. Wine merchants' shops were for the privileged and specialists.

It is difficult to trace all the changes in precise order. Certainly many people took to wine drinking – often because there was no alternative – in North Africa, Italy or, later, France, during war service. Soon afterwards package holidays on the European mainland produced a large number of converts to it who, returning home, persuaded others to follow them: that increased demand. In a whole series of consequences, supermarkets began to sell wine; small dealers with wholesale licences (which allowed them to sell only in dozens) and cash and carry stores followed them. All this in turn brought down prices from the traditional wine merchant whose profits had provided capital for him to mature wines in his cellars. Dealers' tastings were followed by wine appreciation clubs with lectures and subscription tastings for members. So knowledge spread. The number of wine books published increased from two or three a year to dozens. This, in turn, prompted specific wine tours.

Meanwhile technological advances produced an improved standard of world wine production; more good wine at lower prices which were driven lower still by the competition from wine-producing countries for export markets. Between the two wars a good wine merchant would stock French, German and perhaps Italian table wines; and such fortified wines as sherry, port and madeira. Since they were all known to be good and obtainable at relatively low prices, there was no need to prowl cheaper markets for uncertain qualities. In the last twenty years, however, vastly improved Italian, Australian, Spanish and Portuguese wines have fought their way into the British markets; they are accommodated by the vast growth in the number of British wine drinkers.

Britain, though, is not alone. Wine in America suddenly changed from a rich man's hobby to a national enthusiasm; the Japanese began to buy it, at first for their hotel trade. The Dutch, Belgians and Scandinavians had always imported some wine. Now they increased their consumption. All this changed the world pattern. The wine-producing countries had always consumed their own products but generally at a cottage level. Britain had long been a minority quality buyer; now she bought far more. Demand from America, where a long purse went with high-quality ambitions, increased staggeringly; and as overseas demand grew, producers found it harder to meet it.

Now, by amazing coincidence, 1961 in France, especially Bordeaux, was a fine vintage, expected to last well. Opening prices of the premiers crus (Châteaux Mouton-Rothschild, Lafite-Rothschild, Latour, Haut-Brion and Margaux) in 1963-64, long before they were fit to drink, indeed before many of them were even bottled, varied between £28 and £39 a case of a dozen bottles: by the 1968-69 auction season, the figure was £70 to £82; by 1970-71, £145 to £175; this year they will fetch between £2000 and £2600. Neither has this happened only to the premiers crus: the 1961 Château Palmer, a troisième cru, made £16-£20 a dozen in 1963; £80 in 1971; this year a staggering £2300. The Pomerol Château Pétrus 1961, £29 a dozen in 1963, made £575 a *bottle* last year. To complete this varied but fascinating picture, in 1966 Christie's re-emerged as wine auctioneers on a high level, where would-be buyers might bid for the bottles they wanted, and prices would, presumably, find their 'natural' level.

So profits have been made; and are still being made. The 1983 clarets – 1983, not the vaunted 1982 – were first offered for sale early last year. Now they show these rises: Lafite-Rothschild £304 to £528; Latour £296 to £456; Palmer £127 to £207. Vintage ports of 1955, about £13 to £17 a dozen in 1966, now fetch anything from £180 to £680.

It is not difficult to buy and keep wine; whether it makes a profit is a different matter. The rough rule in the trade used to be that only the best clarets and vintage ports were good investments. That might now be extended to include a wider range of the cru clarets, with a few Pomerols and St-Emilions, fine red burgundies (though they do not always last well); even fewer white burgundies; some sweet white Bordeaux, Château d'Yquem, of course, and Coutet, Climens and Guiraud; the rare Trockenbeerenauslese and Beerenauslese of the great Rhine and Moselle estates; and vintage champagne. Not all the others will turn out to be worthwhile investments. The producers have set themselves to take a share of the investors' profits at their end. So margins are much smaller than in the 1960s. The better wine merchants will send catalogues for early purchase of chosen wines; arrange for transport at the right time; and payment of customs duty. Then there is the problem of storage; if the investor has not first-class cellar accommodation (consistent cool temperature, no light, vibration or damp) he will have to pay for space and handling. The best wines, too, take some years – of interest – to mature to optimum condition and, therefore, optimum value. On the other hand, the financial experts warn us that inflation is likely to climb, so that material possessions will appreciate faster than money.

The essential is to taste and understand; young clarets can be harsh and tanninny; the skill lies in realizing their future. Or you can quickly – but quickly – follow the advice of the early expert tasters you trust; you will not then buy at *quite* the lowest price, but you will be in early. Learn which fine wines you enjoy. Taste as soon as you can; and regularly. Watch your investment values through *Decanter* magazine, *Which? Wine Monthly* and the annual *Christie's Price Index of Vintage Wine*. The joy of investing in wine is that, if it does not make money, you can always drink it and enjoy it – so long as you have not left it until it goes over the top!

And, in closing, a few suggestions you should not lose on, certainly not if you enjoy drinking them, and always remembering that such investments is a gamble. Clarets: Châteaux Ausone, Cos d'Estournel, Gruaud-Larose, La Lagune. Sauternes: Châteaux Suduiraut, la Tour-Blanche, Rieussec. The best Moselles of J. J. Prum, the best Rhine wines of Burklin Wolf. In Alsace, the *vendange tardive* Rieslings of Hugel; the Hungarian Tokay Essence, as issued, will usually appreciate. From Italy, good vintages of Antinori Chianti, Tignanello, and Brunello di Montalcino. Spain, the rare Vega Sicilia. From the Rhône, in such great years as 1982 and, especially, 1983, the Hermitage of Jaboulet Aîné and Gerard Chave. Oh! for a cellar of these; to save, to sell, or better still, to drink at their best. What an investment that last would be! *Countrywide* No. 10, 1985

Grace at the Board

April 1951. The blindfold-tasting competitions, of which one sometimes hears, always seem to be rather like cricket played without bats. The power of sight has essential qualities to add to the pleasures of eating and drinking – a fact which some are inclined to deny, but which has fathered some great art.

Indeed, the brightly painted poster which advertises some tasty food or appetizer relies entirely upon the association of seeing with enjoyment of eating, when it makes our mouth water with a picture of a meal.

It must be a *coloured* representation, however, for the colours of food possess almost a texture of their own.

It is, of course, to please the eye that a good cook often employs colouring matter in a dish and always arranges food with such care – even those who deride the practice as an affectation may be heard to object to having food 'slapped on a plate'.

The wine expert can not only deduce much of the origin of a wine from looking at it, but he also takes a sensuous pleasure in the look of wine. Thus, the glass-maker has come to the aid of the drinker with drinking vessels of utterly clear glass so that the eye may enjoy the colour of the wine without interruption. The good wine glass, too, is made in proportions designed to please the eye and, often, engraved to give an associated pleasure to drinking.

Glasses and tankards, however, can add to the drinker's pleasure through the sense of touch. For instance, the firm but delicate touch of thin glass is the perfect 'presentation' for wine; the round metallic strength of pewter matches beer; the cool edge of a cut-glass tumbler seems to add to the refreshing quality of iced lemonade.

Because, from time immemorial, those who enjoyed eating and drinking were conscious that touch and sight added to the grace of a meal, the tables of princes through the centuries have been miniature art galleries.

Benvenuto Cellini's great silver salt-cellar is held to be as great an example of his art as his 'Perseus', and eminent painters decorated the plates and dishes of the French court.

Art on the table has not, however, stopped at the edges of the banqueting tables of the wealthy. Any museum in England can show the unelaborate but dignified and handsome table ware of the ordinary household of earlier days.

One has been looking recently at beer glasses such as were used in the taverns of England a hundred years ago and admiring the crystal brightness of the glass, the fine proportions of the bowls and the wide round feet; and seen, too, the designs of bright simple colours with which the Victorians – by no means so inartistic as is sometimes suggested – decorated plates and mugs so that the eye shared the designer's gaiety.

Wherefore, today, looking at plain plates and squat, heavy white cups, I wonder if we are 'progressing' away from one of the oldest extra pleasures of the table. *The Evening News*

Three Wine Glasses

The sceptic, determined not to be deceived by subtlety for subtlety's sake, is frequently hard to convince on the subject of the finer points of wine drinking: particularly he may be incredulous of niceties expounded by those to whom wine is not native. He will maintain, with some justification, that there is an artificiality in the approach of certain Englishmen to wine – an artificiality not to be observed in the attitude of the French. Indeed, it may be said that the eminently *practical* gusto of the Frenchman accounts for so many of his cultural triumphs lying in the realm of eating and drinking.

Thus, it is with the delight of defending counsel finding a loophole in the law that one discovers an exacting French dictum on the subject of wine glasses. Most convincingly for our purpose, too, it was Maurice des Ombiaux, a Burgundian of Burgundians and deeply attached to his sun-soaked native earth, who declared that, for the proper appreciation of French wine, 'Il faut un beau verre de cristal très fin en forme de calice, haute de pied et de bonne dimension.' Since these are the words of a man not given to extravagance, we may examine the implications of his statement without any sense of affectation. 'Cristal très fin,' we may assume, is the normal demand for assistance in visual pleasure in wine, but it may, too, echo a desire for a complementary elegance – and tactile sensation. 'En forme de calice,' surely, argues a sense of reverence – an imaginative association – for the religious connotation is inescapable. Sternest practicality *may*, however, argue that these requirements are solely those of one who wishes to observe clearly the colour and clarity of his wine, in the first instance, and to inhale its bouquet, in the second. The third qualification, however, cannot be thus argued away – 'un . . . verre . . . haut de pied' is a purely imaginative demand. The foot of a glass is of significance to the connoisseur of glass because it is invested with considerable significance as to the period and method of its manufacture. But, so far as the purely physical factors of drinking wine are concerned, it cannot be relevant. Surely, here, des Ombiaux's entire conception is an image of elevation and importance – 'high of foot' as an automatic interpretation of pride. Finally, the phrase 'de bonne dimension' of a wine glass has no connection, we may assume, with a desire to consume a large quantity of wine, for, provided the bottle be to hand, the size of the glass is, *quantitatively* speaking, of no significance. It may be, in part, an indication of justifiable rebellion against the old heresy of 'A large glass for a poor wine, a small glass for a great wine' which was, presumably, in its turn, born of easy access to indifferent wine for tippling purposes as opposed to the economic obstacle to generous consumption of finer wines. If, however, the entire statement is of the imaginative quality which our third ingredient so strongly indicates, then 'de bonne dimension' is undoubtedly a symbol of the magnificence and generosity of wine and of the immensity of the gesture of drinking it.

'C'est aux vins que l'on reconnait l'élégance d'un dîner' said the Marquis de Castellane and it is this quality of elegance which animates – in its best form – the desire to dine well. Granted the axiom that there are refinements that heighten the satisfaction of each of the appetites, it follows that the glass plays as great a part – if not the same part – in the enjoyment of wine as it does in that of brandy.

The expert judge can usually date a wine glass merely by looking at it and touching it. There are, obviously, innumerable shades of quality in glasses, and to deny the importance of this quality in wine drinking is to deny the sensitivity of the lips as a sensitivity genuinely comparable with that of the palate. Pausing to observe the paucity of historically great glass of French manufacture, we may proceed to argue that the variety, on a high level of quality, of English glass is such that it may provide quite the ideal for every type of wine.

The complete fitness of a particular type of glass for a specific wine is a composite quality. There must, certainly, be physical fitness – the glass must contain an adequate quantity of wine, it must be clear enough in texture to allow the eye to savour the lights in the wine, and it must be of such shape as both to retain the bouquet and to present it readily to the savouring nostrils. Moreover, it should be comfortable to hold and should have a 'toyable' weight – a respect in which the light but elegant Dutch glasses signally fall short of the ideal. Next comes the aesthetic factor. A satisfactory glass is pleasing to the eye: it will avoid such excessive decoration as makes much of the finest Venetian glasswork of Murano of curiosity value rather than artistically pleasing; on the other hand, it should avoid the starker forms of streamlined modernity which elevate hygiene and harshness to the level of artistic aims. The proportion must be good, the shape of itself pleasant, and the decoration – whether it be spirals, engraving or cutting – should, above all, fit the *character* of the glass. Finally, there is imaginative quality, wherein technical knowledge of glass may heighten the enjoyment of wine and, also, where associative values may heighten the emotions which wine brings out.

Because these three ingredients must always be differently blended in different persons, anyone's examples of particular glasses for certain wines must be solely personal. So far as any other connoisseur of wine or glass is concerned, these suggestions must claim to be no more than examples.

My first selection would be a glass for my first wine – claret. It would be an eighteenth-century glass of the 1750-1780 period, with a waisted bowl and an air-twist stem. The air-twist stem may be dismissed as a purely idiosyncratic choice, and the waisted bowl is sufficiently ordinary to provoke little argument. The true quality of this glass is implicit in its dating. The metal of a 1750-1780 English glass contains a high proportion of lead, which endows it with such a remarkably soft texture that even the sternest and most business-minded glass dealers speak of it as 'velvet'. Even to look at, it is gentle – with its *air* rather than *tint* of blue – and it is silky to the touch. The proportions of the wine glasses of that period of taste are immediately delightful: they add their own footnote of refinement to the pleasure of regarding a fine claret in this glass – whose lead-metal subtly enhances and emphasizes *to the eye* that delicate roundness which is the characteristic of the Bordeaux wine. The bowl presents the bouquet adequately, and to drink from it is to feel against the drinker's lips the full lip of a glass which matches perfectly the gentle temperature of correctly chambré claret. The final ingredient which such a glass contributes to enjoyment is partly associative. The glasses of this period were hand-made, and this knowledge gives a relishable background of craftsmanship. Moreover, the creatively minded glass-workers of the period had such a desire for variety that there are deliberate variations between glass and glass – often minute, but always definite to such a degree that one's particular glass or set is virtually unique. This factor is emphasized by the involuntary variations between hand-finished glasses which, lacking the precise uniformity of machine-made products, lack also their monotony – substituting the warmer quality of human-handed difference even between a 'pair' of glasses. This difference, unlike the 'error' of the machine, substituted one minute artistic curve or proportion for another and has left it, down the years, for the eye to perceive and the contemplative mind to relish.

For white wine, my glass is sixty or seventy years younger – a straight-sided Victorian glass of about 1840, engraved with a sailing ship under way, and with a heavy, terraced foot. This glass belongs to the period when the characteristic English metal had moved to the other extreme from the soft lead glass of the previous century. The glass of the bowl itself is thin, yet it has the hardness of a diamond and a startling brilliance. To take a well-iced white wine in it is to watch forming on its sides a mist which seems, such is the clear fineness of the metal, as thick as the glass itself. To drink from it is to feel, cool and hard, a metal as sharply refreshing in its touch on the lips as the wine is on the palate, and the hand relishes the severe, cold cutting of the foot.

Thirdly, for burgundy, I would choose a glass from one of our great modern factories, one with slightly rippled – 'sea-shore' – sides, generously cupped and with a firm, fairly short stem. The modern glass of our best factories – such as Whitefriars – strikes a mean between the eighteenth-century softness and the Victorian brilliance. Brilliant it is, but the hardness of the Victorian glass has been tempered to a metal the feeling of which suggests supple power, the power to contain the deep strength of a burgundy, the clarity to reveal the full depths of its rich colour to the eye, and the generosity to contain its bouquet generously.

The amalgam of the physical, aesthetic and imaginative qualities of a wine glass must be argued to heighten the experience of drinking wine – as distinct from heightening the wine itself. The basis for accepting such an argument may be established by simple experiment in contrasting the drinking of the same wine from an ordinary wine glass and then from an earthenware mug. Once that basis is established, an almost equal difference may be found between a fine glass and an ordinary glass.

At a peak of this pleasure, there is a visionary delight in conceiving it possible to drink the Mouton 1875 – if it is still to be found – from a wine glass of the great, first-century, Roman metal which, still no more than slightly 'crazed', today holds in its faint, distant amber-hints, all the wisdom and patience of its age – an age which its durability seems to deny.

Thus, savouring the work of one great dead artist in that of another, one might feel that a memorable wine and a monumental glass had tendered to one another a due and perfect homage.

The Adelphi, 2nd Qtr, 1952

6
Tasting

Hoc Antique and Krug Moderne

April 1978. Every man's taste is his own: and inalienable. 'I know what I like' only becomes intolerable when it is imposed on someone else against his will. The major, for instance, used to insist on steak for his guests and then order one of the sweeter hocks – without alternative – to go with it. That cured not a few of hock-drinking – and of the major. It has been said, and often repeated, that the term hock was coined by Queen Victoria as a shortening of Hocheimer, her favourite wine solicitously introduced by Albert. The derivation may be accurate, but the attribution is not. John Gay, in his poem 'Wine' (1708), has:

> *Name, Sirs, the WINE that most invites you, Taste*
> *Champaign or Burgundy, or Florence pure,*
> *or Hoc Antique, or Lisbon, New or Old,*
> *Bordeaux, or neat French White, or Alicant*

Old Hock, so called, was recognized as a fine apéritif in Georgian times. Deinhard's price list of 1837, too, offered 'Best Brown Old Hocks of 1822 and 1811'. The great German wines have always aged gracefully.

Although a man must be allowed his taste, it can change his image. It will be hard in future to feel quite the same about Lord Tennyson – the Laureate, not the cricketer – after reading a contemporary note on his drinking habits. It was left by Sir Clements Markham, the man whose copy of his ancestor's 'The Most Honourable Tragedy of Sir Richard Grenville' inspired Tennyson to 'The Ballad of The Revenge'. It runs – 'I went to The Hollies, Clapham Common, to dine with Mr Knowles on March 8, 1873 and met Tennyson for the first time. After dinner we drank hot gin and Liebfraumilch, steamed in large tumblers' (and ate some lotos, no doubt).

Tennyson's son, Hallam, recalled in his Memoir of his father that the launching pad of an opening line – 'At Flores in the Azores Sir Richard Grenville lay' – remained on the poet's desk for years before the rest was written.

In the matter of taste, it should be said that some wine is dull; drinkable, certainly, sound, even – with the food of the country – worthy; but alone, tasted critically, a gustatory nothingness. So it is that many people in the wine world – or half world – often avoid tastings which are a bore to the palate. So a presentation of Turkish rosé, Mexican white, or Venezuelan red – even with lecture illustrated by slides – might draw only a few enraptured British samplers. A man may try such a tipple in private where it is a matter of moments; but, as a day's pilgrimage, it is a poor gamble.

On the other hand, there are some fine vinous occasions. Take for instance the recent introduction – launching is too crude a word, tasting an understatement – of a new vintage of Krug champagne. There you may tick them off – the scholars, historians, critics, merchants of wine – but all devout lovers of that drink, not tipplers, you understand, but men who love wine with an emotion which transcends thirst.

It was the 1971 – the wine of a year of small quantity but high quality and, hence, expensive grapes, especially in the free market where the crucial, fine standard buying is done. That is when Krug, regardless of cost, constantly make a fine wine. The decision to declare a 1971 vintage was taken after the Krugs, Paul and his sons Henri and Remi, had tested many hundreds of combinations and eventually created – and that is the word – a blend of 29 different top-grade champagne wines. The vintage was of precisely 148,000 bottles.

This is a wine to drink with delight, but also with respect. Only one who, with experience limited to wedding champagne (and often not champagne at all), had subscribed to the heresy that champagne is nothing – 'all the same' – can recall the dawning that is the first tasting of Krug: the recognition of a regal white wine; a unique champagne.

The 1971 is deep, golden coloured, with a rich mousse (foam), marked fruity nose and full, balanced taste; yet, in some ways, more subtle than the usual Krug, due probably to the fact that the blend was largely of white Chardonnay and Pinot (46 per cent and 47 per cent) with only 7 per cent of Meunier.

At the introduction, which is less a critical examination – no one ever complains about it – than a generous enjoyment, the true lovers might be ticked off, arriving faithfully, one by one, none more than politely late. Service was smooth, unhurried but efficient. The ample bottles, in their deep imperial purple foil and unobtrusive labels, popped frequently but discreetly; the empty glass was unobtrusively but instantly refilled. The buffet was Lucallan but not ostentatious.

The Guardian

Sharpening Tastes

May 1951. Is the current taste for dry sherry – as opposed to the rich dark browns of the last century – an indication that we are becoming less sweet of tooth?

There is certainly some evidence on this score. More and more people, it seems, abjure sugar in tea, but this, I fancy, may be accounted for by rationing and concern to keep our weight down in a period of much starchy food. On the other hand, the buying of bitter beer – despite its higher price – rather than mild and the apparently decreasing amount of the richer old beer consumed seem to indicate inclination towards sharper flavours. Again, we know that the rich, yellowish champagne usual in the 1840s has long since been completely replaced in favour by the dry.

In soft drinks, even during our own lifetime, there is a shift away from the sweeter minerals like Cherry Cider towards the more piquant grapefruit and lime flavours.

We are apt to think that the Victorians were abnormally sweet-toothed but, by an earlier standard, they were almost half-way towards the sophisticated palate.

We know that the London wits of the eighteenth century tended towards the coffee houses, and that morning chocolate was a fashionable refreshment. We are not, however, quite prepared for the evidence of the fashionable eighteenth and early-nineteenth century palate of France posed by its chief chronicler. Anthelme Brillat-Savarin owes his niche in the wall of literary immortality to his book, *Physiologie du Goût*, which sets out his ideas on food and drink with witty discursiveness; he has been accorded the title of 'gastronomist' by responsible works of reference.

In Brillat-Savarin's time the mixture of sugar, alcohol and flavouring to produce liqueurs was an immense novelty; sugar-lumps soaked in eau-de-cologne were regarded as suitably amusing confections for young ladies. Thus it is understandable that Brillat-Savarin should be much preoccupied with liqueurs, but not, surely, to so much greater extent than with wine.

We are, however, vastly surprised to find such lyrical attention paid to sugar, and the final surprise is the man whom he quotes as saying: 'If only the price of sugar were to drop I would never drink anything but sugar-water.'

After that it is almost refreshing to find that an old English recipe which calls for 'a gallon and a pint of red wine' and 'sugar ii lb' wants also cinnamon, ginger, pepper, cloves and mace – and calls the result 'Ypocras'.
                                                                    The Evening News

Winner by a Nose

February 1974. The ordinary man's tasting of wine is a pleasing, idle or contemplative pastime. The term wine tasting, on the other hand, refers to a skill – which has been as nearly reduced to a precise science as is possible where the measuring instruments are the human senses.

In the classic unwritten Walter Mitty situation, he would lift his port glass to the light, cock a thoughtful nostril over it, swirl it round his mouth, pass a lordly eye over the hushed company and pronounce it, with easy familiarity – 'Delaforce '96'.

Technically, wine tasting is of two kinds – the evaluation of known wine, or the identification of the unknown. The first kind is the more commercially important, whether by an amateur discovering which of several bottles he prefers to buy for his own drinking, or the professional selecting from a group of similar products for his firm's trading. On either side the essence of the activity is the relation of pleasure to price.

The identification of an unnamed bottle is a parlour game which has ruined many a wine expert's dinner. Success depends on palate memory or an extremely deep knowledge of grape growing and wine making – better, both.

Both aspects are dealt with in Michael Broadbent's *Wine Tasting* (Christie's Wine Publications) which has been paid the extremely serious compliment – for an English book on wine – of translation into French and serialization in *La Revue du Vin de France*.

Mr Broadbent, head of Christie's wine department, is one of the 81 men in Britain qualified by examination as Master of Wine. He first set down his ideas on tasting in 1962 as a set of notes for trainees in the wine trade. That has grown through several stages to this – the only English book on the subject – a wise, easily readable, study of technique difficult to define.

Recognizing that a clearminded beginner can generally rank three or four different wines in order of quality, he emphasizes the importance of absolute standards.

'The bulk of the world's wines are of ordinary quality, made from vines which are comparatively easy to grow and prolific yielders. Different grapes are blended; final wine may be blended. Mass-market wines must be blended. Unhappily commercial necessity forces this pace; mixing individual flavours has a similar effect to mixing colours: the more you mix, the greyer the result. Low quality wines are for drinking not for tasting – by far the most revealing type of tasting is one of wines of the same vintage but from different districts, or from the same vineyard but different vintages.'

His order of tasting is – 'Dry before sweet, young before old, modest before fine'. The tasting process itself is – sight, smell, taste. Looking at a glass of wine – preferably against a north light or a candle – shows its degree of clarity and, revealing, its colour. A 'red' wine generally has a purple tinge when young, is red in transition, red brown in early maturity, mahogany when fully mature, and amber-brown in old age. A white, on the other hand, tends to grow darker with age; the basic yellow-green or straw becomes deeper yellow, gold, and in full old age, amber.

The 'nose' of a wine tells the experienced taster the most important fact about it – the variety of grape from which it is made – as well as its acidity, freshness and age or such possible deficiencies as being maderized, oxidized or corky (which has nothing to do with fragments of a badly drawn cork floating in the glass). Finally the taste – not a sip, but a generous pull, enough to flood all the taste buds – identifies flavour, depth, finish, and quality.

With the cynical aside 'a sight of the label is worth 50 years' experience', Mr Broadbent goes to the nub of wine-tasting. 'What has the greatest bearing on the style and flavour of wine? The variety of grape. Is this constant? No, it depends on the soil upon which it is grown. Is the combination constant? Again, no; the latitude, climate, the care of the vine, length of fermentation and, of course, the level of skill at every turn: all these have a bearing.

'The great wines of the world, i.e. those with exceptionally marked taste characteristics and quality, are made from a limited range of "noble" grape varieties.'

He lists his six noble grapes and couples them with wines made from them and in which they can be detected. His first is Cabernet Sauvignon, the main grape of claret – to be smelt at its most characteristic in Château Mouton-Rothschild or, at less expense, in a Lynch-Bages or a Malescot Margaux of a good year. The Riesling is to be recognized in the two most important aspects of its versatility, an Alsace Riesling – Reserve Special, or Exceptionelle – from one of the better growers like Hugel; or a hock of the Rheingau, from Graf Eltze, or von Simmern.

For training in the Pinot – the grape of red burgundy (and champagne) – he recommends a Côte de Nuits from Dau, Damoy, or Vogué; or a Côte de Beaune from Louis Latour or Drouhin.

The Chardonnay – the white version of Pinot – makes the great white burgundies (and champagne); Mr Broadbent's tasting touchstone is a Corton-Charlemagne of Louis Latour or a Puligny-Montrachet from the domaine Leflaive. As a mnemonic for the Traminer – 'the most disregarded of noble grapes' – he suggests an estate bottled Alsace Gewürztraminer of a recent good vintage. He ends the list with Sauvignon Blanc to be tasted in the Loire white wines of Pouilly Fumé and Sancerre.

The man who can detect and identify these grapes 'blind' has mastered the basis of wine tasting. The next step is palate memory – not only for the flavour of these grapes, but for outstanding vintages of great wines. It may strain a palate memory to recall a Château Lafite 1947; but, for the man who has never been able to taste a Château Lafite 1947, that question does not arise; he must reach his conclusion by pure skill.

No aspect of Mr Broadbent's book is more important than its demonstration that wine tasting is an objective, near-science. It is not easy precisely to describe a scent or a taste in words – especially when it is a problem of defining gradations between similar wines. Mr Broadbent includes a glossary of wine-tasting terms in the effort to establish uniformity. He is, though, most impressive with two pages which prove that anyone who seriously wishes to understand about wine must read this book. There he traces the processes of elimination and deduction by which he identified 'blind' a 1966 Châteauneuf-du-Pape and a medium-quality Sauternes.

It is like the man who takes to pieces a piece of complicated machinery, puts it together again and then hands it to you and says 'Now you do it' – and Walter Mitty does.   *The Guardian*

Spit and Relish

May 1983. There is a significant difference between wine drinking and wine tasting. The drinker eyes the glass, estimates – even admires – the colour; sniffs deeply, probably sniffs again, and contemplates the bouquet; swills a gulp round the mouth, cups it in the mouth and inhales over it to draw its full flavour through to the nostrils which are the final arbiters of taste; swallows it, goes on pouring it and drinking it, preferably with appropriate food. The taster goes through all the stages of study but then, instead of swallowing, spits it out. The master spitters can hit a bucket at three yards with no trouble.

In essence, the point of drinking is pleasure. The point of tasting an academic exercise, a commercial evaluation or the parlour game of identifying wines at which, in recent years, amateurs have scored an appreciable number of public triumphs over the experts.

The great tasters are indefatigable. They are able to sample one wine after another, make their notes and their comparative valuations with no blurring of smell or taste. Fritz Hallgarten, for instance, once pounced on a misdating late in a tasting of some fifty wines. Michael Broadbent, the MW head of Christie's Wine Department, has published *The Great Book of Wine* containing 436 pages of his notes from thirty years of tasting.

A recent visit to the Domaine de la Romanée-Conti with him and Christopher Fielden, writer and merchant with a sensitive and well-trained palate, was a considerable experience. In a region where the French laws of inheritance have led to savage fragmentation of so many vineyards, the domain of the Domaine is more than merely impressive. It includes all the small but outstanding Burgundy vineyards of Romaneé-Conti itself; and all the less famous, but consistent, barely inferior, La Tâche; about half of Richebourg; about half of Grands Echézeaux; a seventh of Echézeaux; and handles Marey-Monge's half of Romanée-St-Vivant. Lately, too, it has acquired a half-hectare share of the finest of white burgundy vineyards, Le Montrachet. It is a staggering hand of great wines.

The tasting consisted of two horizontals, all six of those red wines from the vintages of 1971 and 1978, plus a vertical of vintages of La Tâche between 1945 and 1981. The two professionals plugged along for two solemn, morning hours, dutifully eyeing, nosing, swilling, and spitting; often going back over the course to see if one vintage or another had opened up, or faded, and amending their notes accordingly.

So many fine bottles of similar character was a sheer embarras de richesse. Even against a background of some training and experience, spitting out the finest wines in the world was a kind of vinous sacrilege. It is valuable – indeed, invaluable – to know how to taste in order to get a sampling right. Yet if tasting means trying a bottle in a shop or cellar to see if it seems right for supper, that is enough.

It must be said, though, that the two bottles of Le Montrachet were glorious: splendidly rich without being sickly: like dry honey.

Ultimately the approval or rejection of a wine is personal. The doctrine of 'I know what I like' is paramount. On the other hand it is good to know that the liking has a sound basis. To that end, Michael Broadbent's *Wine Tasting, Enjoying, Understanding* (Cassell) is an immense help. Yet even for him, definition is a problem. He admits that he is continually sharpening his terms of reference; especially since the translators of his Great Book – into French (immense compliment for an Englishman) and German (even more surprising) – have pressed him for greater precision.

It remains difficult to communicate taste much beyond the basic. In the glossary of his Tasting, he gives the meaning of the frequently employed tasting term 'supple' as 'easy to taste and sense, hard to define. A combination of sap, vigour and amenable texture'. In wine-scholarly terms, that will do; but it is less acceptable to the body of table wine drinkers than 'Yes, this will go with the steak and kidney'. On the other hand, he performed magnificently in choosing the wines for dinner.   *The Guardian*

7
Going Out

The Gourmet's Guide to Europe

August 1977. 'Perhaps the greatest abasement of the Briton, whose ancestors called the French "Froggie" in scorn, comes when, his first morning in Paris, he orders for breakfast with joyful expectation a dish of the thighs of the little frogs from the vineyards.'

The thought comes from *The Gourmet's Guide to Europe*, by Lieutenant-Colonel Newnham-Davis and Algernon Bastard; 'edited by the former'; and published by Grant Richards in 1903.

It was virtually the first time a book of this kind had been attempted in Britain and it must be accepted as a period piece, for tasting rather than devouring. It was written by a man – for the colonel kept his co-author in place to the extent of identifying his contribution – whose palate was sharper than his pen. He could write, 'Cancale of course has its oyster beds, and the esculent bivalve can be eaten within sight of the mud-flat on which it erstwhile reposed.'

On the other hand, he unconsciously created a picture of a world difficult for his present-day reader to imagine. 'I can dine amply, and on food that even a German doctor could not object to, for less than a louis. For instance, a dinner at the Anglais of half a dozen Ostende oysters, Potage Laitues et Quenelles, Merlan frits, Caisse de poularde Rotie, Salade Romaine, cheese, half a bottle of Graves le Cru and a bottle of St Galmier, costs 18 francs.' The exchange rate then was 25 francs to the pound.

His main interest was in food but he noted 'The great glory of Voisin's is its cellar of red wine, its burgundies and Bordeaux. The Bordeaux are arranged in their proper precedence, the wines from the great vineyards first, and the rest in their correct order down to mere bourgeois tipple. Against each brand is the price of all bottles within a drinkable period and the man who knew the wine list of Voisin's thoroughly would be the greatest authority in the world on claret.'

He tells, too, the story of the Englishman who asked for plum pudding in Voisin's on Christmas Eve. 'The Maitre-d'hotel was equal to the occasion. He was polite but firm and his assertion that "The House of Voisin does not serve, has never served, and will never serve, plum-pudding" settled the matter.'

In Nice he ordered 'a little dinner for two' –

Hors-d'oeuvre
Potage Lamballe
Friture de Goujons
Longe de veau aux celeris
Gelinotte a la Casserole
Salade Romaine et Concombre
Dessert

and observed – 'with a pint of white wine, a pint of champagne, a liqueur and two cups of coffee, my bill was 46 francs'.

In a Monte Carlo hotel he came upon a list of great vintage clarets at extremely low prices. Asking the reason, he was told they had formed the private cellar of a former owner, now dead: they were too old to transfer to Paris and were being sold off cheaply to get rid of them – 'For in Monte Carlo the winners drink nothing but champagne, the losers water or whisky and soda.'

He relates how once the Gambrinus and the Chiaja, the two major restaurants in Naples, 'were at daggers drawn, and a war of cutting down prices raged. In those happy days one could dine or lunch at either place sumptuously for a shilling, but some meddling busybody interfered in the quarrel, brought the proprietors into a friendly spirit and ended the competition.'

His cautionary tale concerns a man who 'returned from a long term of service in India and landing at Naples, concluded that, as he was in Europe, he could get British food'. Accordingly he went to a restaurant where, with great difficulty, even through an interpreter, he ordered a chump chop and then had to wait an hour for it. The bill so horrified him that he protested to the proprietor who explained that 'As such an extraordinary joint had been asked for, he had been compelled to buy a whole sheep to supply it.' The colonel comments – 'This is a warning not to ask for British dishes in a Neapolitan restaurant.'

Not all his restaurants were so simple. 'From the doors of the Maison d'Or, Rigolboche, in the costume of Mother Eve, started her run across the road to the Anglais. There, upstairs in Le Grand 6 Salamanca, who drew a vast revenue from a Spanish banking house, used to give extraordinary suppers at which the lights of the demimonde, Cora Pearl, Anna Deslions, Deveria, and others used to be present.

The amusement of the Spaniard used to be to spill the wax from a candle over the dresses and then to pay royally for the damage. One evening he asked M Verdier whether a very big bill would be presented to him if he burned the whole house down, and, on being told that it was only a matter of two million or three million francs, he would have set light to the curtains if M Verdier had not interfered to prevent him. The 'beau Demidoff', the duelling Baron Espelata, 'Princes Galitzin and Murat, Tolstoy, and the Duc de Rivoli gave their parties in Le Grand 6 and down the narrow steep flight of steps which led into the side street, the Duke of Hamilton fell and broke his neck.'

All that and the esculent bivalve, too.   *The Guardian*

Tate Secret

December 1976. It was never communicated as a secret. Moreover, once the informant, not content with having cased the joint, proceeded virtually to board there, no secrecy could be expected. Anyway, far too many people have found out. Not to beat about the kind of bush good wine does not need, the Tate Gallery restaurant has the cheapest luxury drinking in England.

Fine drink, of course, demands a basis of well prepared food. That is served. First courses on two days included fresh French onion soup, buttered crab, avocado and walnut cocktail, fresh fried sardines with garlic butter (superb), kipper paté, leek quiche and salmon mousse. Among main dishes lobster normande, roast loin of pork, enrecôte marchland de vin, poached lemon sole, roast turkey, veal kidneys florentine. Vegetables are fresh and varied; on the cold table are salmon, beef, turkey, hare pie, and six different kinds of salad. There is a choice of fish, grills, sweets and cheese. The Christmas menu began last week with turkey, baked ham, duckling, guinea fowl.

A three-course meal with coffee, VAT, and service charge comes to about £4.60. Cooking and service have the unstressed efficiency of staff content to work by day, leaving their evening free. Each of the six waitresses is her own, informed, sommelière.

They have no need to advise the regulars. The meal is the basis for the operation by which Tom Machen, the restaurant manager, carries out his original brief from the Trustees – 'Give good value.' Over some years, by highly critical tasting and astute buying, he has built up a cellar which may not be the most elaborate in the country but is established in depth, and from which he sells at prices which are more than merely good value.

Even the house wines – at £1.90 a bottle – are Appellation Contrôlée; the red, Château Lescadre 1971; the white a Mâcon Vinzelles 1974. The wine list is printed unostentatiously inside the brown paper menu-wrapper. The white burgundies begin with Le Montrachet – itself – of the Marquis de Laguice, 1967, at £11.10, not the bottle, but the magnum. A bottle of the same wine, 1969 vintage, is £5.70; of 1966 from the Domaine Baron Thénard, £5.

A Corton-Charlemagne 1970 of Louis Latour is £4.48; of Joseph Drouhin, £3.70. This parade of the two finest dry white wines in the world has distracted the eyes of most customers from the next item which is a domaine bottled Puligny-Montrachet from Roland Thévenin at £6 the magnum. This is a white wine of amazing subtlety; rich and full as honey, yet dry and clean, and with a great rolling aftertaste. To drink it is a considerable experience for anyone with tastebuds. The stock of it, alas, is running desperately low.

So to the claret; and Châteaux Lafite-Rothschild and Margaux of 1964 are – laughably below current auction prices – £10 a magnum.

That is instantly trumped by Châteaux Mouton-Rothschild and Haut-Brion, both 1962, at £5.20 the bottle. Back to the great 1961s, now rare wines and – per bottle – Château Pape-Clément is £4; Gruaud-Larose £5; a Croizet-Bages from 1955 is £4.50. For the solitary luncher – or one who has an afterthought – a half bottle of Château Margaux 1959 is £3; Calon-Ségur 1961, £2.40.

Among the red burgundies, Bonnes-Mares Domaine Clair-Däu 1966 is £4.50 the bottle; Corton Hospices de Beaune 1970, £3.90; the red Chassagne-Montrachet 1971, Domaine bottled, Duc de Magenta a mere £2.70; and the list ends with French bottled Beaune Grèves, Thorin 1970 for £2.60.

For those with stamina details of 1948, 1955, and 1960 vintage port are available on request. It is a vinous Catch 22; at such prices what bibber, however hard up, can afford not to drink?

Why tell? Because no one – not even the Dutchman who naïvely offered 10 per cent on top of list prices – can buy any of this wine except served at the table. Moreover, the restaurant is open only at lunchtime; has only 28 tables, and serves only 125 people a day. At that rate Tom Machen estimates that he has backing to maintain this standard – not, of coure, with these identical wines but with others which will develop to equal stature by the time they are needed – for 13 years to come. That is a comforting permanent thought in an impermanent world, needing only assurance of solvency – and available bookings – for completeness.   *The Guardian*

L'Escargot Bienvenu

Drinking American

July 1982. In the 1950's l'Escargot Bienvenu, in Greek Street, was the most French restaurant in London; indeed, in Britain. It was kept by two generations of the Gaudin family; each retained French citizenship; did national service in the French Army and fought in the First and Second World Wars respectively.

Snails were the main feature; the younger Gaudin once served a five-course dinner presenting them as hors d'oeuvre, soup, fish, entrée and savoury. The wine list was sound – all French of course –

and virtually every bottle supplied by one or another of their French vigneron relations. L'Escargot Bienvenu remained an Edwardian restaurant into the 1950's; but the Gaudins, like so many of their customers, have gone on their way.

Now, after a pedestrian intervening phase, l'Escargot is owned by the Landers. Nick is a Mancunian, and a former commodity trader. His wife, as Jancis Robinson, was the *Sunday Times'* wine correspondent, editor of *Which? Wine Monthly*, and author of *The Wine Book*. Although for the last nine months she has been studying to become a mother, she has continued to take an active part in the choices and decisions which change their wine list every three or four months.

The sommelier is American; Robert Hardy, 6ft 3ins, from Colorado, worked with wine makers as well as in restaurants there before he came to England. At first the Landers concentrated on Californian wines but when these became commonplace, they introduced others from the Pacific north-west, Oregon, Washington State, and Idaho, with considerable success.

On l'Escargot's list of 44 wines, 26 are American. They range from Stone Creek Colombard at £4.95 and Zinfandel £5.75 up to St Jordan Cabernet Sauvignon (£18), two big Chardonnays, St Clement at £14.50 and St Chapelle from Idaho – at £11.

White Loire pleases some customers who find the general run of Californian whites too sweet, and the Chardonnays too big or too dear. There are also some French reds. Only one group – of three French diners – have evinced dissatisfaction with the preponderance of American wines. Indeed, a number of people come there specially to explore them; and they are available by the case at off-licence rates. Six years ago a largely Californian list would have been inconceivable. A variety of other Americans marks a completely new departure; and a measure of the uniquely wide British wine-choice.

The Guardian

London Taverns

February 1979. The term wine bar covers a multitude of sins. Not, though, for the British wine drinker, a fraction so many as the average pub. Unfortunately, wine bars are unevenly distributed. In many provincial areas there are none.

London has by far the greatest concentration and variety. That fact is historically based. The Act 'To Avoyde the Greate Price and Excess of Wines' of 1553 was rigorous in its limitations on vintners. No one person was allowed a licence for more than a single tavern; with a few exceptions no town might have more than two taverns. London, though, was granted 40, the two next cities of the kingdom, York eight, Bristol six.

El Vino, at the Strand end of Fleet Street, is perhaps the best known: a resort of barristers, journalists, editors and those who, incomprehensibly, seek the company of barristers, journalists, or even editors. There Philip Hope-Wallace has been canonized by the fixing of a brass plate to the back of the chair where he has for so long, so impressively, held both his court and his burgundy.

Gordons, at the bottom of Villiers Street, a pot's toss from Charing Cross Station, used to serve on two storeys. On the upper, or ground, floor, Kipling – who wrote *The Light That Failed* there – and Chesterton often worked on their copy in the little parlour; while the lower leads into Embankment Gardens. Local authority regulations dictated the conversion of the upper into kitchen and toilets; and now the only bar is in the basement.

Gordons used to specialize in robust sherries in two measures, adequate and large; Michael Sadleir, who relished its Victorian atmosphere, quaffed large glasses of fino with relaxed speed. Nowadays they serve cold buffet and tapas. Otherwise the main bar remains staunchly behind the times with its nineteenth-century posters, historic newspapers, elderly bottles, and an imprimatur of dust.

The establishment was named for the Gordons who maintained it as a free vintner's through three generations until recently when it was bought, appropriately and economically enough, by another Gordon, Luis, whose family has been in the wine trade for two centuries.

Balls Brothers' business is based on their Wine Centre at 313 Cambridge Heath Road, E2 9LQ; the wholesale list is strong, well chosen, and shrewdly priced. They have nine wine bars and a restaurant in central London and an interesting City escape in their Chelsea Bar,

31 Cheyne Walk, nostalgically sited opposite Albert Bridge where the old Pier Hotel used to stand.

Even in London, wine bar development has not been entirely favourable since Julia Carpenter's first smiling burst of success (she now continues capably, and still smiling, with Bonhote Foster in their Old Brompton Wine Cellars, 150 Old Brompton Road).

Outside the City, Don Hewitson, the exuberant New Zealander, currently chairman of the Champagne Academy, has done markedly well with the Cork and Bottle, Cranbourn Street (beside Leicester Square tube) and Shampers, Kingly Street (behind Libertys). The staff accents are cheerfully Antipodean; the attractions of the bars cosmopolitan: the salads, original, in fine condition and satisfying. Much of the overlapping evening trade – after office and before theatre – is of two or three people splitting a bottle in the original wine tippling fashion. *The Guardian*

The Castle Hotel

September 1978. Extravagance is an indulgence that you can only justify, even to yourself, by sharing it with your spouse. Alternatively, it is a habit of bachelors. What is it worth to sample some 20 fine wines; and to drink as many more with appropriate and well prepared meals? The Castle Hotel at Taunton offers that at their annual wine festival between Friday evening and Sunday afternoon from 3 to 5 November.

It includes a private room for two nights with morning tea served; full English breakfast and afternoon tea; a welcoming champagne party, two dinners and two lunches, for £115 a head. For any wine enthusiast – and especially for married couples or wine enthusiasts – with a wedding anniversary that weekend, it must seem a tempting extravagance.

If it is not cheap, judgement on its fairness must rest largely on the quality of the wines. This six-course Friday dinner is based on five wines from the Hospices de Beaune. The two whites are Meursault Cuvée Jehan Humblot 1972 and Corton-Charlemagne Cuvée François de Salins, 1970; the reds, in ascending order of age, Beaune

Cuvée Guigogne de Salins, 1973; Volnay Jehan de Massol 1950 and Corton Cuvée Charlotte Dumay 1945. The dessert is accompanied by a Blanc de Blancs from the oldest of the Champagne houses, a Ruinart 1971; and the meal is rounded by an Hospices Marc de Bourgogne or a petit champagne cognac.

The Castle, which regularly runs weekend festivals, of music and theatre, is familiar to anyone who knows the West Country. Until the coming of the motorway, anyone going south west had to go through Taunton and take the hinge turn outside the hotel.

Historically, the brochure says, it was built in AD 710 by King Ina of Wessex; and, while the author of a Somerset guide laments that it has been modernized, others may prefer twentieth to eighth-century conditions.

It is a private hotel and Peter Chapman, the cool-looking chairman/managing director, has plunged on its new wine list. He claims that wines have been nursed and served there for over eight centuries; argues that in the first place the cellars were probably stocked with the monastic wines from Glastonbury and he now offers those of four Somerset vineyards, Cheddar Valley, Wootton, Pilton Manor, and Wraxall.

The cover of the list carries a quotation from Aristophanes as unfamiliar as might be expected to one unfamiliar with Aristophanes:

> *'Tis when men drink they thrive,*
> *Grow wealthy, speed their business,win their suits,*
> *Make themselves happy, benefit their friends,*
> *Go, fetch me out a stoup of wine, and let me*
> *Moisten my wits, and utter something bright.*

It offers 220 wines including, before it climbs to splendour, carafe red, white and roseé at £1.80 the half-litre carafe; Findlater's Soave and Valpolicella at £2.45 a bottle; Yugoslav Riesling (£2.80); and a Chianti Classico (£3.10). At the peak it has Château Latour 1934, historically a great wine, indeed, at £75. This is a prodigious (58 château wines) claret cellar for the connoisseur; yet he can buy all château bottled, Trotte-Vieille 1973 (£6.10), d'Angludet 1973 (£5.50), Malescot-St-Exupéry 1971 (£8.80); and as fine a bottle as Cantemerle 1967 for £10.50.

There are five Beaujolais of the splendid 1976 vintage; reasonably priced burgundies, hocks, Loire and Alsace; and even while he drinks the honest carafe with his meal, the enthusiast will find the list interesting as well as appetizing reading.   *The Guardian*

Peacock Vane and Chansons

March 1974. The main obstacle to a gastronomic weekend is a non-conformist conscience. Once that is overcome all is plain wassailing, Wilshawing and widening waistlines. The Peacock Vane at the sheltered southern end of the Isle of Wight was a relaxed, temperate, friendly place for the purpose. The jambon persillé, the hearty potée, the huge snails, the little suckling boar and the salmon were admirable vehicles for a succession of Chanson wines: apart from a renegade claret on the final day, all was burgundy.

There was no better indication of their standards than the humblest bottle of the three days, a simple bourgogne Aligoté, served with the cold meats of a country lunch. The Aligoté is the lowest ranked grape of the region and virtually every negociant of the area puts out a wine of that name. This was the ordinary at its best, crisp and clean with the ideal degree of acidity. The Meursault Cuvée Goureau 1963 of the main dinner was a nutty white wine, smooth but full of body. The red Beaune Clos des Fèves which followed it was rounded, manly but without a hint of heaviness.

The house of Chanson Père & Fils is one of the oldest in Burgundy; Simon Verry began the business in 1750; and since 1847 it has been solely in the hands of the Chansons. Christopher Fielden, a Lancashireman with responsibility for sales, is the first director appointed from outside the family for over a century.

Chansons are not simply negociants; their holdings are among the half dozen most important of the entire Côte d'Or. Their best wines come from their own vineyards or those of uncles, aunts or cousins in their neighbourhood of Beaune. Thus they have a uniformity of character.

In the two tastings they showed five wines of the Chanson domaine – Pernand-Vergelesses les Vergelesses, Savigny, Marconnets, Beaune

Teurone, Beaune Clos des Marconnets and Beaune Clos des Fèves –
all from the same grape variety, cultivated in similar fashion, made in
the same nineteenth-century press house in the Rue du College at
Beaune, and bottled in their own cellars.

There was opportunity to compare a single vintage of the same
wines and then the 1970 with the 1972. The experience was the more
interesting for the fact that all five vineyards lie within four miles –
the last four within one mile – of each other. In fact the two Marconnets are separated only by the A.6 – Paris to Marseilles – motorway.
The Savigny, grown on sandy soil, is the fruitier of the two; the Clos,
on the clay from motorway excavations, the drier and more distinguished.

The comparison between the two years was even more illuminating. The sound 1970 – settled and nearer maturity – were admirable
and satisfying enough: these sell at between £1.90 and £2.90 a bottle.
By comparison, the 1972 – straight from the barrel, for they have not
yet been bottled – already promises to prove an outstanding vintage.
They are the product of the rarest kind of French summmer – cool,
cloudy but dry – with September sun for a late harvest and there is an
unmistakable thoroughbred quality about them.   *The Guardian*

The White Horse

August 1976. Wine can be a necessity or a luxury. In Italy it is accepted so much as a staple part of diet that it is a regular issue with all
meals for convicts. In Britain, where wine drinking is the exception
(10 bottles per annum per head of population) rather than the rule, a
good bottle is accepted celebration for a personal occasion, christening, wedding, anniversary, the winning of an Olympic gold, or the
pools. What follows is an essay in vicarious delight – wine-list reading, which far transcends window shopping: it also provides unusual
information for the wine-seeker.

The British wine enthusiast – certainly one in southern England –
who wants to celebrate with a great bottle can hardly do better than
dine at The White Horse at Chilgrove – in Sussex, on the A2141 between Chichester and Petersfield. The casual diner can buy a bottle of

the house hock, Moselle, claret, red or white burgundy at £2.45 a bottle or £1.25 a half. The more ambitious or celebratory caller has a choice of a thousand bottles between the reasonably priced sound and the memorable. There is not another list like it in Britain.

The landlord, Barry Phillips, fourth generation of his family in the inn catering trade, has been at The White Horse for nearly eight years. He is assisted by his Dutch wife, Dorothea, and Adrian Congdon who has been his chef for seven years. The building up of his cellar is his own work. He will admit one other comparable list in the world – at Burns's famous Florida Steak House; but there a Mouton-Rothschild 1929 would cost $500, at The White Horse it is £45

The cooking at The White Horse is varied, thoughtful, and good. The wines, though, are outstanding. For anyone with a palate who wants one memorable bottle in a lifetime, it must be the first choice in England. Give ample warning. A great wine deserves preparation before drinking. Order a day in advance to give time for decanting – and a sight of cork and bottle – and to discuss the food that will best set off the wine.

What wine? There are 98 from the Rhine, starting with Bereich Nierstein 1973 at £2.45, by way of a Schloss Staufenberg Spätburgunder-Weissherbst Trockenbeerenauslese 1967 at £9.95, to an Oestricher Lenchenbeerenauslese 1971 at £24.50. The Moselle-Saar-Ruwer range is from Bereich Bernkastel Riesling 1973 for £2.45; Dom Scharzofberger Auslese Eiswein 1971, £5.95; to Mulheimer Helenkloster Auslese Eiswein (Max Ferd Richter) 1971 at £28.50.

Even the Alsace list, inadequate in most British restaurants, has 29 items with a wide range from Jean Hugel; a non-vintage Chevalier d'Alsace at £2.65 to the rare – indeed, virtually unobtainable – Gewürztraminer Reserve Exceptionelle, Personal Selection, of 1961 at £6.95. The latter probably is the finest Alsace wine to be found anywhere.

The list swells steadily with pride. White burgundy runs from the house wine at £2.45 to the magnificent Le Montrachet of Baron Thénard at £11.50. There are 20 Hospices de Beaune wines; starting with Volnay Santenots 1962 at £2.65 the half bottle – a splendid occasion for the casual visitor – and ending with Beaune 1949, Cuvée Billardet, £6.25. There is a Pommard Epenots 1928 from the Dr Barolet Collection at £12.75; or, perhaps safer – though one is safe with a bottle served at the table – Vosne Romanée, La Grand Rue, 1962, £11.75.

From the Domaine de la Romanée-Conti, Grands Echézeaux 1961 is £12.45; Richebourg 1947, £27.50; La Romanée-Conti 1959, £19.50; La Tâche 1947, £27. All these are 'once in a lifetime' wines to be remembered with relish through dozens of contemplative bottles of plonk.

The claret section, 18 pages long, is prodigious. It – alone, surely, among British lists – contains a château-bottled Cheval Blanc 1927, said to be the greatest red wine of this century – at £40; the 1929 of the same Château is £42. There are 17 years of Château Lafite between 1893 at £38 and 1968, £5.95; with 1961, £30, in between.

Thirteen Château Mouton-Rothschild range from 1929 at £45 by way of 1959 at £22 to 1968 for £6.75. Twenty-three Château Latour begin with 1934 at £35; 1955 – probably the best to drink at this moment – £24; 1968, still short of its best, is £5.75. Few good clarets are really drinkable under ten years: the great, good vintages, need half as much again. There is a Château Haut-Brion 1947 for £22; the 1955 is £20; 1967, £9.50. The magnificent Château Pétrus, which so often outprices the premiers crus of the Médoc, runs from 1955 at £25 through the great 1961 (probably just ready) at £32, to 1969 at £12.75.

The list itself is worth buying – or stealing. All the foregoing costly wines are recommended untasted but, if wine history is accurate, they are worth a journey – and an 'occasion' budget – simply to taste.

The Guardian

Chip Shop Champion

August 1976. The recital of the costly splendours on the wine list of The White Horse at Chilgrove calls for a balancing note from what none in his right sense would call the other end of the social spectrum. Sausage and mash and bread and cheese are far too easy; almost any wine is proud to go with either.

Fish and chips may seem less simple. First, it is necessary to define fish and chips. According to the Mosey doctrine, fish and chips means fresh, preferably Grimsby-landed, haddock, skinned, filletted and fried in the best Yorkshire beef dripping. The batter must be light between firm and crisp. The chips should be solidly cut, fried in the same dripping and served dry, and firm. He adds: 'This is real fish and chips and none authentic is produced more than 10 miles from Bradford Town Hall.'

Bretts falls within all that specification. It is at North Lane – Nos 12/14 – Headingley. Headingley is on the north side of Leeds and, apart from cricket matches, might be visited by those on their way to the superb small Norman church of Adel; Kirkstall Abbey; Round-hay Park; or the Romanesque St Aldan's, with its Brangwyn mosaics and painted panels by Joseph Heu.

Bretts was founded in 1919 by Arthur Brett as a sideline to his cartage business; he stabled the wagons and horses on the other side of the then semirural lane. It is now run by his son Charlie ('Charles on Sundays') whose wife, and their daughter, Jane, run the dining room.

The 'Special Haddock and Chips, with tea and bread and butter' costs 60p; with a double portion of haddock, 82p. Soup as a first course is 15p; cheese salad or sweet is available, but these are not the serious matters. The fish and chips are; and the claim that 'Bretts is the best fish and chip shop in England' (and therefore in the world) must be taken seriously. The South does not know what this dish means.

The haddock is full and fleshy, with a splendid depth of flavour, utterly clean, with no hint of overcooked fat which so often taints the dish elsewhere. It is delivered straight from Grimsby into the cold cupboard at the back of the shop during the night, and eaten within the day. The chips are flowery, dry, biteable ('I never jib at paying over the odds to get right potatoes.'). A sophisticated variant may be plaice – 65p – but the haddock is the soul of the matter.

What to drink with this splendid plate? Safeway, just over the main road, has a fine, rounded, Appellation Contrôlée, French-bottled Macon Blanc at £1.29, which is good enough for any man – and Mr Brett will allow you to bring your bottle, and will supply glasses free of corkage charges if you come, stay, and leave in orderly fashion. He may even store your bottle in his ice box so that it is chilled for your meal.

For those who regard the Moseian delimitation of the area of fine fish-and-chip production as heretical, the Co-op, in its 3400 nation-wide off-licences, has a Graves at £1.75 a bottle or an Italian Soave for £1.05; drier – and probably better with fish and chips – Chablis is £1.85; the Yugoslav Lutomer Riesling £1.18; Leibfraumilch, £1.22; Moselblumchen, £1.20.

A white Beaujolais – not easy to buy, but Duchy Vintners of Truro have it at £25.90 a dozen inclusive of VAT – fits the plateful like a glove; and it will stay with bread and cheese afterwards if you have not the crust to take red wine with you.

Not all wine travels. Good fish and chips does – but it must be good, and dripping-fried. It should be taken cooked from the place of its birth; re-heated in a dry frying pan, and, though it is not quite the same, eaten with gratitude, and plenty of pepper and salt. Vinegar – hmm, hmm, – to taste – not the best of friends of wine, but part of fish-and-chips with hyphens.

Bretts is at the bottom of the last remaining front garden in North Lane and the dining room – neat and tidy but not large – is through the shop. It is open 11.30 to 2 on weekdays; from 4 pm to 7.30 on Mondays and Thursdays; and well worth a journey.

The Guardian

8
Staying In

Apéritifs for Every Taste

March 1984. The word apéritif as a stimulant for appetite has been absorbed – which seems the appropriate word – into the English language. Let us, though, be clear what an apéritif is. Of course it is possible to have a drink before a meal, and it can be a vast slug of spirits, but that is no more a true apéritif than a cocktail is. Mixed drinks existed earlier, but the cocktail was a product of Prohibition in America – an attempt to veil the taste of bootleg hooch with strong flavours. So, far from sharpening hunger, cocktails knock the taste buds unconscious.

If the universal appetizer is hunger, the finest out of a bottle is champagne. The most versatile, convenient and reasonably priced before-dinner drink, however, is sherry. It is the legitimate descendant of the sherris sack Falstaff – actually Shakespeare, putting the words in Falstaff's mouth – so much relished.

The name sherry covers a multitude of 'vins' – not all good, but some magnificent. There is even 'British sherry' which is not, legally speaking, a wine at all, though for that reason it suffers such a low rate of tax that it probably represents the most alcohol per penny in the business.

Recent research has shown that a number of British people do not realise that sherry is Spanish. Real sherry must come only from Spain – not only from Spain, but from a 32-kilometre triangle around the

108

three sherry towns of Jerez, Puerto de Santa Maria and Sanlucar de Barrameda.

Internally, control over sherry labels is so strict that even the wines of neighbouring Montilla, from with the name Amontillado derives, cannot call its product sherry. Yet all around the world other countries make wines which they blandly call sherry; on the UK market, at least, they are compelled to put their national name in front of it.

The savings on imitations, however, are more than lost in reduced quality. It should be said, too, that sweet sherry – even if it is called cream or East India – is not an apéritif, but a dessert wine.

For our purposes, there are four kinds: fino, Amontillado, oloroso and manzanilla. Fino is pale, clean, light and dry; Amontillado, fuller, yellower, dry and nutty; oloroso, dark, full-flavoured, soft, aromatic. Manzanilla is a fino which has been matured in the estuary town of Sanlucar and has taken in the salty tang of the sea air. The most delicate and probably the subtlest of them all, it is superb, too, with sea foods. Beyond these four, Palo Cortado, not often seen, is something of a divine accident. Somewhere between a fino and an Amontillado, it can develop a mighty 23° of alcohol; a really big gun, it should be drunk sparingly.

It cannot be stressed enough that the cash difference between a pedestrian sherry and a great sherry is extremely small. For instance, the best of all these types – even the rare Palo Cortado – can be bought for £4 or less; indeed, there are some extremely good finos and Amontillados at £3.

Madeira is even more of a connoisseur's wine. Ravaged for more than a century by blight, business apathy and at one stage Napoleon's fleet, it yet survives. Indeed survival is its forte, the best of its vintages (like 1808, 1815, 1822 and 1880) can still sometimes be found, and in this century there have been thirteen fine years. The original Malmsey is the richest; Bual is light and aromatic; Verdelho, soft and drier. Sercial, the driest, is crisp and light. Malmsey and Bual, it must be said, are not really apéritifs.

The French, who have a sweet tooth, often take white port. To use up lesser but government-subsidized wine, they have, too, concocted such branded drinks as Byrrh (wise to ask for 'apéritif Byrrh' or you may be served beer), Lillet (flavoured with herbs and quinine), Dubonnet (quinine again), Suze (gentian), and St Raphael (red or white, herb-flavoured). From Italy, Campari – loved or loathed – is legally spirit but with a wine base. The strongest British entrant in the mixed drink class is Pimm's No 1 Cup (the other five having faded out of the numbering), a decorated gin sling. It can prove heavy, if served over too long a pre-meal period.

Vermouths are generally regarded as mixers, to such an extent that if you order a Dry Martini in most bars you will get not a glass from the bottle marked 'Martini Vermouth Dry', but the cocktail mixture of that vermouth with gin and a garnish of lemon. Many people, though, drink vermouth – often Dry Martini – alone, and since it is not less than 17° proof that is no feeble drink.

It used to be generally accepted that dry vermouth was French; and sweet, Italian. Now, both types and red and white are made in both countries. The finest of vermouths, beyond all question, is the French Chambéry. It comes from the town of that name in Savoy; the only one to be granted Appellation d'Origine, it is made by steeping the Alpine herbs of the district in the local wine. It would be a crime to add gin to as subtly piquant a drink as Chambéry. Chambéryzette is made by using the Alpine wild strawberries instead of herbs.

Nowadays, more and more people serve white wine as an apéritif, often Muscadet de Sèvre et Maine, white Mâcon, Beaujolais Blanc, or even a Moselle. There has been, too, such a growth in the demand for Kir that it is now produced in one-portion bottles. It is named after Canon Kir, the priest, wartime Résistance leader and Mayor of Dijon. It is made, simply enough, by putting a teaspoonful of Crème de Cassis (blackcurrant liqueur) in the bottom of a long wine glass and topping it up with, traditionally, Bourgogne Aligoté but, in practice, with any dryish, white burgundy. Refreshing and appetizing, it's only too easy to drink. *Kitchen Choice*

Soupçon

February 1985. André Simon, the splendid resident Frenchman who led the British from grub towards gastronomy, always asserted that dinner was not truly dinner unless it began with soup. Indeed, he insisted upon it, in preference to anything more elaborate, for his great ninetieth birthday banquet.

Of course, a number of soup recipes call for wine. Indeed, that legendary brew, soupe à l'ivrogne – drunkard's soup – was allegedly made with a bottle of champagne (*cooking* champagne!) and laced with brandy. That was the onion soup the little restaurants which once existed near the old Halles market in Paris used to prepare in the small hours of the morning for late returning revellers. It is, though, a dish that has always been popular, and to this day onion soups include sherry and, often, brandy as well.

Sherry is the most usual wine for soup cooking, and in the case of turtle – the classic sherry-flavoured soup – it is most strictly enjoined *not* to add it at table. As with all wine-cooking it is used for flavour, the alcohol having evaporated during the process.

Other soup recipes calling specifically for sherry are oyster bisque; clam chowder; mussel, crab, split pea, pheasant and chicken soups; consommé; and carrot and sherry, which call most generously for half a pint. Either sherry or madeira can go into cream of chestnut or cream of corn, while some recipes call for madeira in turtle.

Red wine goes into prawn, minestrone and tomato bouillon; and specifically claret into strawberry (an authentic soup), port into wild duck, port and madeira into oxtail. In hare, half a pint of port is called for. The mighty Burgundy soup/stew which incorporates oeufs mollet, belly of pork, mushrooms and garlic needs a litre of red – ideally Beaujolais – for six servings. Red wine, though some American cooks advocate vodka, is also for Borsch. White wine goes in mushroom, lobster bisque (with discretional brandy), melon and cucumber (quite generously in both) and, finally, oyster Billybee (one and a half glasses for four people). White port – or vermouth – is the nectar for avocado. That most reliable cookery writer, Elizabeth Craig, recommends Italian vermouth in both clear and cream soups.

Various alcoholic drinks are put into soups. The classic Spanish gazpacho can take a glass of red wine and one of brandy, not necessarily Spanish. Beer goes well in vegetable, bean and ham, and in lentil soups. Angostura bitters, too, but only add a dash or you have kick rather than flavour. Pernod, again only a trace, can be used in fish, shellfish, and cream of fennel soups. Jellied bloody Mary – mainly of chicken stock, tomato juice, sour cream and lumpfish caviar – will take a dessertspoonful of vodka.

At the end of the course, the French often 'faire chabrot' – pour red wine into the last spoonful or two of soup, and drink the mixture from the plate.

To accompany soup the best all-round drink is undoubtedly manzanilla sherry – light, crisp, dry and distinguished – though some prefer a fino or a slightly heavier amontillado. Sercial madeira or, more unusually, a dry Marsala is possible.

One authority has said categorically that wine is not necessary with the soup course. André Simon did not agree. He was extremely fond of wine, and thirty or so years ago he wrote a pamphlet for his friends, called *Partners*, in which he listed wines to go with different foods. In the section on hors d'oeuvre, he recommended that caviar be served without chopped onions, oysters without vinegar and melon without ginger 'for their own sakes and that of their wine partners'. While 'Grapefruit', he continued, 'like all citrus fruits, is constitutionally unsuited to be the partner of any wine.'

On soups he made no such disclaimer. Some of his pairings were usual enough: sherry – manzanilla with lobster soup, fino with Toheroa, amontillado with mock turtle; madeira – sercial with turtle, verdelho with mulligatawny; ruby port with hare. Then, however, he branched out, ingeniously pairing different wines with a range of soups: Mâcon blanc with asparagus, white burgundy with mushrooms and green pea (potage St Germain); Médoc with Scotch broth, chicken broth, giblet, haricot bean (pureé compiègne) and leek (Parisienne); Pomerol with roûte au pot; St-Emilion with cock-a-leekie, petit marmite and watercress (potage santé); hock with carrot (crécy) and sorrel. Then sweet wines: the Sauternes, Doisy-Védrines, with pumpkin; Côteaux du Layon with celery; Muscat with turnip; Monbazillac with Jerusalem artichoke. Red burgundy, he suggested, with cabbage and oxtail; Beaujolais with lentil, borsch and mutton broth; Chianti with minestrone; Barolo with mill-fanti; Clairette du Languedoc with bouillabaisse.

Occasionally André Simon used to joke about his 'partnerships'. For instance, with a certain commercial brand of meat pies, he, a dedicated champagne expert and drinker, counselled (certainly with a twinkle in his eye) sparkling burgundy, which he abominated!

In the soup selections, however, he is not simply being imaginative, but sympathetic. Again and again the wine is appropriate, even to the extent of locality; for instance the Languedoc is 'the wine of the country' for bouillabaisse.

Not only a great wine man but a superb gastronome, his pairings are well worth trying out and illuminating. In short, he proves himself to be a sensitive matchmaker.   *Kitchen Choice*

Wine to Partner Salmon

September 1984. As far as wine is concerned, everyone should drink what they like, whatever the food on the table. Recent research indicates that the familiar combinations – white wine with fish and white meat, red wine with red meat and game – have sound chemical bases.

Yet that is no reason to submit to 'wine snobbery'. If someone wants red wine with sole or white wine with red meat, the considerate host will probably serve it. Once, though, there was a bright, but by no means conformist, cricket writer and historian who insisted, at his generous dinners, on serving hock with superb underdone red beef. Even his generosity did not keep his more critical guests.

There is one fish dish which no less an arbiter than the great Curnonsky insists must be served with red wine. That is Lamproie à la Bordelaise. The lamprey is a great gastronomic delicacy which that eminent authority, Alan Davidson, describes as a 'slimy and antique creature . . . the most primitive of living vertebrates'. He goes on, 'Boschian in behaviour . . . it rasps and sucks away until it has made a meal of its victim's blood.' We hear little, if anything, nowadays of the Severn lamprey which, especially when potted, used to be regarded as a fine dish.

It is, though, still and most conscientiously, preserved in the Gironde estuary, where it is so strictly protected that it may be fished only on a few days a year. Facially, it looks like a Victorian army colonel, and though its habits are unsavoury, it tastes glorious. Stewed with leeks, in claret and its own juices, and served on croutons, it is so delectable a dish that there can be little surprise that even so clear-minded a monarch as Henry I should have died from a surfeit of it.

113

Curnonsky calls specifically for St-Emilion claret with Lamproie à la Bordelaise.

Braised salmon has even been accompanied by Chambertin. Of course, when it is served in a red wine sauce, red wine is right. A few enthusiasts of red Bordeaux, though, still insist that it should partner salmon even when the fish is not served with a red wine sauce. The argument was once strongly pressed during the apéritif stage of a most enlightened table. The host, a man of open mind, canvassed the choice of his guests and called for the good Médoc they named to be decanted: it was a warm night, and the wine was ready in time for the main course, which was Darne du Saumon Poché.

The claret was served; and, after a glass or two, but well before the salmon was finished, the host asked, 'Would you now like to compare that with this Meursault which I had ready?' It was an expensive demonstration but utterly convincing that Meursault is a better wine than claret with salmon.

This is not to say that salmon is a difficult fish to match. Boiled, with a mousseline sauce, it is happily partnered by hock; grilled, it makes an impressive union with a Bâtard-Montrachet; with different sauces it is happy with Graves, Muscadet, white Hermitage, Vouvray, Pouilly Fuissé. Roast salmon marries well with Sauternes.

Traditionally, the height of luxury was considered to be Le Montrachet, especially with grilled salmon: and, of course, that remains a superb accompaniment. Latterly, however, there has been something of a development of opinion. Chablis has had an odd and mixed history. For many years it was the vast sprawling vineyard which sent Paris its everyday wine. Some of its output was fine; but much was cheaply drinkable, the carafe wine of the bistros.

By early in this century, however, undercutting competition from the Midi, and then the onslaught of phylloxera, had cut down the area under vines by some 95 per cent. Its northerly situation had always meant that the crop was at considerable weather-risk; further damage arose after a series of harsh winters and, even more cruelly, late frosts. There remained the seven Grand Crus and some other worthy vineyards. Largely, though, by the 1930s, Chablis had become 'the greenish white wine that goes with oysters'.

Then, quite unexpectedly in the 1960s, the whole story was set in reverse. Crucially, some wealthy interests from outside the area put in a healthy infusion of capital. New methods of frost control, crop protection and pest neutralization were employed in the winefields; and the most up-to-date production plants were installed. All at once Chablis was outstandingly and sophisticatedly equipped. It still had, too, its priceless basic asset – the Chardonnay grape – which latterly has flourished in many lands; but nowhere more healthily than in Chablis.

Altogether bigger in character than the Riesling, and the guiding influence in the best champagne – especially Blanc de Blancs, it develops, at its best, a strangely contradictory yet captivating blend of dryness and richness. The winefield goes on expanding, and so does the reputation of the wine. If there is not so much of it as there was say, 150 years ago, there is four times the area of vineyards devoted to it as in 1930: and production per hectare is considerably increased. Above all, the wine is much finer than it was. There is still some, labelled Petit Chablis, which is of lower quality, but in the best vintages the Grand Crus and the Premiers Crus undoubtedly make great wines. Even in poorer years the new methods and equipment allow them to make a sound product, while 'Chablis' is a label of increasing stature.

Chablis has, too, the advantage of space to expand into formerly proved vineyard areas. This has enabled its vignerons to hold prices down.

Drunk young, Chablis is attractively fresh, clean and acid-fruity. Given a few years in a bottle – or, better still, a barrel – it reveals all its deep complexity.

The Grand Crus of Chablis are Blanchots, Bugros, Les Clos, Grenouilles, Valmur, Vaudésir. Any one of them will make your salmon dish a distinguished meal. So would one of the most expertly made bottles from the 25 or so Premiers Crus vineyards, if to a slightly lesser degree.

Chablis makes its mark in the season of the best – salmon.

Kitchen Choice

Just Desserts

November 1984. The term 'dessert wine' has at least two meanings, depending on which generation you belong to. But usually it is regarded as the last wine served at a meal – to be taken either with the sweet, with cheese or nuts, or simply alone.

Port has long been known as 'the Englishman's wine' and beyond all question vintage port is a regal drink – as a cautionary note, not one to be drunk lightly. In recent years it seems to have faded out of fashion. Some would argue that the changing tempo of life has militated against the acceptance of a wine which is essentially one to be taken at leisure and in contemplation, rather than in haste. It is true, too, that vintage port, which needs keeping up to twenty years, is expensive. On the other hand, crusted port, or late-bottled vintage, can ease the price problem.

Traditionally, port is drunk with Stilton cheese, often with nuts, but some purists insist that only a good English apple is right with the best. Others believe nothing at all should be eaten with port.

The other fortified, or 'cooked', dessert wines have their advocates, though not in such numbers as formerly. The big sweet sherries and the sweeter Madeiras – Bual or Malmsey, the Sicilian Marsala, the ancient Commandaria of Cyprus – are all worth the serious attention of those with a sweet end-of-meal tooth. None of them is truly expensive; though it is never worth trying to save pence on the genuinely cheap Commandaria.

Those eighteenth- and nineteenth-century connoisseurs – including Lord Nelson, who commended Marsala to the Royal Navy – were not thoughtless. Britain was then the wealthiest market in the world. With such an imperious choice they chose port, sherry, Madeira or Marsala to drink at the end of their meal. Neither were they foolish in electing to drink them in a state of relaxation, encouraging digestion rather than engineering it with pills. Their wines are still to be found, especially in the racks of the old established wine merchants, and at prices low enough to encourage pleasurable experiment.

The fine 'natural' sweet wines are sometimes drunk with fruit or the dessert course or even alone. The greatest are those made wholly or partly from grapes in which the juice has been concentrated by the growth of the fungus, Botrytis cinerea, known as porriture noble – 'the noble rot'. This is the downy mould that forms on some over-ripe grapes in some climates. The best known, of course, are the French Sauternes and the richest German hocks such as Beerenauslese and Trockenbeerenauslese, or even Auslese in a great year.

The great legendary Sauternes is Château d'Yquem. To drink it is a considerable experience, but it is not cheap. Sauternes now, by general acceptance, includes the neighbouring area of Barsac, and between them they produce some most enjoyable sweet wines which, by the twist of fashion, are unreasonably cheap; indeed they may well be produced for little more than the selling price. Such are Châteaux Suduiraut, Coutet, Doisy-Védrines and Climens but they are not at their best when young.

The Germans may often be observed to drink beer throughout a meal but, after it, to sip one of the great Trockenbeerenauslesen, Beerenauslesen or Eiswein (made from grapes picked while frozen) like a liqueur. They have an altogether richer quality than the lesser – or less sweet – hocks.

One immortal dessert wine, described by Professor George Saintsbury as 'the prince of liqueurs', is the Hungarian Tokay – the Aszu variety. Szamorodni may be dry and the Essencia is now rare and expensive. A Tokay of five puttonyos (indicating the number of hods of over-ripe grapes to the vat) can be bought in its traditional half-litre bottle for about £4. Spectacularly rich, this wine never cloys.

There are other fine but less well known dessert wines, notably the Portuguese Setúbal. Although not often seen here, it is gloriously honeyed when you do come across it. The Austrian Ausbruch from Western Burgenland and several from East Burgenland are attractively priced. Then there are good French dessert wines, albeit overshadowed by Sauternes. From the Loire there is Coteaux du Layon, from Anjou together with, notably, Quarts de Chaume and Bonnezeaux; a mature Vouvray of a good year is highly acceptable.

In many parts of France the Muscat grape produces luscious sweet wines. Not generally known, but reasonably priced and not to be disregarded, are those from Roussillon, Frontignan and Lunel. Do not, though, overlook the quite unexpected Rhône wine, the Muscat de Beaumes de Venise, which is delicate and full of flavour.

Italy produces, in Tuscany, the lush vino santo. From Sicily come several rich, almost cloying moscatos (Asti Spumante and Moscato d'Asti Spumanti from Piedmont are sparkling).

No one truly wants to drink one of these wines in any quantity. The Tokay bottle is sized by tradition, but of Sauternes in particular a half bottle is enough for a dinner party of four. Above all, they are drunk at a very slow tempo. *Kitchen Choice*

9
Parties

Liquid Assets

February 1970. Here we have, basically, three occasions: a party, which could be a housewarming, a wedding reception, or a twenty-first birthday. Each deserves different treatment so far as drinks are concerned, the important thing being to match the occasion and the tastes of the guests. Throughout I shall assume that no spirits are to be served, not only because they are diabolically expensive, but because just as much effect and enjoyment may be obtained by offering carefully chosen wines. First the housewarming or 'general' party: with one eye on economy.

When the guests arrive, welcome them with a glass of white wine. Champagne or Sparkling Moselle would be ideal, but if you feel that these are too expensive, settle for a nice medium-dry Hungarian or Yugoslav Riesling. You can expect the first phase to last for anything up to an hour, for only when the party has been going for some time will people begin to turn their attention to the pleasures of the cold table.

With the food some of them may want to continue drinking the medium-dry white wine, but others will enjoy a change, so see that there are some bottles of red wine available. Choose something fairly young and not too heavy. A Beaujolais Villages would be ideal, but if this is above your price limit then a Bulgarian or Chilean Cabernet or an inexpensive Valpolicella would be quite suitable. The red wines will go particularly well with the terrine de campagne, the pâté of chicken livers, and the roast jellied ribs of beef, while the white wines will enhance the galantine of chicken, the turkey, and the baked sugared ham. With the cheese a glass of Ruby or Tawny Port would be welcome, or alternatively some more red wine. Wind up the evening by producing lemon, lime, or orange squash, and beer, all of which are very good for the thirst.

A wedding reception is usually a less leisurely and more crowded occasion than the kind of party visualized above, so keep the drinks simple.

Champagne is still the traditional wine for drinking toasts and long may it remain so, for it is a wonderful invention. It is also an ideal wine for drinking throughout the reception, but regrettably, it is expensive. Sparkling Moselle or Sparkling Saumur are less expensive and often nicer than cheap champagne. Alternatively, serve a medium-dry white as your main wine and bring on champagne for the toasts. Any of these alternatives will go well with the buffet. Finally, don't forget small bridesmaids, expectant mothers, and maiden great-aunts: the two former will need some soft drinks and the latter have been known to enjoy a glass of sweet sherry. And incidentally, so may you, at a wedding, in mid-afternoon, with fruit salad or a nice piece of cheese.

Lastly, the twenty-first birthday party: on this occasion the average age of the guests will be lower than on the other two, and there are unlikely to be as many dyed-in-the-wool wine drinkers present. For this reason it could be more successful to think in terms of an exciting cup as the main drink, with a glass of champagne for drinking the health of the newly-come-of-age, if long-enfranchised, young man or woman. If there is a request for beer to be served throughout the evening, our instinct tells us that it should be resisted if only to discourage members of the rugger fraternity and their vocal villainies.

Whereas it is easy to sing 'If I was a marrying man, which thank the Lord I'm not sir!' with a tankard in the fist, it is much more difficult to do so with any conviction while the fingers are entwining the slender stem of a wineglass. Here are recipes for two cups and a mull:

SANGRIA

To one bottle of sound red Portuguese or Spanish wine add 4 slices of lemon, plenty of ice cubes, 2 tinned peaches, and ¾ tumbler of soda water. Tasting carefully, now add some of the syrup from the peach tin and finally adjust to the desired sweetness with sugar, if necessary. This is a popular warm-weather drink in Andalusia.

WHITE WINE CUP

Peel and dice a generous slice of ripe melon and put it into a large jug. Sprinkle with castor sugar and add 4 dashes of Angostura Bitters, a small measure of brandy and a small measure of Cointreau or other orange Curacao. Leave for 30 minutes if you can spare the time. Then add a bottle of well-chilled sweet white Portuguese wine, some large lumps of ice, and a good garnish of fruit. Just before serving, add ¾ tumbler of soda water.

GLUHWEIN

Hot spiced red wine from the Alps. Infuse in half a pint of hot water a large pinch of nutmeg, a sprig of mint (dried or fresh), a stick of cinnamon, the juice and rind of one lemon, and two tablespoons of sugar. After 15 minutes, strain into the wine (any sound, inexpensive red wine will do) in another pan, and heat well without boiling. Serve with a large ladle. If you use a glass jug, the chances are that you will crack it.

At parties it is safe to allow half a bottle a head for every two hours. All white wines should be served chilled. Most red wines taste best at room temperature, but Beaujolais is sometimes preferred chilled – but only if it is the genuine article, i.e. a fresh light wine. Your local wine merchant will probably agree to hire you glasses and to give credit for any unused, unopened bottles.   *The Guardian*

Small Measures

September 1981. Teenage parties should not be underestimated, for they are regarded by the young with an anticipation and seriousness greater than some parents, in their anxiety about their glassware and carpets, fully appreciate.

To categorize the young may seem adult arrogance. It is, though, possible to generalize about drink, Indeed, Research Associates United Kingdom, who are long experienced in these operations, have lately produced for the United States market a study of *How Young Adults Form Drinking Behaviour and Choose Brands*. They questioned Americans between 16 and 24; male and female; white and non-white; in various parts of the United States. They comment: 'Young people believe parents accept drinking when they realize their children can handle it without causing trouble.' They found that most drinking by 16- to 24-year-olds was done at parties (40 per cent); at home (28 per cent); then, well down, in bars (14 per cent). 'They look to alcohol to assist social encounter; mainly at parties – the easiest way to drink in a safe and generally acceptable manner.'

There are basic probabilities about teenage drink parties. First, some will certainly try to drink too much; which can be embarrassing, messy, and, where young drivers are involved, perilous. Two crucial safeguards, therefore, are that non-alcoholic drinks should be available; and that 'blotting paper' food should be plentiful (many, though they will not admit it, will eat more enthusiastically than they drink).

The non-alcoholic drinks should be generous, prominently and unashamedly displayed; and attractively presented. They should not – and certainly need not – appear drab. Served well-chilled, and in good-looking glasses, a 50:50 mixture of orange juice and ginger ale; blackcurrant juice and Perrier water; grape juice and soda; apple juice (Schloer); tomato juice (varying the Worcestershire sauce for kick); a mixed cup of orange, grapefruit, and lemon juice with ice and soda water; are all interesting, palatable, and refreshing.

The food ought to include plenty of carbohydrates: teenage lads will steam through canapes and such featherweight delicacies like a swarm of locusts. So produce solid sandwiches; French bread and cheese; three times as many potato crisps as you would think possible; sausage rolls and not-too-small chipolatas. Baked potatoes are ideal if the labour can be organized, and cake and ice cream are also good ideas.

Alcoholic drinks of course cannot be excluded. The Research Associates report observes 'boys like the macho image of party drinking'. 'There is little rebellion against parental attitudes except when alcohol is banned without adequate explanations.' The drink should be responsibly controlled, ideally by one of the young of the host family. The minimum of adult supervision – or even presence – is desirable.

The drinks should pander to the generally sweet tooth of the young. Among the lightweights, shandy is usually acceptable; stepped down Kir – one of Ribena instead of Crème de Chassis to four of dry white wine – is invariably successful.

A keg, pin, or party size can of beer is a necessity. The Research Associates sample asked 'When you can afford to drink what you like, what will it be? The largest overall vote (21 per cent) was for beer, though that included only 13 per cent of females, 28 per cent of whom wanted mixed drinks or cocktails. The strong second choice (27 per cent) of the non-white youngsters was non-alcoholic drinks: while the white preferred mixed drinks (23 per cent); beer (22 per cent); wines (12 per cent) and vodka (9 per cent) before the non-alcoholic (8 per cent).

If wine is to be included, and every extra drink complicates organization and increases labour, the white Portuguese vinho verde, dry, light, clean, slightly 'spritz' and low (9 per cent) in alcohol is ideal and not expensive. Moselle, similar but more distinguished – and a little dearer – is always well received; white wine is the usual choice of under-20s. If it is to be red, then Beaujolais can hardly be bettered.

If persuaded with reasonable subtlety, young visitors will usually clear and wash up. On the host's side, it vastly eases the conscience if guests who ought to sleep on the premises rather than try to make their way home can be accommodated.   *The Guardian*

The Morning After

September 1952. There is no more depressing atmosphere than that of one's own home on the morning after it has housed a party.

Congratulating ourselves on feeling rather well, we come downstairs. At once we do not feel so well – not by several degrees. There is a fretted blue pall of cigarette smoke over the sitting room, which grows in staleness as the curtains are moved.

Here and there – but always in the most unconcealable places – someone has dropped a lighted cigarette on the carpet. A few sandwiches have dried up to the point of curling their edges in an echo of the distaste produced by the sight of them. The saddest of all sights – an unemptied glass – confronts the householder from several corners.

Now one of the greatest contributory factors to all this is punch. Recipes for punch are numerous: they are invariably well thought out, reasonably economical, pleasant to taste and planned with a good palate for the blending of flavours.

The trouble is that punch, and punch recipes, however good, are never accepted as quite honest. The attitude varies between guest and host. The guest, coming, so he deceives himself, at considerable personal inconvenience to grace his friend's house with his company, is loftily contemptuous of punch.

'Ha,' he says to himself – or perhaps even to a fellow guest, 'punch – just some fruit juice, a little white wine and a smell of the gin cork – teetotal stuff.' He feels that he is being given weak liquor – either out of parsimony on the part of his host or a suspicion that the guests cannot carry their liquor.

Then there is the host's point of view. He has been to parties himself and knows what guests usually think of it. 'Now,' he says, 'I will mix them such a punch as never was.' Stinting fruit juice and soft drink, lest he be suspected of putting up a weak drink, he tosses in an extra bottle of gin.

Then he suddenly remembers the bottle of highly potent but nauseatingly unpalatable spirit brought back from Eastern Europe.

This makes the whole mixture a little too rough for pleasant tasting so he adds a little icing sugar and just a squirt from the siphon. At once he wonders if he has weakened it too much: perhaps it would be better to sweeten it with a liqueur, so in goes the rest of the long-hoarded and sticky bottle from Italy.

By now the exotic nature of his own freehand composition has gone to his head and he tosses in the last of the age-old cognac which was his pride – a gesture he will regret for weeks to come.

Intoxicated with power and the fumes from the bowl he adds a bottle of sherry – and bears the brimming bowl proudly in to the party.

The non-drinkers think it harmless enough – 'like Aunt Annie's claret cup'. The seasoned drinkers regard it with manly contempt. Everyone promptly drinks too much.

PARTIES

Some of the visitors think it is time they left. Others ought to have gone long before and have to be given places to sleep because 'the heat makes me feel faint'.

At last the party is reduced to a few strong stayers with nowhere to go afterwards and who vaguely hope to have a meal cooked for them. A fatherly suggestion of coffee all round is greeted with roars of laughter and the entire family rations of eggs and bacon are eaten with abandon.

Eventually it is all over. Stowaways are unearthed from spare rooms and the family, ashamed of itself, goes to bed.

Punch is the danger. Punch is potent. In future, all visitors should be given a portion of fruit juice and directed to help themselves from a barrel of absolute alcohol bearing a printed list of the drugging, dangerous and fatal doses, and the carpet should be soaked, in advance, with fire-extinguishing fluid. *The Evening News*

10
Champagne

The Facets of Champagne

Champagne is, supremely, an idea. In languages far remote from French, people who have never seen – leave alone tasted – the wine of Champagne, use the word as an image of gaiety. In Lurcat's 'Song of the World' tapestry, 'Champagne', the grapes and vine roots – against a black background – burst from a barrel with beams, butterflies, blooms and branches in a blaze of brilliance. A schoolgirl said of her first glass 'It's like icicles of rainbow in my mouth'. Talleyrand called it 'The great civilizer'. Here, here, Master, see how it puns and quibbles in the glass' says Farquhar's character, Club. For Art Buchwald 'It tastes as if my foot has gone to sleep'. Its quick streamers of bubbles, racing through their golden prison out into the world, make it the most visually exciting of all wines. To some it is a symbol of luxury or extravagance. It is pre-eminently the wine of celebration: and the finest apéritif ever conceived by man or provided by nature.

Originally, Champagne ('the Land of Plains') was the province of the Counts of Champagne, bounded on the north by Belgium and Luxembourg, on the west by the Ile de France and Picardy, to the south by Burgundy and the east by Lorraine. In 1790 it was divided between the départements of Ardennes, Marne, Haute Marne and Aube, and into parts of Seine-et-Marne, Aisne, Yonne and Meuse. It is a huge area – some 27,000 square miles – but, bled by Paris and largely given over to agriculture and woodland, its population is only about 1¼ million.

Many people – most of them French, but many British, American and German – still remember Champagne – though perhaps not by that name – as the battle-ravaged terrain over which the armies of centuries, from Ghengis Khan to Hitler, have advanced from the east on Paris. A Frenchman will point to a copse a few yards off some unremarkable strip of road near Chemin des Dames and say 'A thousand men died there in a day in 1917.' It was the field on which the First World War was won and lost. By 3 September 1914 the Germans were in Reims; by the 7 September they were across the Marne. This was the last line of defence for Paris and for four dreadful years dogged, savage battles were fought there. A single stone marks the centre of an area where five villages were so shattered by the interminable artillery bombardment and trench warfare that it would have been desecration to attempt to rebuild them. Memorials recall the French, British, Commonwealth, American, Moroccan, Russian and German troops who died there. The first battles that checked the German advance were waged among the grapes ripening for the 1914 vintage in vineyards some of which were so pulverized by weight of shell-fire that they have still not recovered. By May 1940 the Germans were back into France, again by way of Champagne, and this time they clung on until 1945, first as a demanding army of occupation and finally as a malevolent rearguard.

To the world in general, though, champagne is the wine and the district – much smaller than the ancient province – that produces it. That is a square of about 40 miles north-south from the Aisne above Reims to the N33 and, east-west, between Châlons-sur-Marne and Dormans. It is in every way – topographically, geologically, viticulturally, scenically, socially and historically – the most interesting part of the otherwise monotonous plain of Champagne *pouilleuse*. Some millions of years ago a violent paroxysm of the earth's seething interior forced up a series of bluffs in the centre of that area. Crucially, the minute marine fossils which, as a result, became the effective growing soil of these hills, are formed of belemite chalk and – secondarily – chalk with fossilized micasters (sea urchins). The 25,000 scattered acres of these soils are ideal for the propagation of the grapes which, combined, create the greatest of all sparkling wines.

The axes of this little kingdom – *la Champagne viticole* – are Reims and Epernay; contrasting in every way; rivals yet united in the common cause of their wine. Reims is dominated physically – and all the champagne area spiritually – by the great cathedral. Gravely damaged by German bombardment during the First World War, it has been faithfully restored. Every day work is in progress on the prodigious tracery of its stonework. Every day pilgrims, trippers, sightseers, students come to visit it, to spend their minutes or hours in wonder and go on their way with a new experience implanted in their consciousness. Reims has largely recovered from its series of batterings. New industries have stabilized its economy and produced fresh growth. The nearness of Paris precludes it from reaching such size or influence as Marseilles, Toulouse or Bordeaux; but with a population of about 180,000 it is sixteenth in size of the provincial cities in France; and its prosperity is clearly to be seen.

Epernay, the other major champagne town, is smaller than Reims – about a sixth of the size – and even more closely involved with champagne. Creditably for a route town, it maintains a civilized tempo. The Avenue de Champagne, an amazing architectural extravaganza – with an occasional triumph like the French garden and the orangery Jean Baptiste Isabey designed – presents the palaces of the nineteenth-century champagne princes in an elaborate and successful publicity frontage. There is, too, in the Place de la République, a dramatically simple memorial stone to the dead of the Resistance: an urn set in concrete bears the names of Auschwitz, Buchenwald, Dachau, Mauthausen and Ravensbrück. Less tragic is a Parc de Maigret; a generous Rue de Reims (Reims replies with an Avenue Epernay), and the excellent champagne museum and library.

Smallest of the champagne towns, and the most completely committed to the wine, is Ay – strictly, Ay-Champagne – set among vineyard terraces; trees and vines lapping up to its walls; its generous church spire hoist high above the huddle of houses and close streets. In the sixteenth century not only the kings of France but Henry IV (proud to call himself Lord d'Ay) and Henry VIII of England, Charles V of Spain and Pope Leo X all owned vineyards there. The scale of prices for the crus of champagne used to be based upon the 100 per cent of Ay. Its population is still less than 8000 but it is mightily busy and it sustains a number of champagne houses, outstandingly, of course, Bollinger; but also Ayala and Deutz et Gelderman.

Châlons-sur-Marne, substantially larger with a population of 54,000 and good communications, competed actively with Reims and Epernay for the champagne market in the early nineteenth century. Indeed, Joseph Krug, founder of the family business, entered the trade there. Gradually, however, the town became more deeply involved with other activities and now has a bare half-dozen marques, only Joseph Perrier of appreciable stature.

Champagne is too, a people, the Champenois. There are, of course, some ancient families among them but, in the main, they are the mixed race to be expected in a region which has been one of the main European highways of commerce, armies and ideas for more than two thousand years. They are largely a peasant people, less extrovert, less bibulous than those of most French wine regions: shrewd, quiet, notably industrious. They have been constantly under attack, much on the defensive; and have always proved resistant and resilient. In 1911 at Ay, though, growers from the Marne vineyards attacked and wrecked the cellars of makers they suspected of using grapes from outside the area in their champagne. So effective was their ferocity that the dragoons stood by reluctant to interfere, as the streets swam with champagne. The Government soon accepted their arguments to the extent of over-ruling the senate on a bill to control champagne making. Subsequently, too, official excise returns confirmed their suspicions.

The Champenois tend often to drink still wine. Formerly, of course, there was a considerable production of still wine in the region: a white Côteaux Champenois (formerly Vin Nature de Champagne) and the long-established red Bouzy can be bought nowadays. Some growers make still wine for their own domestic use – though the controls are strict – and an appreciable amount of vin ordinaire is imported. Despite erosion by standardization, the Champenois retain a number of dialect words ('parler champenois'), many of them connected with drinking or the table – 'c'est ta fête, c'est toi qu'arroses' (It's your treat – your turn to buy a round'); 'godailler' is to go on a café- (or, in English, a pub-) crawl; 'cul-net', to drink down in one gulp; three expressions for a drunk are 'churleur', 'rondibus' and 'sac-à-vin'. Among the best of these terms are 'jus de chapeau' for bad coffee; 'machoiller' – almost impossible in English – to eat without appetite; 'couleuse' is an important, though sad, Champenois expression for a bottle that has lost its gas – and some of its wine: and, best of all as a final note, 'luter' is to drink well. Thus the Champenois, if not over-vocal, can be individually expressive.

They have, too, established a coherent and definable gastronomic character. The visitor does not merely drink the local wine; he eats the local dishes. The most famous of them is the potée Champenoise, a multi-meat casserole as vastly satisfying in impact as a Languedoc cassoulet. It is defensibly claimed, though, that the matelote (fresh fish stew) of Champagne is the finest of all in France. The Montagne de Reims may seem little more than a hillock to some from high mountain country, but there are still wild boar in the woods that cap it and the young (marcassin) are a cook's delight. Salmon poached in (still) champagne is incomparable; chicken similarly prepared and served with a fresh, utterly dry, sparkling champagne, is a memorable dish. Breaded and grilled pigs' trotters (à la Saint-Ménehould) is perhaps the unique dish of the region. Boursault cheese; pâté de grives (made from thrushes); jambon de Reims; andouillettes (sheep's-giblet sausages); and salade au lard (with dandelions, potatoes and vinegar), too, are specialities of the district, found in most of its restaurants. The biscuit de Reims is made to be 'dunked' in champagne. Monsieur Boyer's La Chaumière restaurant in Reims and Hostellerie du Château at Fère en Tardenois, (46 kilometres towards Paris) have two stars in the Michelin; the Royal Champagne, picturesquely sited at Champillon near Ay, Berceaux at Epernay and Cheval Blanc at Sept Saulx have one: the Restaurant de la Gare at Epernay, too, still has its nostalgically faithful friends.

The landscape is not spectacular, but it is pleasing and, with familiarity, beguiling. Often it recalls the English Downland. In many places hills of this height – less than 280 metres above sea level and only about 180 from the surrounding plain – would be unremarkable, but in such flat country they are impressive, dominant, stimulating; they give character to the countryside. Below them the Marne follows a reluctant, twisting, yet stately course and the N3, the Marne-Rhine canal and the railway join its east-west line in near-parallel. This countryside is quiet, softly rounded, for the sharp edges of the hills' violent birth have been weathered smooth: yet, looking down from the Mountain of Reims or Hautvillers to the Marne, the scene is unforgettably rich. The glory of this country lies in its vines; not merely for their wine – which is supreme – but for the sight of them, like a vast, serried green army – their lines set at different angles to distinguish one grower's strip from another's: and, as the vendange approaches, heavy, thickset with their crop. The villages are widely spaced, for it is not the fashion of the peasant grower to waste good vineyard land on buildings. When they do appear, the church spire flourished like a pennant over the sea of vines, they are modest, drably coloured, inward-looking – showing few windows – yet at one with their surroundings. Most of the villagers work in the vines or in the cellars of Reims or Epernay and, at the vendange, there is hardly a lane, alley or courtyard of the village where pressing is not in progress, identified by a thin trickle of grape-juice running into the street or under a wooden gate. Then the vineyards are full of pickers, the roads of every kind of vehicle bringing the fruit down to the presses and brokers, manipulants, technicians, tourists and the local tradesmen are involved in the comings and goings of this crown of the wine year.

One important aspect of the Champagne region and more significantly of the wine territory is not immediately apparent. The cellars of Champagne are unique; some of them were described in the last century as 'wonders of the world' and they still attract some thousands of visitors today. They are cut out of the chalk and they play a crucial part in the making of champagne because it is essential that sparkling wine is matured over a substantial period at an extremely low and consistent temperature. These cellars remain at a steady 12 centigrade – 10 at the lowest level – even in the hottest weather. Because the ageing process must take place in bottle, the champagne makers need relatively more cellar space than other vignerons.

The chalk works easily and the Champenois have become expert in tunnelling it. In many cases the workmen simply sank a shaft on the shipper's land and then, like coalminers, dug galleries and corridors at different levels; though these are much wider and higher than those of coal mines. Some of the bigger cellars have two or even three tiers of galleries, all piped and wired for water, drainage, ventilation and electric lighting. Many of them are so large that formerly horses and carts were used as they might have been in the streets above;

bicycles are normal and, in modern times, not only fork trucks, but cars are used in the frequent removal of bottles and men.

The most remarkable cellarage is that of the Butte Saint Nicaise now occupied by the shippers Ruinart Père et Fils, Charles Heidsieck and, most spectacularly, by Pommery et Greno where the different architectural styles, wall carvings and a vast staircase create a place of fantasy. These were originally quarries worked by the Romans to provide chalk building blocks. To protect the workings against rain or frost which would impair the quality of the chalk, they were not worked in opencast fashion. Instead, the diggers – presumably slaves – made their way in at ground level through a hole small enough to be covered against the weather. Then they proceeded to dig downwards and outwards until finally they had made a huge pyramid-shaped excavation. Since these diggings were connected by tunnels and had stairs by which the slaves could make their way to and from the surface, they serve admirably as wine cellars.

The whole townships of tunnels under Reims, Epernay, Ay and parts of Châlons-sur-Marne are said to extend in all to some 450 kilometres; and to be capable of accommodating more than 200 million bottles of champagne.

This underground showpiece is not simply ideal storage space for wine, but it is an immense tourist attraction giving the shippers admirable value in publicity, public relations and even a captive audience at a 'point of sale'.

Champagne demands more of its makers than most wines. Its production method took longer to develop than any; and, ultimately, it is the most complex of all in terms of production.

In Bordeaux, Burgundy or Alsace a man may produce his own wine in virtual isolation. His vines grow within the walls of his own vineyard; he presses the grapes in the press house attached to his home; matures them in his own chai; bottles them there and sends them away without having to step off his own land. The champagne maker is in an altogether different – indeed, almost opposite – situation. In Bordeaux and Burgundy, especially, it is regarded as a major virtue in a wine that it is made from the grapes of a single vineyard only, and authenticated by being made, bottled and labelled on the premises. Champagne, to do itself justice, must be a blended wine, made from different kinds of grapes, from different vineyards in different micro-climates. So, during the nineteenth century, a system developed in which growers and makers were separate – sometimes opposing – groups. Nowadays some growers sell their own champagne as récoltants-manipulants. Others have formed powerful and efficient co-operatives which some use only for vinification, others for the entire process to bottling and sale. Meanwhile an increasing number of makers have substantially extended their vineyard holdings. Traditionally, however, the makers travelled the various parts of the vignoble inspecting, negotiating, supervising pressing, before they returned to their celliers to direct the blending and subsequent processes. The growers, for their part, have always sought to disperse their vine plots in the attempt to avoid damage from the usually localized, violent summer thunderstorms characteristic of the area. Although their holdings are small (three quarters of them own less than a hectare – 2½ acres; a third less than half an acre) they often have plots as much as five or six miles apart. So the vignerons of champagne have always been mobile. In Bordeaux a négociant with an office in Bordeaux might never go to St-Emilion, or vice versa; but in Champagne, although there is rivalry between Reims and Epernay, there is close contact between them. The office of the Comité Interprofessionel du Vin de Champagne (CIVC) is in Epernay: but the champagne growers' club is in Reims: and the much-used road between the two passes, straight as a dropped stone, over the Montagne de Reims.

It is important to recognize that champagne as we know it is a modern wine; young by comparison with the historic still wines of Bordeaux and Burgundy. It is little more than a century ago that it first became possible consistently to produce clear, sparkling champagne in safe bottles. Technical changes still go on in its manufacture. There is often reference to the traditions of champagne – and, certainly, under the law it must be vinified 'in accordance with the traditional methods of the region'. Yet it is an industry in flux, the standards which makers regarded, and growers accepted, as established and invariable a hundred years ago become yearly less constant. Its structure contains some inbuilt political, economic and psychological conflicts which do not occur in other winefields. They have been recognized and partly understood for more than sixty years but are no nearer being resolved now than they were then. They involve not only the people of the region but the character, quality and image of the wine itself.

For the visitor to the district the Comité Interprofessionel du Vin de Champagne has devised three Routes de Champagne: the blue route runs from Reims round the Montagne de Reims to Ay; the red along the Marne Valley and back to Epernay; the green from Epernay through the Côtes des Blancs. They now are the routes of tourism; but the Champenois have followed them for centuries. Their new, secondary but important, value lies in leading tourists off the fast roads and into a countryside which grows into the mind through the eyes – green, fresh, uncomplicated, simple, earthy.

Such are the facets of the concept of champagne – le champagne, the wine which is an idea and an image; la Champagne, the ancient kingdom; les Champenois, the people who give it life; and la Champagne viticole – the vineyard region.

Krug: House of Champagne, 1976

11
Summer, Winter and Christmas

Avoid the Wasps

Sip some Nectar in your own Bath

May 1982. The essential purpose of summer drinking is cool refreshment. Like football fixtures, it falls into two phases – home and away. At home, all is simple, perhaps too simple. Away – at picnics – simplicity should be the prime aim.

Temperature is crucial. If the summer party is held indoors, the room should be cool at the start; the presence of a number of people in warm weather will so increase the heat that either the guests swelter, or the windows and doors must be opened wide to let in gusts of evening wind.

Temperature of drinks, too, is important. At home, use of the refrigerator is all too easy – and potentially dangerous. Do not leave drinks long in a refrigerator; never in a deep freeze. Too many summer drinks are ruined by being served so numbingly cold that they freeze the roof of the mouth and are wasted because they cannot be tasted. Ideally they should take their temperature from not too long in a bucket of water with ice in it: what the French call 'frais' (which recalls the head of one of the Grande Marque houses sending back a bottle of his own champagne because it had been too long in the ice for its flavour to be appreciated). If a cooling bucket is used, it will rarely take a long-necked bottle adequately; so, to avoid the first glass being tepid, immerse it cork first in the ice – and water. Tepid wine is an abomination; a double abomination at a summer party.

For picnics, always, but always, load a corkscrew first; and take another in case of mischance. Make sure a freezer bag or box – or both – are ready; that the freezing sachets are in the refrigerator overnight. Allow one more box or bag than you think you will need. You can always drink the contents after you come home; but you cannot conjure them out of the air in the depth of the country. Better still, hold the picnic in your own garden; using no petrol; suffering no sand in sandwiches; no wasps that cannot be defeated by retreat indoors; no long homeward drag; no deprivation of siesta. Best of all, on a very hot day, enjoy it in your own cool bathroom or cold bath.

Always ensure that there is provision for teetotallers, dieters and drivers. Iced tea, iced mint tea, iced coffee, as well as the perpetual orange juice; cool tomato, grape or apple juice with soda. The laced drink is a sick joke. If some want beer at a picnic, ensure that they undertake their own porterage and open their bottles where they will not fountain over other people and their food.

Now your conscience is clear – assuming someone else is coping with the food – you may settle to the matter of your own civilized drinking. The best of all is properly chilled champagne. If that seems too expensive (and it does) there are reasonably priced French non-champagne, and Spanish sparklers; and for those who like their fizz sweet, there is the Italian Asti Spumante; which, according to research, is much favoured by *Guardian* readers.

There are some cooling and reviving cocktails but they are for the enthusiastic home barman or those who can afford a professional. There are a few simple ones; Buck's Fizz merely calls for the juice of an orange in a glass topped up with champagne (or substitute fizz). Pimm's needs the addition of a slice of lemon, a sliver of cucumber, some leaves of mint, ice: and top up with soda, champagne – or.

The Spanish Sangria is basically a bottle of red wine, sliced lemon and orange, a sprig of mint, a glass of brandy and fizzy lemonade or soda to taste. Some like to dust the top surface with cinnamon; others to add mixed fruits; substitute champagne for mineral water, or give it a slug of Cointreau.

Aligoté, dry to sharp, is a good summer drink by itself; so are most dry to medium white wines. No need to go for the dearest; but chill them properly – the French Muscadet de Sèvre-et-Maine, Mâcon Villages, the Alsace Riesling, or Sancerre; the German Moselle; Spanish white Rioja – notably the Marqués de Cáceres – Italian Soave; the Californian white – now in a pleasing carafe – from Paul Masson.

White wines generally are best for summer tippling; one red, however, makes splendid hot weather refreshment. Beaujolais – said to be the only alcoholic drink that truly quenches thirst – is superb to swig. It should be cellar cool. *The Guardian*

Turning on the Heat

December 1982. Nothing spurs the urge for a warm drink so sharply as the British winter, when the damp, sleety, wind-driven cold sinks into the bones. It is never keener than when one comes home after a day's work. Then the body cries out for the comfort of warmth in the belly. Some drinks are warming; for instance hot sugary coffee, tea – even cocoa – Marmite or Bovril. Not, though, alcohol. A whisky or a brandy may feel warming as it goes down. To an extent it is, for anyone just in from the cold to a warm house. The truth is, though, that so far from warming the body, alcohol has the opposite effect of dispersing its heat. Indeed, a drunk is a hypothermic risk: liable to die from exposure.

Food warms: and, happily, many drinks accompany it. The instant warmer is soup; beef or game, mulligatawny, giblet, turtle (tinned, good); thick vegetable; perhaps best of all, French onion. None of them is the worse for a glass of sherry in and/or with it.

Many warming dishes are enriched by the cook's addition of wine or brandy. Cooking drives off the alcohol but retains the flavour. Such a warmer is – pre-eminently – oxtail stew. Rashers, onion, carrots and meat browned in butter; casseroled in a bottle of red wine; ten minutes before serving, add celery hearts and a glass of brandy.

Some dishes contain wine by definition: coq au vin, boeuf bourguignon, entrecôte marchand de vins, kidneys in Madeira. There is gigot en chevreuil – leg of lamb marinated 48 hours in full red wine (a bottle), onions, bay leaves, and a little olive oil before roasting. Or hare Piedmontese jointed and left two days in a marinade of Chianti, celery, onions, peppercorns, bay leaves, garlic and bouquet; browned in butter with chopped rashers and casseroled; stir in the hare's blood and a glass of Armagnac a few minutes before serving.

So, to eat the dish – with wine. The most warming wines come from regions whose people are generally warm enough. The most northerly wine regions, Germany, Champagne and England, have white wine; white may warm, but does not feel as if it does. The real warmers, as should be expected, store the heats of sunny lands; Burgundy, the Rhône, Provence, Italy, Spain.

Prise open lips stuck together by the richness of oxtail; and the accompaniments are legion. The automatic reaction – which is right – is to go for reds. If, though, the dish is fatty (worth skimming) a young fresh wine, like a Beaujolais or a young Rioja or Chianti, is the wisest choice. Otherwise the big reds: no more than room temperature: the warmth is built in. Châteauneuf-du-Pape is obvious; but not all of such broadly namd wine is good: the cheaper bottles should be viewed with caution. Safer with the fine Côte Rôtie – not too old – the powerful, deep Gigondas or Cornas; Hermitage, full, round and majestic; or a Crozes-Hermitage, cheaper and little the worse with a big, rich, oniony, meat dish.

With hot pasta the Italians offer Barolo – weighty from the Nebbiolo grape – or Chianti (worth buying the Reserva, in the straight-sided, Bordeaux-type bottle). With spicey, gamey, Spanish food like the hugely warming chorizos, served with beans and peppers – any good Rioja; especially once more, a Reserva. Alternatively, one of the Torres heavyweights from Penedés – like the Tres Coronas or Sangredetoro. With peppery – paprika – meals, the Hungarian Vilanyi Burgundi. Egri Bikaver – Bull's Blood – can be good, but usually reaches Britain too young. It is worth cellaring for four or five years, when it can be a big, deep revelation.

To finish, Welsh rabbit with burgundy, or port; sleep well – and warm. *The Guardian*

Dear Boy

December 1982. Here, with love, is your Christmas present (money as you would wish): not as much as I would like, but more, I hope, than you expected. Now, before the courtesies, to the annual rough stuff. At this time of year there is plenty of good drink and much bad drinking; the time to drink at home, when too many drink away from home; when too many drive instead of walking after drinking. It is time, too, when the unaccustomed fall to the perils of mixing drinks. Beer to whisky, wine to brandy; cider to Calvados; the paths should never cross. 'Mixing drinks makes you drunk,' Raymond Postgate was once heard to mutter, 'but he must have been drunk to mix them in the first place.'

Now, about enjoying Christmas drinking. As a host, have plenty of soft drinks to hand; not simply ordinary fruit squashes, but, instead of laughing him out, something to tempt and please the driver who likes to drink but knows he should not. Good minerals, like Perrier; Schloer grape or apple juice; tomato juice; use a liquidizer and ingenuity (cabbage gives a peppery bite to a fruity drink); perhaps a drop – but only a drop – of tabasco.

For those who like alcohol, provide their kind of drink but a step or two upmarket from their usual level. That is the true way for them to enjoy drinking: to understand what they are enjoying, and why. The amount of alcohol is not important: pleasure – bouquet, taste, contentment – are. Not necessary with beer because 'better' too often means different; just get in a barrel, well in advance, and treat it well. For the whisky drinker, buy him a few single malts to try; but keep his usual blend in the sideboard. Gin is simply gin: get plenty; and the mixers; simple.

The hard stuff, though, is not for a long party; no alcoholic drink is. Beer is over bulky except for the case-hardened; and even wine can be too much of a good thing. If you are bent on an evening-long party make sure there is plenty of blotting-paper food; hefty open sandwiches, sausage rolls, baked potatoes, quiches, pizzas may not look particularly elegant but they soothe the alcohol-stressed stomach.

For the big parties buy litre or two-litre bottles. Go along to an honest wine merchant and ask to sample. A dry red and a semi-sweet white will probably see you through for a youngish party and most wine merchants will loan glasses.

Be prepared, though, for people taking too much – it would be a remarkable party in any age group if no one did. Try to ensure that no one goes out on the road – or the street – under the weather. Much better a make-shift bed; or billet them on neighbours at the party. Only time hardens us – but not completely – to the potential horrors of a party. Always look under furniture at the end; there are often surprising things – and people – to be found there.

Importantly, have hangover cures to hand. Pints of cold water helped out with health salts before turning in will always help; but those wise and clear-headed enough to remember that do not truly need it. After the fact, more water – above all, sleep, and more sleep, is the healer. Onion soup; hot stew; mashed potatoes; more even than the ingredients that produce a hangover, the effective cures are completely idiosyncratic. Some can face Fernet Branca; Underberg, even two – neat – can produce something near recovery.

The prairie oyster is controversial. All agree on the basics; take a tumbler, crack a raw egg into it without breaking the yolk; add a spoonful of Worcestershire sauce and a dash or two of black pepper. Then argument begins: some add, and perhaps it is safest, a small brandy. Swallow, again without breaking the yolk. Then wait; it is a depth charge. The hair of the dog works for some people. Heavy beer drinkers have been known to take a bottle of beer to bed; open it before going to sleep and drink it flat when they wake. Arghhh!

Better, perhaps even cheaper in the end, and certainly safer (drink parties by no means always make or keep friends), ask a young woman in to help with the cooking and have another couple in to dinner. At least that reduces the number of problems; you can plan your drinks – apéritifs, red and/or white wine, desert wines – and enjoy working out the list.

So far as apéritifs are concerned, cocktails – the American alcoholic jump-starter that stuns the palate – is not for your drink-understanding generation. Champagne is the best before-meal drink: but the finest can cost as much as £20 a bottle, some £9; but you cannot afford it and you do not get it at home. There are, though, many cheap sparklers (£2.65). It's safest to stick to the dry. Safest of all to buy one or two and sample in advance. It is not an unpleasing experience.

Some of your guests will prefer sherry. If that is your appetizer, see that you have three kinds. A good dry (£3.50) is the best apéritif – usually fino. Manzanilla is less usual, and distinguished; medium (£3) is preferred by many who say they like dry. Some people prefer sweet (£3) – and who are you to tell them what they like? If you fancy vermouth, Chambéry (£3.50) is far, out and away, the best: but do not desecrate it with gin.

Some guests, when asked, say merely that they like white wine which, like red, covers a multitude of vins. Safest to give them Moselle (£3-£4.50); light, cheerful, fresh; slightly tingly; edge of fruit but not too sweet. Buy young; be careful about the 1980. Or, increasingly popular nowadays, the Loire Muscadet de Sèvre-et-Maine (£3) is fruity, clean, not too dry, nor too sweet. Do not be frightened to try the Californians. Their Chardonnays (£7) can be fine and big – sometimes almost too big. If there is to be seafood, or someone likes dry white, think of Alsace Riesling (£3.70); Meursault (£8); Chablis (a premier, not a Grand, cru) £5. Some like rosé: two are good, both from the Rhône; both crisp and dry and of some stature: Tavel and Lirac (£3-£3.30). The rest are pink confections for pink confection drinkers.

Beaujolais, as you know, has been called the beer-drinker's wine. Certainly it does not call for a sophisticated palate (£2.30). Make sure it is young, so that it retains its freshness; and take the upmarket step to Beaujolais Villages (£2.70) or even a specific village, like Morgon, Juliénas, Moulin-à-Vent, Chénas, Brouilly (£3.80).

There can be appalling snags with the more serious red wines – especially claret. For the enthusiast, make sure of the right vintage; better a minor wine of a good year than one with a prestigious name from a bad one, or a bottle so recent that it is not ready. You will generally be safe with a 1970, 1971, or 1973 (£10).

With burgundy you can come on to 1978. If you are entertaining your boss, or your intended's father, you might spring a Chambertin (£14), a Morey-St-Denis (£7) or a Corton (£8). Burgundy is costly because it is in short supply and high demand. Côtes de Beaune-Villages (£3) is cheaper and ususally safe.

If you are frightened by the prices of the smart clarets and burgundies, go for the Rhônes: Hermitage (£6.50), Côte Rôtie (£6) or Gigondas (£5) – not too young – will always be good value. Or, saving money without loss of taste, serve a Spanish red Rioja. They are all safe and reasonably priced. Paternina, Marqués de Murrieta, Marqués de Cáceres; Rioja Alta Ardanze (£3). If you want to indulge, go to the top of that vine. Buy a Reserva (£5) of the same name; it is simply older and was considered worth maturing when it was made. Their still whites, with a few exceptions, are not impressive. But the area about San Adurni de Noya makes some good, and good value, méthode champenoise sparklers (£3.75).

If you want a sweet wine with the Christmas pudding or any other dessert, you will find an ordinary sauternes (£3.75) rich enough for anyone, and vastly cheaper than its upmarket superiors; or try the neighbouring Monbazillac (£2.80) or the rich, distinguished Muscat Beaumes de Venise (£5.30).

If you believe in port with the cheese, vintage port is beyond your purse, age or need. Vintage character or late bottled (£6-£7) saves trouble and lacks little in flavour.

After dinner? A Madeira – Bual (£6.40); or Malmsey (£4.80). Or try one of the richer hocks, generally better drunk like liqueurs than with food; not less than a Spätlese (£6) to enjoy it to the full.

What of brandy? Well, the Delamain Pale and Dry (£13) or a 1948 Otard (£29).

What are we both talking about? Go to bed. Remember, though, if you pay much above these prices, you have overspent; much less and you have taken a quality risk. Sleep well.

Your affectionate father.

P.S. Have re-read the letter; times have changed; here is a cheque for another £20. *The Guardian*

12
Touring and Tippling

Grand Tours

September 1981. Those experienced in wine tourism know that it can pose its own particular problems. In its most serious or concentrated form, when one tasting is poured upon another, it can resemble a crammer course. That may be ideal for the student with a thirst for knowledge but often no pleasure for a spouse of milder enthusiasm. It is valuable, though, to have facilities – which the casual traveller through vineyard territory can rarely discover – arranged in advance. That applies especially to tasting and conducted tours of cellars. The agents, too, can usually rely upon sufficiently expert advice to offer an informed balance of visits to the major and differing wine centres.

The question of climate and timing, too, are important. The European high summer is no time to trail round dusty vineyards. The time of significant activity is that of the vendange and the making of the wine, during the long, and generally mild, continental autumn.

It is that period which the evocative French Republican calendar of 1793 divided between Fructidor, Vendemaire and Brumaire – mist, mellow fruitfulness *and* vintage. It is the most pleasant time to travel Europe or, at least, the romance countries.

If writers ought to declare an interest it is, in this instance, finding the French, Italian, Portuguese, and Spanish autumn nostalgically and romantically irresistible. It runs long, too; the splendid German Eiswein has been made from grapes left on the vines until their juice was turned to ice by night frosts of mid-November; (they are pressed while still in a state of frozen concentration).

Because autumn is the most interesting time in the vineyards, presses and cellars, it is also the time when the vignerons are most busy, and visitors least welcome. The gent who can arrange an – apparently – welcome conducted visit at such a time has done well.

Ideally a wine tour should combine that kind of opportunity with broader interests. A specifically wine tour of Tuscany may suggest Philistinism; but a Chianti will never taste better than in the Villa Antinori in Florence; and the visitor to San Gemignano is appropriately refreshed by a few glasses of its Vernaccia. Even the journeys between vineyards – fairly humdrum in some wine districts – in Tuscany, are memorable with the background scenery of some of the greatest religious oils ever painted.

Blackheath Travel (13 Blackheath Village, London SE3) have laid out a beguiling autumn programme of understandingly balanced, non-pressurized, wine tours. The week in Tuscany includes vineyards, tastings and the Enotica; but also sightseeing in Florence, Siena and Pisa. Four days on the Loire encompasses both wine and noble châteaux; and the long, picturesque drive to Paris. One of the three north Portugal trips – all of about a week – takes in Oporto, Vila Nova da Gaia, Aveleda, (vinho verde), Barcelos, Braga – the sanctuary of Bom Jesus – folkfood and folksong. Another goes to the Douro Valley, Vinho Verde country, and Oporto: the third to the Dao and Douro valleys: and they all include samplings in some of the great port lodges.

Only in spring, unfortunately, do they take a party to the Lisbon coast; Lisbon itself, Sintra and Cascais: and the Setúbal dessert wine district, though most importantly, to Colares, where vines, rooted in coastal sand, made it virtually the only vineyard to escape the plague of phylloxera which destroyed the grapes of Europe about the turn of the century.   *The Guardian*

Touring and Tippling

October 1975. The wine tourist has only lately been accepted in the vineyard scene. At first most French and German vignerons tended to regard him suspiciously, witholding their wares jealously from someone not concerned with the wine trade who wanted to taste them – surely a scrounger. Soon, though, they came to see him from a directly opposite viewpoint, as a naive enthusiast, only too anxious to buy wine, romantically, from the very vineyard where it was made, with little critical appreciation of quality or price.

If the Beaujolais and Champagne were the first areas to exploit that situation to any substantial extent, growers throughout the French wine producing areas now sell their wines by the tasting-glass, bottle or case at such profit margins as justify their appreciable expenditure on antique-tarted caves de dégustation.

The beginner-visitor can waste much time and money in finding his way and ascertaining values. So 'Discovery Tours' of the wine regions can be genuinely valuable.

The Burgundy vineyards are eminently touristic country and Inghams (329 Putney Bridge Road, London SW15 2PL) have been sending four- and five-day trips there at vintage time. Early morning departure from the local airport involves seeing the dawn come up over Luton which is a salutary experience: like apoplexy suffusing acne. That salutary experience is eased by – on this sample – the relations between the Britannia staff and passengers, notably more pleasant than on some British airlines: herding is efficient. The party bus from Dijon to Beaune takes the touristically planned and evocatively place-named Route des Grands Crus through the Côte d'Or and Côte de Nuits, and pays a visit to the Clos de Vougeot.

Beaune is a major asset among the wine tours; an ancient, historic, warm – and, above all, walkable – walled town with attractive shops. It offers, too, the Hôtel Dieu, endowed with a legacy of vineyards whose wines are sold at the great annual auction of the Hospice de Beaune, and the generous wine museum in the mansion of the Dukes of Burgundy. They occupy the second morning; the Côte de Beaune the afternoon. After dinner a local expert – in this instance Paul Bouchard of Bouchard Aîné – tasted a wine simultaneously with the party and announced his findings and reactions for general discussion; a skilful and brave performance.

The third concentrated day – the paying party were gourmets for informative punishment – covered the Mâconnais, Beaujolais, and the abbey church of Tournus, with the evening 'free'.

The four-day party (£55-59) had time for shopping in Dijon before they flew home; those who had taken a fifth – for another £8 – spent it in Beaune, which still had much fresh interest to offer and then went back by way of Dijon.

A convincing testimonial to the effect of these tours lay in the conversation of two young men fortuitously encountered in a bar – on an unscheduled visit – who first went to Burgundy on one of the wine tours of Inghams' forerunners, Clarksons. Since then they had driven down twice a year to stay in Beaune and study the surrounding vineyards.

The couriers' good manners and highly necessary sense of humour lightened a determinedly educative, but perhaps over-concentrated tour. Next year it is – wisely – planned to leave the tourists a little more spare time by extending the visits to five and six days.

The Guardian

Alsatian Flight

February 1976. Of all French tours, the Route du Vin d'Alsace is scenically the most spectacular – and gastronomically impressive. Both the region and its wines are increasingly popular with British tourists and drinkers. The regular British Midland Airways flight between Heathrow and Strasbourg used to be almost solely a commuter service between London and the European Parliament. Now, however, it regularly carries both wine-tourists and merchants seeking agencies from Alsatian vineyards.

The publicity map shows the Route du Vin d'Alsace as a green line running unbroken from Thann north to Marlenheim; where a small, adjoining patch of map, with Wissembourg at its centre, has no sign of the Route. In fact Wissembourg is by no means so near Marlenheim as the map shows it. It is 56 kilometres north, up the narrow and busy N63 through the sugar beet, cabbage, tobacco, maize, asparagus, and hop fields of agricultural France. Such a journey might well discourage the wine tourist: yet it is well worth while, and Cleebourg is at its end. These are the most northerly vineyards of France, producing almost 10 million bottles of high quality wine a year, yet constantly left off wine maps and rarely mentioned in the reference books. Wissembourg itself is over the border into Germany; and so are some vines of the outlying Cleebourg vineyards.

When the Second World War began, the Cleebourg vines – of Rott, Offenburg, Steinseltz, and Cleebourg – lay precisely and grotesquely between the Maginot and the Siegfried lines. That was no place to make wine. The occupying Germans compensated the growers for their vines, which ran rank or were cut up by military operations, and all production stopped until the end of the war. Then Alsace once more became French territory and the growers claimed compensation from France to replant their vineyards. So, they were paid twice; which was, in truth, not unreasonable.

The leader and spokesman for the Cleebourg vignerons was Georges Rupp. He was said to have cooperated with the Germans in negotiating compensation for the vines, and was put into a concentration camp. His fellow vignerons, however, protested so reasonably, justly, and vehemently that he was not only released, but awarded the Legion d'Honneur. Thereupon he founded the two local cooperatives for wine and fruit.

The Cleebourg vineyards are in three respects unique in Alsace. Because they occur at the point where the Vosges mountains turn west, they are the only vines of the region on purely south facing slopes. Their complete post-war replanting ensured that they had none of the lesser Knipperlé, Chasselas, or hybrid grapes as other Alsatian vineyards have. Importantly, too, it is the only wine district of the region where every vineyard owner belongs to the cooperative.

Cleebourg produces all the classical Alsace types of wine – Riesling, Tokay d'Alsace, Sylvaner, and Gewürztraminer – except Muscat, which the director does not think grows at its best in that setting.

The director is Georges Rupp, son of that Georges Rupp who founded the two cooperatives: he has succeeded his father also as Mayor of Steinseltz. Letters to him are addressed, somewhat unusually – Monsieur Georges Rupp, Maire, Rue Maire Georges Rupp, Steinseltz. *The Guardian*

A Tipple on the Quay

July 1983. The Sixth World Wine Fair opened at Bristol yesterday, appropriately enough, in the thirstiest weather of the year.

It continues to succeed as the best possible presentation of the wines of the world to the honest drinking public and is the only one of the current national fairs not confined to the trade. It has developed a happily clubbish atmosphere among the parties which often come by coach to sample its exhibits. There are over 300 exhibitors offering products of more than 30 countries – from the latest novelties to the established wines of the world.

The formula is now established. The visitors come in – admission £5, which includes eight tasting vouchers – and make their haphazard way round the various stands on two floors and at the water's edge. They can taste for vouchers or for cash. There are experts to guide them and discuss; tastings and lectures; above all, countless opportunities to sample and learn.

It appears that the solid bank of support is for the semi-sweet white wines; but inquiries and tasting range widely. There is a thirst for knowledge which must hearten everyone with a hope for wine drinking in British life. Nothing is more impressive than the look of wonderment on the face of a primary student – tempted to wine drinking, perhaps, by a package European holiday – at the impact of some rich, Rhenish wine; a steely Alsace; or a profound Spanish Reserva. Unless it be the bliss of someone enjoying a glass of well made and well-chilled champagne at 11 of a muggy morning.

The organizers are fortunate in having lost most the duller stands of old, which contributed little public information and nothing at all to the fun of the fair.

The setting is fortuitously handsome – beside the Bristol waterfront. The ancient wine wharves, formerly derelict although officially protected, have been converted into a series of shops, cinemas, restaurants and bars, to form a handsome approach to the fair itself.

Once inside there are many surprises. A Chilean pavilion was hardly to be expected, but it is expansively ambitious. Upstairs, a Russian stand offered Shampanskoe (officially КРЫМ) sparkling wine – red or white, sweet, semi-sweet, and brut. Unfortunately for a pleasant young woman in charge of the stand, no one could find her sufficient ice to present her wares fairly.

There was the usual refreshing Portuguese pavilion; and an impressively wide-ranging one from California. Eurocave showed their alternative-to-wine-cellar cupboards, a boon to flat-bound buffs.

The sharpest of the novelties were undoubtedly the sorbets based on the Boudier liqueurs and Eaux de Vie, quite the most alcoholic ice creams ever conceived. They more than justified their introduction. Close behind came Fracasse, a somewhat startling melange of sparkling wine flavoured with liqueur framboise and Crème de Cassis made at Nuits St George and retailing at £4 a bottle.

Less novel, but still interesting, were the Franken wines in bocksbeutels, and the original Rüdesheimer Rosengarten Riesling Kabinett from the historic vineyard surrounded by rose trees – it had a charming floral nose and taste. Even the purists could find no hint of metal in the canned Beaujolais – but canned in France.

Robin Butler showed wine-related antiques, silver and glass, in a covetable display. The Madeira stand competed with majestic wines of almost comparable antiquity. There was plenty of food: from baked potatoes for the hungry: beer for the heretics, strawberries and cream: a bar and a dining room on board the Lochiel tied up at the quay. George's of Bristol displayed their surprisingly generous shelves of wine and cookery books.

Despite the oppressive humidity, it was a friendly, freshly revealing occasion for the British wine enthusiast.   *The Guardian*

By a Nose

November 1977. Yesterday at the Dijon gastronomic fair, the Wootton English table wine was placed first in a competition of English vintages judged by a panel of eminent French experts. Two others – the Biddenden Manor Müller-Thurgau from Little Whatmans, Biddenden, Kent, and Pilton Manor Riesling Sylvaner, from Pilton, in Somerset, placed second and third – were considered to have a rich, full 'nose' and to be well made.

Almost 14,000 people from Dijon and the rest of France, plus about 50 from Germany, 60 from Tunisia, and 40 from Britain (including Glasgow) walked the lanes, visited and tasted the exhibitions. Between them they ate 15,000 oysters, 23,000 snails and 28,000 mussels (the latter turned out as moules marinières by one man at a rate of 3,000 an hour). It is all happily, gravely, enjoyably informal.

The competitions, however, are extremely businesslike. The Judges, who, for the English wines, included a government frauds department taster of professionally highly sensitive palate, said their initial reaction was one of curiosity: but they were 'not disappointed'.

The 16 wines submitted were recommended by the English Wine Growers' Association. Their choice was, on the whole, sound, though it is sad that neither Adgestone (Isle of Wight) nor Cavendish Manor (Suffolk) was entered.

The judges accounted all the wines entered 'honnête' – a highly viticulturally professional compliment. They thought at least half of the 16 wines entered were, 'by Burgundian standards' – and they have no higher standard than that – 'quality' wines. They thought only five of them 'bad'.

At one juncture a seasoned taster withdrew his quizzical nose from the tasting glass and said, drily, 'This wine smells like a woman you have to pay for.' His precise meaning was debated for some time, but he refused to be drawn.   *The Guardian*

Bar Knacks

August 1980. In legal theory at least, the bona fide traveller is entitled to fair treatment in British public houses. Often he receives his due: if he is a wine drinker that is much less than probable. It is common to be charged 65p for a five-ounce glass of wine; that is merely unjust pricing. It is, though, quite intolerable when the wine in question comes from a bottle which has obviously spent the time since it was opened, a week or more, standing directly under the strip lighting, and is consequently undrinkable. Some houses keep their white wine pleasantly cool on the same chilled shelves as their lagers and minerals. There, too, though, the barman will often shake the last dregs of an elderly bottle into the glass before he tops it up from a fresh one. This constantly happens in pubs where the beer is treated with the reverence it deserves; rested before it is broached, and served from the barrel, at perfect temperature.

A reasonable licensee in amiable conversation will ask, 'But what can do, I sell about four or five glasses a week: I can't throw it away when it's off, that's not economic; no, there's nothing I can do for the wine drinkers unless they want to buy a bottle; but if they do, I must sell it to them at by-the-glass prices.'

That argument is indefensible. It is possible to serve good wine fresh from a small bottle. R & C Vintners have recently extended their Single Serve Moussec range. They now offer 10cl bottles of three French wines in their Vin de Table range – red, white and rosé – plus two quality wines, a Liebfraumilch and an Appellation Contrôlée Côtes du Rhône. Any one of those bottles will make two fair glasses; and a publican can buy them through his wholesaler at about £3 a dozen for the vins de table; £4 for the other two. At that rate he could sell them to his customers, without the slightest fear of falling into bankruptcy, at 40p or 50p a bottle.

John Lipitch of R & C Vintners, who has been interested in this single serve problem and has marketed these measures for some time, lately came upon an alternative method of providing fresh wine to the one-glass drinker. In the new and smart Bistro de Bordeaux he found a wine service of high-class French wines by the glass. The house had a highly expensive counter rack of some dozen bottles from which they serve by the glass. The wines – crus classées of the Médoc, and fine burgundies – were kept fresh by a nitrogen sparge floated over the surface so that a bottle could be kept open for a fortnight without noticeable deterioration in quality. To be sure a glass of 1934 Château Palmer cost some 23 francs (about £2.20 a glass) but it would have been equally expensive by the bottle; and by this arrangement someone lunching alone could savour some four or five fine wines for little more than the price of a bottle.

A similar, if less high level, kind of service has been launched in this country by Gales of Horndean, doughty defenders of the principle of real ale. In that field they have little respect for beer served under pressure. Clear mindedly, however, they recognize that what may be sought for the booze is not necessarily right for the vino. They have collaborated with Teltschers, the major Yugoslav importers, to provide a bar service of top condition wine.

The show bar is Donald Powell's Hog's Lodge at Clanfield, a few yards off the main A3 London to Portsmouth road. There, after experiments with red and rosé, which kept well but did not sell enough to justify stocking, they have compounded for a semi-sweet Yugoslav Riesling, served cool – but not too cold (a controlled 55°F) – and in perfect condition, for 46p the five-ounce glass. The wine will keep, at need, six to eight weeks in good condition. Consumption, however, runs at a fairly steady nine gallons a fortnight so that the storage period is kept far short of maximum. Gales have extended the availability of this wine through a dozen of their houses. If their first modern reputation was for real ale, they have perceptively followed it with a service of honestly drinkable wine.

Other chains and pubs could accept this example if they genuinely wished to give the wine drinker a fair deal. In general, though, they do not. Many landlords, no doubt, offer lip service to the concept of wine by the glass. The staff, though, generally do not.

The Guardian

Vinotabulaphobia

August 1973. Vinotabulaphobia – or horror of wine lists – is a major and justifiable cause of anti-wine attitudes. The constant question 'How do I read a wine list?' cannot be completely answered; but it is possible to offer some cautionary advice.

The first problem is that wine lists are not uniform; some few include tasting notes or advice; most have no more than group headings, names (often without years, shippers, or other relevant information), and prices. The Victorian books on wine merely advised the beginner to 'be guided by the wine waiter'. That was sound advice then, but not now. Only a small proportion of those who serve wine in the current British restaurant explosion understand the subject, and not all those can be relied upon to act in the customer's interests.

They may have a declining wine, an overstock, or an over-priced line to unload.

Anyone uninformed about wine, entertaining an unfamiliar guest, and faced with the wine list, can feel lonely. At least he can observe two negatives. Do not hastily observe the old 'way out' and point to the third item down the chosen class. While in most lists the prices increase from top to bottom of each group, in some they do not; check the prices. No one ordering wine at the table should ask for the most expensive of even an average list: an outstanding claret, burgundy, hock, or champagne ought to be ordered in advance of the meal so that it can be chambré, chilled, or allowed to breathe.

It is safe, though not mandatory, to take red wine with red meat, white wine with white meat or fish. Red wine will serve equally well with white meat, though not with fish – except, perhaps, claret with salmon.

The chief possibility of embarrassing error is ordering a dry wine when a sweet one is wanted, or vice versa. Thus a white Bordeaux, German, Italian, Portuguese, or Spanish wine may be dry, medium, or sweet. Unless the list indicates the degree of sweetness, the diner-out who is not familiar with the wines would be wise not to take the risk of ordering drink which positively clashes with the food.

This is why so many people order the 'safe', rule-of-thumb Mouton Cadet, Liebfraumilch, or rosé. Dining out, however, should not be a matter of safety, but of pleasure. No red Bordeaux, burgundy, or Rhône wine will ever be anything but dry, and will always partner meat well. All white burgundy, Rhône, or Algerian on an ordinary wine list will be dry. Under the heading 'White Bordeaux,' Graves will never be so dry as a white burgundy: all Sauternes or Barsac will be sweet. Hungarian Tokay is a sweet dessert wine, Tokay d'Alsace is piquant. Muscatel is generally sweet but Loire Muscadet and Alsatian Muscat both have a dry finish and will go well with fish, shell fish, or as an apéritif. Other wines from Alsace and the Loire can be rich. It can be both pleasing and economical to choose a low priced white burgundy as an apéritif.

Once you have reached a decision as to red or white, Bordeaux, Burgundy, Rhône, or champagne, and if none of the wine names rings any bell in the memory, decide purely on what you can afford. Barring the risks of overconfidence, these notes should provide adequate

safeguards against error until drinking breeds familiarity and familiarity knowledge.   *The Guardian*

Wining Faith

March 1974. Is it safe to order carafe wine in a restaurant? There is no simple answer. The question itself, though, is significant. Many occasional diners-out view wine with suspicion, and with some reason. While there are many honest merchants and restaurateurs, opportunities to defraud, or at least exploit, customers are dangerously plentiful in the wine trade; and nowhere more than in restaurants.

The customer can be in some peril. The temptation to make virtually undetectable illicit profit on drink is strong – even for the almost-honest – through masking bad wine (and there is a vast difference of principle between bad and poor); mixing in left-overs from tastings, or filtered dregs; or even serving the 'claret' which, according to some recent writers, can be made from grape concentrate, rose petals, honey, bananas, and elderberries; or for that matter, by some recent reports even chemicals and almost no grapes.

The best guarantee against most of these practices lies in the fact that, except for the most unscrupulously mercenary caterers, the return is hardly worth the – slight – risk, or the trouble. 'Real' – though poor – wine can be bought so cheaply that it shows a margin which should satisfy even the greediest man.

Carafe service is normal in the wine-making countries. It is the logical way to serve wine from the barrel – wine which probably came from the restaurateur's relations in the country – or his vigneron neighbour in the village – in cask and has simply never been in a bottle. Indeed in France, Italy, Spain, and Portugal far more wine is brought to the table from the barrel than from labelled bottles.

There are perhaps more grounds for suspicion in England, because wine from the barrel is rare here. Usually in this country a carafe wine comes from a container of a size somewhere between a barrel and a two-litre bottle. Invariably, too, it is cheap; and derives dignity from a decanter rather than from its label – if any.

Crucially, its price is so much lower than the bottled wines of the establishment that, while still showing a substantial profit margin to the seller, it makes dining out considerably cheaper for the customer; or, for some, possible.

The doubting customer has three possible safeguards. The first and best is knowing and respecting the proprietor of the establishment. Indeed, dining out is almost entirely a matter of trust. If you can safely assume that you will not be given 'off' fish or meat masked by highly flavoured sauce, synthetic cream, tinned fruit (especially grapefruit), instant coffee, or Argentine steak masquerading as 'Angus', then you will also assume that the wine is 'honest'. The qualification here, however, is that profit margins on wine are often extremely high in establishments where prices are otherwise fair.

In a strange restaurant it is perfectly reasonable to ask the wine waiter 'What is the carafe wine?' If he hesitates that is ground for suspicion. The best recent reply to the question was 'Chianti – not so good as our bottled Chianti – that's why its cheaper – but it's what the guv'nor gives us.'

Finally there is the test of the palate. If it tastes good it probably is. Then it does not matter if it is a blend of something the owner has bought extremely cheaply and sold at a large profit. If in doubt, however, buy the lowest priced bottle of wine on the list and ensure that it is opened at your table. It may be dearer: but it is cheap if it makes the difference between confident pleasure and queasy doubt.

The late Sir Cedric Hardwick used to recall sitting near the service door of a famous New York theatrical restaurant when, as two waiters passed, he heard one say to the other, '*And* he ate it – the lot.' Wining out, like dining out, is a matter of faith.   *The Guardian*

13
France

Holiday in le Beaujolais

May 1983. There is a vast difference between a holiday in France and a French holiday. It is possible to go to France and have an English-type holiday plus sun; but it is also possible to spend a *French* French holiday. This is addressed solely to enthusiasts for the second kind.

Fly to Lyon (possible from all European capitals) or take the 160-mph TGV from Paris to Mâcon (about two hours). On first entering France acclimatize yourself with a Pernod; only one; the water dripped unhurriedly; the whole drunk equally slowly: it is a kind of (temporary) naturalization.

Hire a car. Seventeen kilometres north-west of Lyon you will cross the river Azergues; ten south-west of Mâcon, the Veyle. In either event you will then be in the Beaujolais; note, not Beaujolais, but *le* Beaujolais. It is not large; 48 kilometres north-south, 16 east-west; it has virtually no main roads, unless you count the D37 which meanders east-west from Belleville to Beaujeu. That may sound like walking size but the roads are so twisty as almost to treble crow-flight; and some of them are extremely steep.

The guide books and the tourists ignore it. Climb any of the hills of the Beaujolais and look outwards to the east, though, and you will see the traffic and trains hurrying north-south along the Route Napoleon, Paris-Marseilles.

The French, of course, appreciate it; they visit it increasingly to enjoy the essence of their own rural countryside. The Beaujolaises, in

156

their own defence, do not widen their narrow and difficult roads. Chesterton's assertion that the rolling English drunkard made the rolling English road may not be true, but there can be no doubt that those responsible for the roads of the Beaujolais were familiar with the local tipple. Against foreign visitors who determinedly do not speak French they are defensive, but courteous to those who try.

It is a land of vineyards and villages. If you come to a large town – Villefranche, or even Belleville – you have strayed out of the Beaujolais. To the north you may climb the hills – not exceptionally high at 3300 feet – but impressive in scale and, in winter, often snow-topped; you look away to the winding Saône, the mountains of the Jura, and, on a clear day, the Alps.

At Beaujeu, capital of the Beaujolais (pop. 2301), there is a folk museum with – no surprise – a tasting cellar built into it. At Salle there are ancient cloisters in the priory; a superb panorama from la Terrasse; a twelfth-century Augustine abbey at Belleville; massive old fortresses at Chenelatte and Bois d'Oingt.

That, though, is not what you have come for; you have come for the life and the people of a region which is pre-eminently wine country, its name synonymous with the wine which prompts the saying that the city of Lyon – where it was first exported on any large scale – is washed by three rivers – the Rhône, the Saône, and Beaujolais. Probably the Romans had vines there; but, at the time of the French Revolution, there were few; it was a lonely, infertile, strip of sheep country. The great estates were broken up, and now, from 50,000 acres of land, about 10,000 growers produce nearly 150 million bottles a year of the simplest, cleanest, most easily drinkable wine in the world. Made from the once banned Gamay grape, it is one of the few red wines better served cool. Indeed it is said to be the only wine in the world that truly quenches thirst.

From June until the picking, the tiny villages hoist their houses and church spires out of a vast green sea of vines that laps up so closely to their walls that the graveyards are never extended; that would cost good vine land.

In the south, the Bas (polite recent abbreviation of the former Bastard) Beaujolais produces run-of-the-mill Beaujolais and most of the popular Beaujolais Nouveau. There, too, is probably the most companionable town of the region, Bois d'Oingt; a business place warm with good humour and companionable drinking.

To the north, where the Gamay loves the granite soil, you climb through, first, the vineyards of the Beaujolais Villages; and of the nine felicitously named great growths – St-Amour, Juliénas, Chénas, Moulin-à-Vent, Fleurie, Chiroubles, Morgon, Brouilly and Côte de Brouilly. There are tasting cellars in most of the villages, and at most of the many cooperatives: and there is usually a reassuring glass for the motorist who loses his way in the tangle of roads. It is claimed that, at the Maison du Beaujolais, out on the N6, it is possible to taste every wine of the district: recommended only to visitors with happily teetotal drivers.

If wine is the labour and the staple diet of the Beaujolaises, their sport is boules. See them there, the serious players; faces ruddy red from sun, wind and wine; peaks of their berets pulled so sharply forward into peaks that from a distance they look like pecking birds. This is the game; watch it; appreciate it; it is skilfully played in those parts.

The life is broad, earthy and expansive. Gabriel Chevalier most accurately placed that raciest of novels, *Clochemerle*, in the Beaujolais. The actual village was Vaux-en-Beaujolais, where there is now a splendid Cave de Clochemerle with magnificently bawdy paintings, an Auberge Clochemerle; though the film was made in the nearby St Lager.

Book your hotel early; they are few and small; at a pinch, though, someone will always find you a bed. Above all, you will eat simply but magnificently. The three-star restaurants are not here; but they are near at hand, in and about Lyon. Here you will eat the folk dishes of people to whom eating is important; and the midday meal sacred. Every village serves meals but do not be late for lunch or the restaurant will be full. The wise, inexperienced and small-stomached will picnic from the pork products, brawns, sausages, hams (especially the parslied ham) from such charcuteries as that of the legendary Mademoiselle Marguerite Chabert at Fleurie; and a bottle of the local wine. Then in the evening you can 'sleep where you eat' after one of the huge local meals. To complete the scene, you will eat well: for you are at the heart – in Burgundy and the Lyonnais – of the best of French food and cooking. Choose from onion soup with cheese, fresh fish stew, beef in Beaujolais, chickens or beef from nearby Bresse and

Charollais; snails in sauce meurette; kid meat; breadcrumbed and deep-fried tripe ('fireman's apron'), baby eels, eggs poached in wine, quenelles of pike; and, unless your will-power is strong, the vastly rich gâteaux, nougat with chocolate, meringues, chocolate with almonds. Wash it down with the wine of Beaujolais, the easiest wine in the world to drink. You will return fatter; but, in mind, heart and understanding, more French than ever before. *The Mail on Sunday*

Jura

January 1978. Many factors have contributed to the widening scope of British wine catalogues: in the past decade the most important, probably, economic, as the fine wines have gradually been priced beyond the purses of all but a few. Touring, though, has played a considerable part, especially in introducing the wines of Spain, Italy, the Midi and the Languedoc and, to a smaller but growing degree, Alsace.

The next wine-tourist region to become popular could well be the Jura. The vineyards, of about a dozen square miles, run through attractive, fresh, green, and varied foothills of the Jura mountains; while Arbois, centre of the best wine, is a pedestrian-busy, ancient, small French town of good family shops, old houses, little bridges, and a small stream. It was Pasteur's birthplace and there he carried out the experiments with Jura wines which changed the whole shape of wine-making.

Twelve million bottles a year is not a large output by French standards; but Jura vineyards, hard hit by the phylloxera, have shrunk from 18,400 hectares in the last century to less than 1000. Still the area under vines produces red, white, rosé – some of it called 'grey' – still, and sparkling wines; about 30 per cent of them appellation contrôlée. They are not merely widely varied; they are, in two kinds, unique.

Of the unusual *vin jaune*, the most famous is Château Chalon; not a wine château in the accepted sense of the word, but an appellation granted to the town of that name and three of its neighbours. It is basically a white wine made from the Savagnin grape, like sherry, but not fortified.

After slow fermentation, it is stored in wooden casks with air space at the top where, by some freak unknown anywhere else except in Spain, a *flor* of the sherry type forms naturally on the surface of the wine. The French law specifies that it must be kept in barrel for at least six years. It tastes like a deeply flavoured fino sherry, and will go on improving in bottle for at least fifty years.

The accidents to which it is subject during its long – and therefore expensive – maturation period ensure that it can never be cheap; and it is on the whole rare (not more than 60,000 bottles a year of all *vin jaune*). O. W. Loeb, of 15 Jermyn Street, London S.W.1, have a 1970 Côtes du Jura Vin Jaune at £6.14.

The *vin de paille* is called straw wine because, traditionally, the gathered grapes were laid out on straw to dry. Nowadays they are generally dried by other means before they are pressed – sometimes as late as January or February – to produce a distinguished rich dessert wince of about 15° alcohol.

It is generally held that the best Jura wine is the Arbois rosé; some rank it with Tavel as the finest of all rosés; but it is slightly sweeter and less coherent. The reds cover a range of colours from near rosé (sometimes referred to as 'pélure d'oignon' or onion skin) to an extremely dark ruby from the Trousseau grape. The white, generally made from the local version of the Chardonnay, is fully flavoured, clean, and best drunk young.

Most of the wine production of the Arbois district is controlled by Henri Maire, whose name is more widely paraded there even than Pasteur's; in some areas the wall signs suggest he is standing for President. A local map shows that he has 18 vineyards there, as well as an impressive tasting house in the town itself and a most up-to-date winery – to use the appropriate Australian term – and the office complex with its vast filing, mailing, and addressograph system to ensure that his tens of thousands of customers across the world unfailingly receive his literature and notices of his latest offers and packages. His deep, ruby, Henri Barberousse, arguably the best Jura red, is £2.70 French bottled from Justerini & Brooks (61 St James's Street, SW1A 1LZ) who also sell the clear, crisp Côtes du Jura 'Blanc de Blancs' at £2.30. Henri Maire has done much to promote Jura wines outside their own particular district. A major check to his plans is the fondness of the local people for their own wines: they are happy – even proud – to drink most of current production themselves. In Britain Loeb offer the lively 1968 L'Etoile Blanc at £2.64; and three Côtes du Jura from Arlay – the 1967 rouge at £2.74, 1964, £3.14; and 1966 blanc at £3.15. It tastes best with the well flavoured food of the unpretentious, but sound and reasonably priced, restaurants of its native territory.   *The Guardian*

Wines of Alsace

April 1973. Anyone who has drunk Alsatian wine in the places where it is made will never be able to taste it without recalling those associations. The food is distinctive, the company earthily cheerful, and the wine villages splendidly set, their church spires cunningly placed, dark and sharp against a light sky, or white to stand out on the sombre background of the fir-cloaked slopes of the Vosges.

Yet for anyone who has never been to Alsace, these wines are still unique, and their makers are at constant effort to retain and even emphasize their specific character. In Burgundy, for instance, the vignerons will leave the cellar doors open to encourage malolactic – secondary – fermentation of their wine; in Bordeaux it occurs rarely and is not regarded as important; in Germany it does not matter, for the wine is by nature fairly acid. In Alsace, however, the growers are fiercely convinced that the process destroys the true Alsatian flavour and they will go to all lengths – sterilization, centrifuge, and early-bottling – to prevent it.

The distinctive flavour of their wine is never more apparent than in a Riesling – it need be no more than two or three years old – with Alsatian matelste cooked in a Riesling. That is a pairing hard to follow; better, probably, to end the meal there, and turn the flavour on the palate and the memory.

Only their white wines reach this level of distinction. The fact that some red wine is made from the fine Pinot Noir grape is, gastronomically speaking, no more than a technical quibble. One good restaurant in Colmar listed a local red, but when the wine waiter was asked for it he said firmly: 'There is no red wine in Alsace, only rosé.' Under pressure he produced it; it was red – though only just – and we should have taken his advice. It was, however, illuminating as an unforgettable, if rather exaggerated demonstration of what the French call 'goût de terrier'; but the taste of the soil was too strong for enjoyment. The same waiter, asked to name his favourite Alsatian wine, replied unequivocally: 'Beer'. Yet he was later observed taking the local white carafe wine in the true Alsatian long-swigging fashion.

Halfway up the picturesque cobbled main street of Riquewihr are the shop, offices, and cellars of the family Hugel who have made and sold wine there for twelve generations, since 1636. In their main cellar they have the oldest wine cask still in use in the world; made of oak in 1719 and elaborately carved, it contains 8800 litres – a thousand dozen bottles – and was acquired by one of the family after the French Revolution. They are realists – 'if you are an Alsatian winemaker you change your nationality and lose your market every 25 years' – as well as idealists about their wine. Jean Hugel, now the elder of the household, believes that 'people all over the world want – and should be able to buy – a bottle at the price that ought to be its value'. There are, he argues, three essential ingredients to a good wine – the grapes, the technical ability of its maker, and the integrity of its maker.

He added, too, that the most important man in any cellar is the one who can make the most of the grapes he has; even a poor wine can be made drinkable; the man who really counts is the one who loses least of what it has.

This has been the philosophy of Alsatian wine-makers ever since the end of the First World War when they set out to re-establish the long-suppressed standing of their product. They have succeeded; now they are waiting for the slow palate of world fashion to recognize the fact.

January 1978. It used to be said that some wines 'do not travel'. That applies to few nowadays since modern methods of vinification virtually guarantee stability. It is true, though, that most wines are at their best drunk in the district where they are made, and with its food. 'Drink the wine of the country' is the soundest of maxims for travellers and tipplers.

The vast increase in wine tourism drives its truth home, nowhere more than in Alsace, in a way a place apart. Every quiz student knows that it is the most northerly French wine region; but not everyone realizes that, with the exception of Perpignan, it is also the driest; (during the German occupation it was said to be the driest in Greater Germany). Set in the eastern lee of the Vosges it is, too, remarkably warm. Within 60 miles going west and crossing the mountains, the daytime temperature dropped by 20 degrees.

Inside its natural boundaries of the Rhine and the Vosges, tugged, taken and ceded by Gauls, Germany and France, Alsace has tended to become a self-contained unit. So its foods are as unique as the wines to accompany them. Virtually no smart German hotel or restaurant serves sauerkraut; on the other hand, no Alsatian establishment at any level – including the Auberge de l'Ill, one of the best in France and a street ahead of any in Germany – would fail to have choucroute; and most have the splendid choucroute Royale – and a fine Alsace Riesling – which is quite unlike any German Riesling – to go with it.

So the Alsatian Zweibeltorte (onion tart), knepfl (savoury dumplings), Schiffala (smoked pork shoulder), Baeckaoffa (mixed meat casserole), Marknepfle (poached meat balls), Ill creamed pike, Kougelhopf (fruity bun) and Birewecke (fruit bread) are unlike any other dishes to be found anywhere.

Above all, while foie gras is produced elsewhere, there is none like the foie gras de Strasbourg served hot, en brioche. Nowadays the goose livers may be imported from any one of half a dozen countries; but the process of marinating in old Alsace wine gives the Strasbourg foie gras its unique flavour. Only fine wines can live with such rich food; but the Alsatians hold their own.

Even the wine route of Alsace, the most picturesque of them all, steals attention from the wine. Riquewihr is all sixteenth- and seventeenth-century houses, no traffic – well, hardly any – no television aerials – well, hardly any – a place to walk in, soaking in the middle ages through the pores, and surrounded by fine vineyards. You will do well, too, in autumn there, to take the vin bourru (new wine) with fresh walnuts.

Eguisheim, the circular sixteenth-century town; Ribeauvillé with its three mountain-top castles; Obernai, flowers and towers; Bergheim within its walls; Barr, towers and wooden houses; Turckheim, of the three gates – not simply wine villages but tourist centres in their own right – form a major background to a life of which the wine is a part, a part blending in so perfectly as to become an unobtrusive ingredient of a splendid whole.

Perhaps, too, many visitors are unused to the Alsace wine pattern, which is unlike any other. Certainly local pride in it is unexpectedly fierce; an official wine-trade handout reads, at one point 'Betrayed and adulterated during the long German occupation from 1871 to 1918 it was only used to improve the wines of Baden and Moselle.'

Since then, interrupted by yet another German invasion from 1940 to 1945, the Alsatians have steadily improved the quality of their wine. Now it must be as good as it has ever been, even in the fifteenth century when over 20 million gallons from more than 400 villages were exported every year; and it is quite unlike any other in the world.

The wine generally is known by the name of grape from which it is made – Riesling, Muscat, Tokay, Pinot Blanc, Sylvaner. Vineyard names are rarely used; most bottles bear the name of the maker – many of whom, quite unlike general practice elsewhere in France, may make four or five different kinds in most years.

These wines have progressed on the British market steadily, if not so rapidly as the producers hoped, for more than a decade. For some years there have been moves afoot in Alsace to establish an aristocracy of wines; not merely by separating 'noble' wines from the lesser, or even establishing grand cru level, but to admit officially prestigious site and vineyard names – some already known in this country.

Lately some shrewd members of the trade have suggested that, relatively soon, the Alsace may be the only French dry white wines of genuine AC quality to be bought in this country at reasonable prices. If only for that sound economic reason they should be investigated further.   *The Guardian*

Médoc

February 1978. Leaving England under snow and tasting claret in warm sunshine before lunch was a bright start to a visit to the Médoc. Château Chasse-Spleen was given its name – which, of course, means chase away spleen – by Lord Byron. Madame Bernadette Villars who now administers the château belongs to the Merlaut family, who are vineyard owners. She is also an historian who admits sadly that research has convinced her Byron never visited the place; if he named it, it was as a result of drinking its wine in London.

The 1977 vintage at Chasse-Spleen proved a happy surprise. After early frost and a wet summer it was so nearly given up for lost that it was decided that no more harm could come from picking late. The chance came off. The long late sunny spell ended with a wine which shows the vineyard's strongest characteristic – an intensely deep red colour – to perfection; although, of course, it is not remotely ready, it is already deep and well balanced. *The Guardian*

Bordeaux Wine Harvest

Although wine is to be drunk and appreciated anywhere, it is not to be *known* except in France and, even there, perhaps, it is only known completely by the French of the wine-growing regions.

Come to the great square of Bordeaux. You may sit at a table at the Café de Bordeaux and study the stone ladies on the portico of the civic theatre in their differing stages of grime and undress – which vary according to the whims of current cleaners and original sculptors. Simultaneously, and with the barest movement of the head, you may be informed by the civic timepiece or the civic barometer, both of which are part of the structure of two massive central lamp-standards. Content with the provision of refreshment, civic elegance, beauty, chronology and climatic prognostication, it is possible to overlook the half-furtive activity which takes place at the small *tabac* opposite. There, men come and go, hover or relax; they are men who drink coffee without respite and talk furiously in short bursts. These men are dealers in wine, the solitary indication to the traveller who takes refreshment in the main square, that he sits at the hub of the greatest wine-growing district in the world.

There are, of course, wine cellars – some of them extremely vast – in Bordeaux itself, and virtually all the wine of the district passes through it commercially, yet the atmosphere which pervades the wine-growing districts of the surrounding Gironde vanishes at the outskirts of the city, and is not to be recaptured there, except in the single corner where Haut-Brion brings the vines within sound of the trams.

Nevertheless, the character and flavour of the town of Bordeaux are a necessity, for, without the rationalizing touchstone of its urban-provincial air, the newcomer could be overborne by the mystique of the vine which persists among the vineyards. For this mystique – and it is difficult to rate it lower – is the temper of the wine-growing districts. The suspicion that it is all elaborate deception is dispelled almost as soon as entertained. There are, indeed, certain mildly deceptive facades erected to take the eye of the visitor and to persuade him into an interest which he might not otherwise feel. On the other hand, the true character of the wine-country and its people is at once its finest justification and its most artless side.

It is, I am convinced, its genuine profundity and its extreme complexity which have mitigated against any completely satisfying study of the wine country of France ever having been written. To write a pleasantly chatty 'travel' book of the vineyards is relatively simple to anyone experienced in topographical description; to write a pastoral study of the workers there is not beyond the compass of the adequate country writer; to examine the wines from the point of view of the connoisseur, or of the châteaux from the viewpoint of the architect or the historian is, again, limited only by the amount of work the expert writer is prepared to spend on his task. But, every one of these aspects must contribute to the full study of the vineyards, since they are all essential ingredients of the life. Moreover, they must be fused not only with the highly complicated technical and commercial sides of the business, but also with the unique but barely analysable mental attitude which exists in the vicinity of the great vineyards. Such a study calls for a blend of the scholar, the novelist and the native of wine country such as literature has not yet contained.

If any attempt is to be made to present the vines and wines of Bordeaux, it must illuminate surfaces on many different levels of thought, for while complicated matters of fact can be presented straightforwardly enough, they must, for the English-speaking world, be related to their general setting. Such a work must be a huge one; the present essay can only hint at its scope.

The visitor leaving Bordeaux to drive to the wine châteaux has at once to make two major adjustments. The first is in respect of the Bordeaux wine châteaux themselves. In the English countryside, a great residence every two or three miles is a generous allowance. Through the Médoc in particular, however, one may quite frequently see some five or six châteaux within comfortable sight. Secondly, an adjustment has to be made as to the extent of named wines. To have dined in a first-class English hotel is to have seen a wine list bearing, perhaps, the names of some 20 Bordeaux wines. Now to find several hundred names on bottles of genuine worth is to begin to take the fairest long view of the claret industry. Yet, simultaneously, it must be borne in mind that about one tenth of French wine bears the name of its vineyard, while the remainder, at best, goes under the name of its district, even though, as may well be the case, much of it is sound wine.

To tour the Gironde district is to take a journey through vineyard after vineyard, and to bring back an impression of the immense extent of the area under vines. Alternatively, one may visit a single château and, there, move from the broadest outline to the smallest detail of the growth of the vine and the production of wine. Any attempts at compromise between these two extremes brings the realization that both types of visit are necessary for any real understanding, and that the study demands a capacity for absorbing facts, theories and impressions topographical, geographical, historical and agricultural, as well as a thousand conflicting points of viticultural method.

To a far greater extent than in English farming, the active cooperation and goodwill of the wine grower is a necessary adjunct to even the barest study of French wine. The knowledgeable agriculturist in England can walk to the side of a roadside field, crumble the soil between his fingers, calculate the quality of the soil and the fertilizer used and, with a glance at the crop, assess reasonably accurately the quality and the methods of the farmer and the standing of his crops. One cannot, however, gauge the quality of a wine by such methods. The handling of the soil does no more than confirm the fact that the finest grapes grow on land virtually too poor – in its sandy or gravelly character – to produce any other worthwhile crop. Next, while the experienced eye will assess the age of the immediate vines, there is no certainty that their grapes will in fact provide any important part of the vineyard's current output; particularly this is the case if the vines are very old or very young.

Finally – and perhaps this is at once the most revealing and the most baffling part of the vast puzzle of wines – it is difficult to believe, after travelling the vineyards, that the grapes themselves are more than one among many almost equally important factors deciding the final quality of a wine. This statement, of course, needs qualification, but not *essential* qualification. That is to say, among the good wine-making grapes of a particular region, there is little to suggest that such wide differences exist between the qualities of the various grape crops as between the wines made from them. Thus, we may walk along one of the narrow paths which alone separate one vineyard from another, and observe apparently similar grapes – certainly of identical species and the same age – growing in roughly the same condition on either side of the path. These, on the one hand, may be the fruit which produces a wine famous throughout the drinking world, its label a gastronomic guarantee. Thence it is difficult to realize that these similar, neighbour grapes are pressed to a wine so undistinguished that it has no local name of its own but is sold merely as 'Bordeaux' – the lowest level in the order of the region's wines.

Whole books have been devoted to the subject of how wine is made. In fact, it can be told in one sentence – in so far as constants are concerned. As soon as the writer departs from constants, ten books are not enough. Basically it is true to say that the grapes are taken from the vine, that their juice is extracted and allowed to ferment and that it is then barrelled and later bottled. Apart from this process, it would probably be true to say that in the many hundreds of wine making establishments of the Gironde, no two follow an identical course, or achieve an identical result, in any given year.

The average French vigneron will explain his technique – not, perhaps, to the last detailed trick of the trade but at least fairly extensively – and then in three chais within a mile of the teller's, you may find different and absolute contradictions of his methods.

Let us examine something of the passage of the grape from the vine to the bottle, and observe the factors which govern its development. First of all, we shall need to know who controls the château and the wine making. Is there a resident owner and, if so, is he an expert in the field or in the chai – or both? If he is not an expert, is he struggling to learn and making mistakes, or has he an expert in his employ? If the latter – which will also apply if the owner is not resident – in which direction does the expert's own interest lie – in the production of vast quantities of wine or in improvement of quality? Will his failure – particularly in a bad year – be understood, or must he return a profit at all costs? Again, if the owner is a visitor only to the château, does he take over at the time of the vendange and, if so, does he do so with an adequate background of knowledge of his own, or on good advice?

This may appear a complicated approach to so elementary a matter as the ownership of a château, but it has strict bearing on the aim of any particular vendange and, hence, with the methods adopted and the wine produced.

Recall that many of the greatest wines – each with its own distinctive, even unique, character – come from vineyards a mere two or three miles apart, and it will be appreciated that there are basic differences which will produce, over the entire district, a variation between wine and wine which is quite distinct, even to the non-expert, in comparative tasting. These differences derive, in the first place, from the soil, then from the type of grape used and, thirdly, from the rate of replacement of vines, the age to which they will be allowed to produce grapes before they are replaced by new and, at first, unproductive vines – and by whether the ground is allowed a fallow period, and, to some degree, the micro-climate.

The grapes at different vineyards are gathered at varying stages of ripeness between peak juice-content and that mouldy-raisin-like state which, at Château Yquem, is exhibited as 'la pourriture noble' – the noble rot. Every vigneron has his own idea of the exact state at which his grapes should be gathered. Once that is decided, the speed at which they are gathered is dictated by the amount of labour available in the shape of vendangeurs, and also by the weather, which may hasten the gathering by threats of rain or, by actual rainfall, inflict a waiting period, the duration of which is, again, a matter for the vigneron himself to decide.

Gathering is, of course, not uniform: at Yquem, the grapes are detached one by one from the stems; in most vineyards, however, they are gathered by the bunch. Local policy and the quality of overseeing will decide whether they are hastily and roughly gathered, or handled with care – and also the extent to which grapes which fall short of the local ideal of pressable state, shall be included. Again, the labour available and the capacity of the chai will decide the time over which the picking is spread and, hence, the variation in the juice content and sugar content between early and later pressings. Thereafter, the number of vats available is an important factor in the decision as to whether pressings likely – through the state of the grapes or the weather – to produce a different standard of wine are mixed together, and if, for instance, the wine of the young grapes is kept apart from that of the mature growth.

Throughout the entire process, the often conflicting aims of quality and quantity decide many points. For instance, how many pressings shall there be and, if more than one, shall the wine of the subsequent pressings be added to the first or not? Once in vat, temperature, humidity, sugar content and intensity of pressing will produce a fermentation period not always to be foretold even by the most expert. Here, too, there is variation in the degree of use of sulphur salts to combat alien bacterial growth and the employment of yeast cultures to aid fermentation.

The complexities of the manufacture and preparation of barrels, the sulphur cleansing and hot water cleaning are, from time to time, sufficient to convince the newcomer that they are an all-important factor, whose effects may be altered by the minutest inflections of rigid rules: thus, one is amazed to find, at the next cellar, a completely fresh set of rules.

Through the wine country, however, one finds two inflexible rules as to wine in barrel. The first is the high standard of cleanliness observed, especially in respect of the bungs – many of which are made of glass to facilitate cleansing in the early cellar period. The second is that, after wine for tasting has been drawn from the barrel by means of the cellarman's pipette, put into the glass and tasted, the undrunk wine left in the glass is replaced in the barrel for, it is courteously explained, no germs can live in wine.

For the rest, the wine in barrel lives different lives in different cellars. Not only do the fining agents vary – fish scales, white of egg, glue, gelatine, clay, insinglass – but cellar standards are by no means constant. In one, stalactites hang from dripping walls and the proprietaire boasts of the fine effect upon his wine of this humidity; at the next, dusty cobwebs hang from sand-dry walls and the belief is expressed that cellars must be bone dry. At a famous showpiece château, with its electric candles and modern antiquities, one could suspect that the dramatically draped cobwebs which occurred at regular intervals along the otherwise spotless cellar walls, were ingeniously manufactured and only recently hung.

The number of barrels and cellar-labour available dictates the speed and frequency with which the vital space between the 'losing' wine and its bung is refilled with wine through the early stage of barrelling. The wine's progress, economic demand and the supply of bottles all have effect upon the point at which it is bottled. Many considerations conflict in the decision as to whether the wine shall be 'mis en bouteilles au château', or bottled locally, shipped in barrel or mixed with another wine, and whether it is given the name of its vineyard, its commune or its region.

These variations are, certainly, part of the mystery of the vintage, part of the fascination of wine. They make it appear remarkable that any two Bordeaux wines are ever even remotely similar, yet they all have that Bordeaux character which the expert's palate distinguishes even as it observes the particular quality of the vineyard. That his palate does distinguish differences between extremely similar wines is not to be doubted. This fact is frequently challenged when in truth, the fallacy which should be challenged is that which credits expert taste to roughly a hundred times as many persons as really possess it.

The true experts are the men who live with wine. Many of them rigidly abstain from smoking because they accept the sacrifice as part of the bargain by which they taste wine more fully and more subtly than those who smoke. Tobacco is a general enjoyment which they are not prepared to dispute, but they account themselves fortunate that the trade which they follow provides them with a greater pleasure.

The genuine wine châtelain of the wine growing district – if one may venture upon a generalization about so large and, obviously, so varied a community – is a wine enthusiast. If he were anything less, he would not embrace so risky a profession – except in the few cases of the wealthy dabbler prepared to pay for his losses in return for the pleasant life of the château. On average, a single decade gives a vineyard one great year, one good one and, perhaps, two fair ones but, even then, the wine of all four saleable years will not necessarily age well. Recent years have been immensely rich for the wine growers of Bordeaux. 1947 was a great year, 1945 only a little less good, 1948 and 1949 were above average and 1950 promised well both in quantity and quality. Human memory cannot recall so fine a run of vintages in such a short period. For the vintners, however, this is not, immediately, an unmixed blessing, for storage, bottling, prices, exchange and currency difficulties, all present acute complications of his major problem – which is that of selling wine to cover running costs.

Wine in his cellar allows the châtelain to entertain lavishly at his own table, and to no class anywhere in the world is that power a greater delight. It allows him also, to make those presents of wine to other château proprietors which are both an established courtesy and the reason for the variety of wines at château tables. On the other hand, wine in the cellar meets neither wages bills, household expenses nor taxes. In such circumstances as exist at the moment, the vignerons may well be wondering if this, the most lavish blessing of good vintages in their history is, in fact, so desirable as the rarer good year. In the year of poor vintages, the stored wines of greater years command prices high enough to contribute towards making good the bad year. A succession of good years, however, tends to keep prices down. Thus, many have kept the wine of 1945 – rich in achievement and promise – against its rising value with increasing age. But, 1947, two years younger, is generally accepted as a greater wine. Moreover, if both 1945 and 1947 maintain their high price-places, 1948 and 1949 – both good wines – must sell more cheaply. 1950 has not yet come to any authoritative judgement but it is certain that, if it is as good as expected, then it, too, becomes a level to be used against the values of the four older wines.

Yet, while one rarely hears wine merchants discuss wine without reference to prices, who has yet heard a vigneron so much as mention the price of wine? Their talk of wine is an eternal 'shop' which is concerned far more with their life than with their living. Their life passes from vine to bottle without diminution – or indeed change – of attitude. The châtelain takes his glass, looks at the wine against the light, savours its bouquet, tastes it. Then, appreciatively, 'Margaux – 1934'. That is sufficient. Everyone of his acquaintance knows the characteristics of the Margaux wine, and everyone knows exactly how the summer of that great vintage year impressed itself upon that basic character. Thus, any further remark as to body, strength, suppleness, bouquet, is superfluous. Places, châteaux and dates are the mental shorthand of a lore which is so extensive in its ramifications that few men in the world can compass it all. Yet its emanations are in all the air of each autumn's vendange, in the hospitality which makes the proffering of wine a courtesy the châtelain will not forgo. Only the most insensitive visitor could fail to recognize the gift of a vigneron's wine as something far more, in the estimation of the giver, than mere proffering of refreshment.

Therein, the man who produces wine feels the truth about it. It is, in fact, more than mere refreshment. The culture of the vine and the making of wine are sciences – not sciences which may be reduced to invariable and foolproof formulae, but sciences flexible, in experienced hands, to defend themselves against the weather and all the enemies of the grape and its juice. The distinguishing of different qualities as between wine and wine is often ridiculed – yet it is borne out in the hardest of all spheres – that of buying and selling – to the extent of making the price of a specific wine six times that of one produced only a few yards away.

The attraction of the lore, tradition, craft, humanity, of wine growing, the hierarchy of the classification of the Médoc wines is great – but it is also fraught with a considerable danger to those of other nations than the French. The wine snob is a product of enthusiasm. His interest in labels, châteaux and years and, particularly, with their translation into terms of the palate is apt, however, to rob him of pleasure. Thus in his devotion to named, and, particularly, to château-bottled wines, he frequently deprives himself – as no Frenchman, however wealthy in bottles and knowledge of wine does – of the simple pleasure of humbly nameless but eminently drinkable French table wines. Simultaneously, the wine snob tends to discredit wine in the eyes of those who know his subject less well than they know the connoisseur himself. Possibly the great tragedy of French wine in England and America is the establishment of wine drinking, in the public consciousness, as a wealthy and socially upper-class habit. Yet, three or four people may take with dinner a bottle of ordinary table wine – roughly nine tenths of France's wine production – as cheaply as they might with beer.

It would, obviously, be an affectation to suggest that tradition, skill, mystery and fellowship can be tasted in a glass of wine but it is, surely, not extravagant to suggest that Bordeaux wine – even in the relative anonymity of a simple 'Bordeaux' label – has a background which heightens appreciation of the eminently civilized pleasure of taking wine with a meal.   *The Fortnightly*, 1951

Châteaux in the Air

June 1951. Perhaps it was the film 'Passport to Pimlico' that began it, or perhaps it was the depression which always sets in among Englishmen when their meagre annual summer is delayed. Certainly it struck an answering chord to hear two men across the bar wishing they had vineyards in Bordeaux.

For 300 years Bordeaux was capital of the English possessions in South-West France, and we have our roots there even today. The legend still persists that Château Haut-Brion was originally named after an Irishman named O'Brien.

Touring the great wine country of the Médoc and driving up to Château Langoa, the tourist is amazed to find that the proprietor, Mr Hugh Barton, speaks the most polished and perfect English. Although the château has been in his family for over 120 years, Mr Barton was educated in England – his son is at school here now – and he remains, like all his ancestors, a British citizen.

Once to have stayed in a French wine château is to remember it for ever as a greater ideal than a South Sea island, and to count Mr Barton – for all the professional worries of the wine grower – one of the luckiest of Englishmen.

The Bordeaux wine châteaux are among the finest examples of domestic architecture in the world. Sparklingly clean – since grapes are the cleanest of crops – and cool, each is a cross between a manor house and a large farmhouse. The château land can comfortably be scanned from the house itself, for the vineyards are relatively small – a mile across would mean a fairly large one.

This is precious soil, despite its apparent gravelly, sandy or pebbly poverty, for it is the land on which grapes grow best. Therefore it is given over almost entirely to the grapes except, perhaps, a small fallow parcel which feeds the château cow for a return of milk and butter.

There through that April to October carnival of sunshine which is summer in the South of France, the grapes grow until the bustle and excitement of the grape harvest. The châteaux' cellars are the histories of great summers. They hold not only the recent vintages but bottles from all the great years of the vineyards and, also, the wines of the other châteaux of the area which the vignerons courteously present to one another.

Rarely could one share the happiness of another so much as one day at a St-Emilion vineyard. The châtelain had been round his cellars: the grapes were in, they had been pressed; the wine was vatted: there was a fine quantity of it and, as nearly as could be said, it was good.

We went into the château: the whole family, the grape pickers and the cellar workers were there; the meats were smoking on the table. The owner of the vineyards smiled, reached under the table and brought up the first of the assembled bottles of the best years of his wine and poured it for his guests.

In a refinement of simplicity we drank the toast of the harvest *in* the harvest.   *The Evening News*

The Rose from the Co-op

August 1951. The Maison du Vin, at Pauillac, is the finest of the wine show-houses of Bordeaux; its business is to present food and drink in perfect harmony to demonstrate the quality of the wines of the region.

At the banquet there which marked last year's wine harvest the second wine served was called La Rose Pauillac. All the other wines of the day bore the names of long-known and respected châteaux, but La Rose Pauillac – its name barely known to the visitors – was duly tasted and found quite worthy to hold up its head in the company of more famous bottles.

Interested enough to trail the bottle, one had not far to go. Near the centre of the tiny riverside town, among the vineyards and houses concentration, there is a busy, sun-drenched concrete building to which, all the wine harvest through, ox-carts, donkey carts, panniers on wheels, ancient lorries bearing more panniers bring the grapes of the little growers of the district.

A bespectacled and wise-cracking former Commando weighs and scans the grapes, rigidly rejecting any that are not of good quality, grading the others. In case of appeal he turns to the kindly old man who is the chairman of the Cave (*Vault*) Co-operative of Pauillac.

The little men who grew grapes in their own gardens used, of old, to sell them to the big wine vineyards or, sometimes, to press them themselves. Now, however, they have formed themselves into a co-operative – strictly non-political – which presses their wine, grades it and markets it. The local committee, after taking out expenses and putting some of the receipts by against a bad year, shares out the profits among the members in strict accordance with the quantity and quality of the grapes each has delivered.

One man found including some poor grapes in his panniers was fined half the value of the entire delivery, for the co-operative, with a reputation to build up, must produce good wine all the time.

These co-operative caves are shrewd French peasant common sense – producing better wine, from modern equipment, more economically than the members could do independently. The first was opened in 1935 and now there are 70 of them in the south-west, with a membership of over 10,000 small-holders, producing nearly 400,000 gallons of wine a year.

These are the wines that have already shouldered their way into the wine lists of even the most exclusive French restaurants and are now stepping out, with well-founded confidence, into the wine markets of the world. *The Evening News*

Wines of Burgundy

January 1973. The 'Rivalry' between the wines of Bordeaux and Burgundy is not apparent in Bordeaux and Burgundy. The wines of Bordeaux are, as a general rule, not seen in Burgundy nor those of Burgundy in Bordeaux. Only occasionally does one recognize the existence of the other but it happened at the rsecent banquet 'Aux Chandelles' in the bastion of the walls of Beaune – a major occasion of the wine year in Burgundy. One Burgundian approached another whose guest was a known devotee of Bordeaux with the words 'I presume your friend has brought his own claret – but I trust he has had the courtesy to put it in burgundy bottles.'

The wise drinker will enjoy the wines of both regions; it has been said that, at the perfect dinner, calling for both white and red wines, a white burgundy and a claret would be served.

Where Bordeaux is a wide expanse of vineyards grouped round the city, Burgundy is a series of small, almost isolated strips strung along the Route des Vins, with Chablis as the distant north-eastern outpost, the Côte d'Or with Mercurey close at hand and then the essentially separate 'southern Burgundy' of the Mâconnais and, with its distinctive Gamay grape, the Beaujolais.

In spite of the differences of character – and they are considerable – between the Burgundy districts they have a marked unity in comparison with Bordeaux. The wine region of the Gironde, the biggest single wine producing area in the world, is a block of land surrounding the city of Bordeaux.

The Côte d'Or – with only the barest break in the vineyards between the Côte de Nuits and the Côte de Beaune – a 30-mile vineyard strip on a ridge not nearly so high as the South Downs, is nowhere as much as half a mile, and often less than a quarter, wide. Whereas the Bordeaux vines generally centre on châteaux of varying size, the Burgundy vineyards are essentially agricultural – vinefields in fact – with, so far from châteaux, hardly so much interruption as a wall.

Because of the French law of inheritance which divides property equally between children some of these *climats* are almost ludicrously subdivided. The famous Clos de Vougeot, the largest vineyard of the Côte d'Or, covers 124 acres, but the average holding in it is less than two acres. When it was a single vineyard belonging to a monastery, the monks used to blend the wines from the top, middle and bottom of the hill to produce a balanced wine in all but the worst years. Now, in any one year, nearly 70 different wines can be produced all entitled to be called Clos de Vougeot, so that two utterly different wines may bear the same perfectly honest name and date.

This is country to make nonsense of wine theorizing. Look up the slope outside Vosne Romanée and wonder why the tiny, four-and-a-half-acre Romanée-Conti should produce the most expensive of French wines and La Tâche, only a few yards to the south, one almost as dear, while La Grande Rue – literally only as wide as a street – running all the way up the hill between them is rated a growth lower, and the adjoining part Les Reignots one lower again. They may retort in Courtépée's dictum – 'No ordinary wines are to be found in Vosne.'

Perhaps most baffling of all is the sight of the hill of Corton with nothing at all to show the line where the vines which produce one of the greatest red wines in the world (Corton) give way to those of one of the greatest whites (Corton-Charlemagne).

Many of the Burgundy holdings are so small that they have no adequate cellaring arrangements, and one negociant takes a portable bottling plant round to the various vignerons to bottle their wine on the spot, which enables him, legally, to call it domaine-bottled.

Both the splendour and the bewilderment of Burgundy wines lie in their variations. A wine made of grapes from the bottom of the slope of the Côte may fetch less than half the price of one from near the top; and when expert French buyers make these distinctions in francs it is no matter of wine snobbry or chi-chi. Or notice how a great vineyard, economically the most valuable land in France, suddenly ends part way up the hill, and the scrubland inches away is left to run to waste.

Nothing in all Burgundy was more impressive than to go into a small, unpretentious, indeed poor, tabac in a Beaujolais village, ask for a vin rouge and be poured, from an unlabelled bottle, for a couple of pence, an unquestionable and extremely palatable red Beaujolais.

The Guardian

The Men of Burgundy and Their Work

A fine wine can only be made from correctly chosen grapes grown in the right soil and in an ideal weather sequence. Even given those ingredients, though, the quality of the final product depends on the human element at every stage. Wine is a living thing and as such it is vulnerable to ill treatment. From the selection and planting of the vine shoots to the ultimate stage of drinking and enjoying a mature bottle, a whole chain of people – vigneron, broker, merchant, cellarman, retailer or wine waiter – have their separate responsibilities for its welfare.

The wines of Burgundy, more than any others of comparable eminence, are individual creations. The vast majority of the vineyards where they are made are family concerns. A man, his wife and son – or perhaps father or daughter – are quite capable of tending the average vineyard of the region. Some of the larger domaines have their own labour forces, but that is exceptional. In the past all the work had to be done by hand and horse. Now, as labour becomes more costly, an increasing amount of mechanization has been introduced, the tractor has replaced the horse almost everywhere, while the helicopter and even the aeroplane can be summoned at need. No machine, however, can replace the human skills demanded for pruning the vines. Machine picking of grapes is common in California, Australia and even the Cognac area: but the slopes of Burgundy are at many points too steep for it and, even more conclusively, the vignerons regard their fruit as far too precious to be subjected to such

179

risks. For the better wines too, a loss of 12 per cent of the grapes, the accepted norm for a machine, is too costly.

The vineyards of the Côte d'Or are at their most beautiful, a rolling sea of russets, reds and golds, immediately after the vintage, when work in the vines is only just beginning – for next year's harvest. As the last grapes are gathered in, fertilizers of nitrogen and potassium are spread to fortify the vines against the stresses of the winter. (While horses were still in general use their manure was one of the most useful by-products; if only for that reason the tractor can never be a complete replacement.) At this time, too, the land that has been lying fallow and is due to be replanted must be deeply ploughed.

The vine in Burgundy can have a useful life of 50 or more years, but as it grows older, it suffers from the law of diminishing returns. Although the wine it produces improves in quality, the yield decreases from year to year. So they are generally uprooted after about 30 years. The land is then planted with a different crop for three years, before it is replanted with vines. It is then another three years before the grapes can be picked for appellation contrôlée wine. In Chablis, because of the poor nature of the soil, the land was sometimes allowed to lie fallow for 15 or more years; but probably during the depressed times for the wines of that area, the growers did not think it financially worthwhile to replant quickly. Nowadays (can it simply be due to the efficacy of recently developed fertilizers?) the Chablis vineyards are replanted more promptly. In any case, throughout Burgundy, the intelligent grower rotates his replanting so that he never has too large a proportion of his vineyard non-productive.

In November and December a preliminary pruning takes place to remove dead twigs, which may be burnt on the spot or taken home for kindling. One of the most attractive sights of early winter in the region is of thin columns of grey smoke rising to the sky from the braziers in the middle of the vines. Before the frosts arrive, the fertilizers must be dug in and the roots protected by earth piled up around them.

During the months of winter there is little to do and, apart from a certain amount of maintenance work, the grower can take his rest. On 22 January, each vineyard village celebrates the feast of Saint Vincent, the patron saint of the vine grower. On the following Saturday, under the patronage of the Confrérie des Chevaliers du Tastevin, the Saint Vincent Tournante is celebrated – each year in a different village of the Côte d'Or or the Région de Mercurey. Every village – and there are 50 or more of them – sends its representatives with their statue of Saint Vincent, to join in the procession, which is enlivened by all the best brass bands of the region. Afterwards the Confrérie, in their robes of scarlet and yellow, attend a solemn mass of thanksgiving, honour those who have worked long and well in the vines, and then retire to Clos Vougeot for a traditional banquet.

The main pruning is begun towards the middle of February. The shape into which the vines are pruned, and thus grow, varies from area to area, even within Burgundy. The main determining factor is the grape variety. In cooler vineyard areas they generally prefer a form of pruning that gives a low plant which will benefit in full during the night from the heat stored in the soil during the day. One disadvantage of this form, though, is that it increases the risk of damage by spring frosts. So far as the Gamay grape is concerned, all the buds on the shoot are productive, so it can be pruned severely. On the other hand, in the case of the Pinot, the buds closest to the trunk are less productive, so the pruning is less rigorous.

In the Beaujolais, the vines grow separately and are pruned *à gobelet*, each with its individual stake. In the Mâconnais, the traditional method is the *taille à queue*, where the producing branch is bent over in a semicircle. On the Côte d'Or, the *taille guyot* is general: the main branch is trained along a wire about a foot from the ground, with a double wire above it to hold the shoots in place, and then a final, single wire above that. The vines are planted a metre apart, with a metre between the rows.

On certain places on the Côte d'Or, you can also see plantings following the Austrian Lenz Moser system. This is allowed, on an experimental basis, for the lesser appellations. The rows of vines are planted considerably further apart than is general in France and they are allowed to grow to a height of six or seven feet. This makes for ease of cultivation and for better aeration of the bunches of grapes. (It also makes for much less suffering on the part of grape pickers.) The number of such plantings is strictly limited, and one old grower said, 'They will carry out tests for fifty years or so and then forbid it.'

Pruning is a very specialized job and the good vigneron knows every vine and how it should be treated. He will be familiar with its production over past years and will adapt the pruning to its potential and its limitations. The purposes of pruning are to assure the fruitfulness of the vine, to increase the production of best quality grapes and to give the plant a regular, planned form.

At the end of the winter and the beginning of spring, the earth that was piled round the roots for protection is dug up and spread out. At this time, too, selected shoots are grafted on to American rootstock. The selection of both the shoots and the rootstock is of the greatest importance. Immediately after phylloxera, the most common phylloxera-resistant stock used was pure *riparia*, but now there is an increasing preference for *riparia x rupestris* no. 3309 and *riparia x berlandieri* no. 161.49, both of which have a success rate of approximately 70 per cent in grafting. The shoots are chosen from individual vines with successful production records.

The more important domains have their own nurseries, where the young vines are kept for a year in sterile conditions, to protect them from danger of disease during infancy. As phylloxera arrived in France by way of England, it is perhaps fitting that the method of grafting usually used is the *greffe anglaise*, which matches the stock to the French shoot in z-shaped cuts.

In April the vines begin to grow and the young shoots have to be trained along the wires. If the weather has been fine and dry, the vines can be attacked at this moment by the red spider, a comparatively recent addition to the problems of the French vigneron, released by newly-developed insecticides killing off those insects that used to prey upon them. The spider, which is often invisible to the naked eye, feeds on the green parts of the vine. As a result, development is slowed up, or possibly stopped. The spider is impervious to DDT, and even sprays developed specifically to deal with it have had only limited success.

Other pests that develop at this time are the grubs of three insects: Pyralis, Eudemis and Cochylis. All three have different life-cycles: Pyralis has one generation during the season; Cochylis (whose grub is called the *ver rouge* on the Côte d'Or and the *ver coquin* in the Beaujolais) has two; and Eudemis three. In common, they all feed upon the leaves and, later in the year, upon the grapes themselves. Certain treatments carried out during the winter have had limited success in destroying the chrysalids, but spraying with DDT and Parathion during the spring is more general.

At the beginning of May each year, the Service de la Protection des Végétaux offers a prize of F50 to the first person who brings them vine-leaves suffering from mildew. This appears in hot, humid weather and causes the leaves to dry up and fall. As a result the grapes cannot receive the nourishment they need from the leaves, so some of them wither or rot and give an unpleasant taste to the wine. As the mildew fungus exists in the tissue of the vine, no treatment can eradicate it, but can only restrict its effect. The usual treatment is by spraying with Bordeaux mixture (two kilos of copper sulphate and one kilo of lime dissolved in 100 litres of water). This is normally sprayed on by tractor, but if the vineyards are too muddy for convenient working, a helicopter can be called in. The slopes are spread with signs in blue, yellow and white to show the pilot where to spray.

The end of April and the first week of May are also the time when frost can cause the most damage. This is particularly the case if there has been a mild spring and the vines are far advanced. Generally frost strikes just before dawn and the grower will set his alarm to be up in time to take protective measures. It is not unknown, though, for frost to strike in the middle of the night and it can attack just a patch of vines, leaving a band of damage, where one row might be affected and the next not. In Chablis, where the problem is most real, some vineyards have propane heaters installed or even a system for spraying the vines with water, so that they are protected by a layer of ice. On the Côte d'Or, smudge pots or burning tyres are more generally used to safeguard the vines with a cloud of smoke. On rare occasions industrial fan-heaters can be seen in the vines. Vineyards on the plain and in hollows, though, are most likely to suffer from frost and thus the great *climats* of the Côte d'Or are rarely affected. If there has not been frost damage by 15 May – Sainte Denise's day – the danger is considered to be past.

At the beginning of June the vines flower, and the vintage is traditionally taken to be 100 days from that day. The weather at this time is important, because, if it is cold or wet, either the flowers or the grapes might abort and not mature. The former problem is called *coulure*, the latter *millérandage*. Whilst the grower can do nothing to prevent the bad weather that causes these, there are other dangers he should foresee. The Chardonnay is particularly liable to coulure and when he grafts this plant the vigneron should take special care to choose his shoots from vines that have not suffered from it. Over-use of nitrogenous fertilisers and any contact whatsoever with hormone weedkillers are also potential sources of damage. Perhaps the most serious cause of coulure, however, is the virus disease *court-noué*, for which there is no other treatment but the complete rooting up of the vine, cleansing of the soil and replanting with completely healthy vines.

As well as treatment against mildew during June and July, the grower must be on his guard in warm, damp weather, against another fungal disease, oïdium. The leaves and grapes take on blackish scabs and develop a mouldy smell. The recommended preventive treatment is three sprayings with powdered sulphur, one before flowering, the second at the time of flowering and the third two or three weeks before the grapes change colour. The most effective cure, once oïdium has attacked, is spraying with a solution of potassium permanganate.

During the summer days of July and August, the tops of the vines are trimmed back, so that grapes derive maximum benefit from the food brought up through the roots. Whilst sun is always welcome, rain, too, is needed from time to time, to swell out the grapes. Too much sun can present almost as many problems as too much rain, since the grapes can shrivel up for lack of moisture. That happened in 1973 when, just a week before the vintage, about 24 hours' rain was needed to fill out the grapes. The rains came but, unfortunately, they continued for a week. All the moisture was thirstily absorbed. As a result, in a matter of hours, what might have been one of the best vintages of the century, with an important quantity of wine, became one of only average quality, but with the largest crop since records began.

Hailstorms in the summer are another grave threat. Although they generally cause damage over only a limited area, within those limits it can be total. From the eighteenth century until the First World War, the fashionable preventative was the *canon grélifuge*, which looked rather like a vertical foghorn of up to 15 feet in height. The makers claimed that firing this at the hail-clouds caused enough turbulence in the air to protect an area of up to 60 acres. When this weapon became unfashionable, vineyard owners turned to prayer – and insurance. More recently rockets have been developed to explode at a height of four or more thousand feet, in the cumulo-nimbus clouds where the hail forms, causing the stones to liquefy and fall as rain.

For the last three years the growers of the Côte d'Or and the Mercurey region have joined together to take apparently even more successful steps against hail. During the summer two or more aircraft of Air Alpes are based in the area, at Châlon-sur-Saône. These can take off at a moment's notice to seed the storm clouds so that just rain falls. From radar detection of cloud formations they can be alerted in time to reach the clouds whilst they are still over the Morvan and break them up before they reach the vineyard areas. It is too early yet to say how effective this watch is, but in 1973 when the climatic conditions would normally have made for a considerable incidence of hailstorms, the damage was minimal. Only a few miles away in the valley of the Saône, on the other hand, there was considerable damage to crops. In 1974, however, an August hailstorm caused considerable damage in certain villages of the Côte de Beaune, and to another in the southern Beaujolais. In the Beaujolais, there is at least one plane on hail alert; it is based at the Seagram property, Château de Pizay, at Morgon.

Vineyards that have suffered from hail damage produce wines with an unmistakable smoky taste which can be detected, for example, in some wines of the 1971 vintage from Pommard, a village that suffered particularly in that year. A violent hailstorm can have even more enduring effects, damaging the vines so severely that their production can suffer the following year.

September sees the final preparation for the vintage, which normally begins towards the end of the month and continues for a fortnight. All the materials and equipment for the pickers are prepared. The vathouse is thoroughly cleaned out; the oak vats scrubbed and filled with water to swell the wood; and all metalwork is repainted.

The vintage in Burgundy is not such a glamorous affair as in Bordeaux. As the majority of the vineyard holdings are small, the picking is generally done by the family and friends. Unfortunately, in 1973, some government official decided that picking grapes was not suitable work for young children, so the work force, which used to be swelled on school holidays, has suffered. No longer do swarms of gipsies descend from the Morvan, singing, according to Camille Rodier,

> *Let's be off to the vintage*
> *To earn five sous,*
> *Sleep in the barns*
> *And gather some fleas.*

There are few places now where pickers come in from outside and eat and lodge together. The former team-feeling may have been impaired as a result of each vendangeur nursing his stiff back alone in the evening. Nevertheless, every year many visitors from other non-wine growing countries come to Burgundy for the experience of a grape harvest.

In early times the day for the beginning of the vintage was declared by the feudal lord or, later, by the commune; and there were severe punishments, such as the confiscation of their crop, for those who began picking too early or who sought to recruit their workforce before the due date. Nowadays sample bunches of grapes are analyzed to establish the sugar content and when this is at the optimum, picking may begin – each grower starting when he feels so inclined. Sometimes the date may be brought forward if the weather breaks and there is a danger of the crop being ruined. This is the age-old dilemma of the grower. Shall he leave the grapes on the vines in the hope that they will get more sunshine and thus produce better wine – and, if he does, will they be damaged by rain or hail?

Since many domaines have vineyards scattered along the Côte d'Or, the grapes in some cases have to be transported several miles to the press-house – yet each load must be accompanied by a government certificate – even at this stage the system of appellation contrôlée has begun.

Most vineyard owners in Burgundy vinify their grapes themselves, though, as has alreaady been mentioned, the cooperative cellars have an important role to play in the Beaujolais, the Mâconnais and to a lesser extent in Chablis. On the Côte de Nuits, particularly, it is not uncommon for a grower to sell his grapes directly to a négociant, who will then vinify them himself. In exceptional vintages, like 1972 and 1973, this is even more common, for the grower might find himself short of both vat space in which to vinify and cellar space in which to store the wine. In 1972, when the price of young wine rose considerably during the following year, many extremely profitable deals were made by those who purchased grapes cheaply at vintage times. (In Alsace, where the purchase of grapes is more widespread, the growers insist on a clause in the contract of sale, which allows for additional compensatory payments to be made during the following year, in the event of the price of the wine rising. No doubt this will come in Burgundy, though it is unlikely that growers would be prepared to make a reimbursement if the value of the wine fell.)

When the grapes arrive at the press-house, the juice is tested for its sugar content, for this will give the ultimate alcoholic degree of the wine. (In cooperative cellars, the grapes are also weighed, for payment is generally made on the kilo-degree; that is to say, on the combination of the quantity of grapes and the strength of the wine they will produce.) Before the grapes are de-stalked they are sprinkled with sulphur dioxide, which acts as an antiseptic, killing off harmful bacteria.

On arrival at the press-house the tubs of fruit are tipped into the *fouloir-égrappoir*, which looks like a large mangle with ridged rollers. This machine crushes the grapes and separates them from their stalks. It is important, though, that the operation is not so violent as to crush the pips since that would release oils which give an unpleasant astringency to the wine.

The question of the proportion of stalks to be put in the fermenting vats to add tannin is much discussed in Burgundy. One thing is certain, the term *méthode ancienne*, used by some shippers to describe a long first fermentation, with a high percentage of stalks, is misleading. It is, in truth, by no means traditional and seems to have come into fashion only at the end of the last century. This may have come about because burgundy was difficult to sell at the time and therefore had to be able to support a longer period before it was consumed. One thing is certain, the traditional way of making burgundy is with a short fermentation of five or so days. Each grower and shipper tries consistently to produce a style of wine of which he is proud. These styles can vary considerably, yet each, in its own way, is correct. It is a peculiarly British (and perhaps Danish) fallacy to consider that burgundy should have the consistency, and colour, of an unfortified ruby port. Some growers make such wines (often to please their customers) but others produce wines lighter in colour, yet which have more finesse and in no way lack such depth and keeping qualities as there might be in their deeply coloured brethren. Depth of colour should not be equated with the potential of a wine. It may be true that, because of increasing demand, some growers vinify to produce wines that mature more quickly and are therefore more rapidly marketed. This situation is not peculiar to Burgundy, but one that occurs equally in Bordeaux. It is regrettable that over 80 per cent of Côte d'Or wine shipped to the United States, presumably for immediate consumption, is three years old or less. Thus the chances of a wine from such a great vintage as 1971 being drunk at its best – with years of bottle-age – must be rated as negligible.

From the de-stalker, the juice and pulp is pumped to the fermenting vat. Traditionally this is of oak with an open top, but more and more it is replaced by a closed, enamel-lined tank, which is easier to maintain, and which can be used during the rest of the year, if needed, for storage purposes. The depth to which the vat is filled is of primary importance, as in certain vintages, such as 1972, the fermentation can be so violent that there is a risk of the must overflowing.

On the skin of the grape there is a dusty bloom which contains the natural yeasts that will precipitate the fermentation. On the extremely rare occasions when the process does not start spontaneously, strains of local yeasts may be added to the must, or, more commonly, the must is slightly heated to set off the ferments.

The length of time that the fermentation takes depends on the grower, but it is important that each vat is carefully tended. The temperature must be taken at regular intervals, as fermentation takes place most comfortably between 22°C and 30°C (72°F and 86°F). If it falls below the lower figure, there is a danger that the fermentation will stop – and it is difficult to restart it – so part of the must is heated, generally by passing it over pipes containing hot water, and then returned to the vat. If the must becomes too hot – usually because of too active a fermentation – it must be cooled down, either by passing it over pipes containing cold water, or by circulating it in contact with the air. Each vat will also have its individual graph, which shows two lines apart from the temperature; one is the decreasing amount of sugar in the must and the other the increasing amount of alcohol. Since, in all the wines of Burgundy, the sugar is fermented out completely, when the first line reaches – or approaches – zero the first fermentation is considered to have finished.

Whilst the must is fermenting in the vat the oenologist has to decide whether the resultant wine will be sound and balanced, and, if not, what treatment is necessary. As Burgundy is near the northern limit of the vine, it may happen that there is not sufficient sugar in the grapes to produce a stable wine, therefore the process called chaptalization is permitted for every vintage. Basically this gives the producer the possibility of adding sugar to the must so as to increase the strength of the wine by a maximum of 2°. (In Bordeaux, chaptalization is only permitted in exceptional circumstances, and then after an official decree. In the Midi it is completely forbidden.)

Whilst, officially, chaptalization can only be carried out after notice has been given to the necessary authorities, and only strictly limited amounts of sugar can be purchased to carry it out (200 kilos per hectare of vines is the maximum), there is no doubt that the process is open to abuse. The good wine-chemist will never chaptalize beyond the necessary limit; and in some years, when the grapes are rich in sugar, he will not chaptalize at all. Each vat, each wine, must be considered as a separate case and the correct amount of sugar must be added. Some growers, who consider that a high strength is the only criterion for a wine will, therefore, sugar to the maximum. They even go beyond the maximum in some cases, for it is not difficult to buy an extra pound or two of sugar for the family every week; nor is there any control over the distribution of the officially permitted allowance between vats. In any case, the allowance is not granted on how much you produce, but on how much you might produce.

The question as to whether chaptalization should be permitted has long been debated in Burgundy. The idea was orginally proposed at the beginning of the nineteenth century, as a means of using up the excess production of beet sugar. Even as early as 1845, though, a congress of vine growers in Dijon passed a resolution condemning it as being a harmful practice. 'It cannot be disputed,' they said, 'that sugaring denatures wines, taking away from them that which is most precious to them; that incomparable bouquet and delicacy that is their true mark.'

Whilst some over-chaptalized wines taste 'exaggerated' on the palate, it is generally only by analysis that it can be traced. Even having over-chaptalized wines in one's cellar is a serious offence in France, punishable by heavy fines and prison sentences. With the introduction of the Common Market regulations, a decision was apparently taken to make an example of some offenders. As a result one or two prosecutions were launched against those who had in their cellars over-sugared Beaujolais of the 1973 vintage.

Other problems, such as lack of acidity, tannin or colour in the wine can also be rectified to some extent whilst the fermentation is taking place. The addition of unripe grapes to the must will increase acidity; a higher proportion of stalks will add to the tannin. To make the colour deeper, some of the must, together with the skins, is heated, which releases the pigments.

During the fermentation, all the solid matter is thrust up to the top of the wine, where it forms a thick crust, or *chapeau*. Some growers consider that this crust should be regularly broken up and immersed in the must; and in traditional cellars teams of men clamber into the vats to trample it in. The term for this operation is *pigeage*. Nowadays, gym-shorts are the dress for the event, but formerly it was generally carried out in the nude and, as witness, a photograph in the wine museum at Beaune shows a line-up that would not disgrace *Oh! Calcutta*. Other growers will twice a day pump over a proportion of the must to break up the crust – this is the process of *remontage*.

After five or six days, or longer as desired, the juice is drawn off from the bottom of the vat and the *marc* (or mass of pulp) is shovelled into a horizontal press. In Burgundy the marc is pressed just once and the resultant juice (the *vin de presse*) is added to that which has already been drawn off (the *vin de goutte*). The resultant blend is put into oak casks to continue its development. During the coming six or more months, the wine undergoes a secondary fermentation, known as the malo-lactic. During this time, the bacterium *gracile* converts the natural malic acid (the acidity of apples) in the wine into lactic acid (the acidity of milk). It is not difficult to judge that the second acid is much less prominent than the first. This secondary fermentation also liberates a certain amount of carbon dioxide, which gives a prickle to a wine if it is bottled before the process has ended. (In certain circumstances if the wine is bottled too cold it might also have the same prickle, for, although the fermentation has been completed, the gas has remained in suspension and has not been liberated. A simple warming of the glass in the hand will make the prickle disappear.)

Whilst the malo-lactic fermentation traditionally took place in oak casks, certain growers now return the wine to the metal fermenting vats and let it take place there in bulk. The thought behind this is that the process occurs rather more quickly in large quantities and that there is less likelihood of any problems in an enamel-lined vessel. It has yet to be seen whether the character of the wine is altered in any way – or whether it will be shorter lived, for not having absorbed the six months' tannin from the cask.

So far, we have studied only the vinification of red wines – for the white it is different. As soon as they arrive at the press-house, the grapes are crushed and immediately put into the press with the stalks, where they are usually pressed twice. The jus de presse and the jus de goutte are then blended together and put straight into casks. These are not filled completely, nor are the bungs hammered home, since the fermentation takes place slowly during the winter months in the grower's cellars. It is important, though, that the fermentation should be continuous, so often it is necessary to light a stove in the cellar to keep it warm enough to maintain the activity of the ferments.

The amount of time the wine spends in cask again depends on the grower, or, more often, the négociant, who is more generally responsible for the *élevage*, or upbringing, of the wine. The average length of time in cask for a Côte d'Or wine is between 12 and 18 months, though some shippers think it wrong to bottle great wines under two years old. For wines from the Beaujolais and the Mâconnais, a period of three to nine months in cask is generally considered adequate.

After the wine has spent six months in wood it is fined to remove any impurities resting in suspension. When the finings have dropped to the bottom of the cask, the first racking takes place; that is, the bright wine is drawn off its deposit and placed into a clean cask. As the level in the old cask drops, it is gently tilted forward and the cellarman continually studies the clarity of the wine in his silver tastevin, or tasting cup. As soon as there is any trace of cloudiness, the tap in the caskhead is closed. This racking takes place every six months while the wine is in cask, though an extra one or two may be necessary if the wine has some foreign taste which might disappear on exposure to the air. To avoid oxidization, white wines are normally racked without coming into contact with the air. In all cases, the receiving cask has always either had a sulphur candle burnt in it, or has been rinsed out with a sulphur solution as an antiseptic measure.

The lees, or deposit, are either sold for distillation into Fine Bourgogne or else sent to one of the great restaurants in the region or in Paris for use in preparing such local specialities as *jambon à la lie*.

To avoid oxidization, every two weeks or so the cellarman carries out the operation of *ouillage*, or topping up. To do it he uses a vessel like a watering can with a long spout, which turns down at the end. Also at the end a holder is fitted to take a candle to light up the bungholes in the casks, which may be stacked three or four high.

Before bottling, a sample of each cask is analysed to see that the malo-lactic fermentation is finished and the wine is generally filtered, though some traditionalists prefer to bottle directly from the cask-head. After bottling, the vintage should spend some months resting, to overcome the shock, before it is consumed. Certain shippers pasteurize their wines to minimize possible problems once it is in bottle. Some feel that this caponizes the wine and prevents it developing naturally; others argue that it preserves the wine at the peak of its condition. Certainly pasteurization is an artificial process which must destroy some of the natural attributes of a wine.

Although the grower is a considerable man of Burgundy, however, he actually bottles and sells only a small proportion of the production of the region. Over 80 per cent of the wine sold outside the area passes through the hands of the négociants. Before it reaches them, though, the *courtier* or broker plays his considerable part. He is the important middleman between the grower and the merchant. It is his job to introduce the wines of the vast number of growers to the small number of shippers.

Generally speaking, each merchant works through a limited

number of brokers; perhaps one for wines of the Côte de Nuits, two for those of the Côte de Beaune and one each for the Mâconnais and the Beaujolais. Each broker knows what style of wine his customer is looking for and the price he is prepared to pay for it. He will know what stocks the growers have available for sale, and what price they are seeking. He will submit small samples of those wines he thinks suitable to the négociants with the quantity on offer, the price and the name of the grower. If the price is too high, it is his job to negotiate on behalf of the merchant, without letting the grower know the name of the potential purchaser. Thus, whilst the shipper might buy from the same producer year after year, he has an interest in working through a broker, so that he may maintain a certain anonymity in his bargaining. The courtier is responsible also for fixing terms of payment, arranging the transport of the wine from the grower to the merchant, and overseeing the racking of the wine into the merchant's casks. Formerly, for his services, he was paid a fixed sum per cask, but now he usually works on a percentage commission on the sale price. Generally this is 2 per cent, paid by the purchaser, though it is not uncommon for the seller also to pay a commission.

The profession of *courtier de campagne* is both skilful and honourable. Unfortunately, the 'wine explosion' of recent years has attracted some to the profession who consider it an easy way of making money. By peddling useless sample after useless sample round the merchants and failing to accept the full responsibilities of the job, they bring not just themselves, but the whole profession into disrepute. In a time of increasing prices and demand for wine, a good broker can make a handsome living. However, the wine trade moves like a pendulum and the good years may have to support many lean years in the future.

Increasing awareness of the wines of Burgundy overseas has produced a new style of broker: he deals directly with the foreign customer. By cutting out the négociant, there are certain savings to be made, but these bring with them certain risks. Naturally such a broker is frowned upon by much of the traditional trade, even though he may have spent many years studying the wines of the region. More dangerous is the outsider who attempts to exploit the situation.

In Burgundy, the grower and the shipper tend to live in different worlds, for they each have different problems and requirements. The good broker is a valuable bridge between them: he keeps them informed of the condition of the market; he is their eye upon the world. In many ways he, of all the men of Burgundy, should be the best instructed.

Why is the négociant so important in Burgundy? We have shown that his original role was that of salesman for the wines of the area in the more distant corners of France and abroad. That is still true today, though it is only one aspect of his function. Where there exists such a multitude of producers, many of whom do not make enough wine to commercialize individually, it is the function of the merchant to blend their output so that he can offer reasonable quantities of any given wine on the market. It is important to realize that burgundy is a blended wine, and that this, so far from being a disadvantage, is its strength.

For example, the shipper might buy Gevrey-Chambertin from ten different growers; from some, just one cask or two, from others six or even more. Some of this wine will have been purchased immediately after the vintage, perhaps even as grapes; some may have been bought a year or eighteen months later. All the time he is striving to produce a Gevrey-Chambertin in the style of his company, one that will do credit to his label. Weaknesses in some of the wines he has bought will be cancelled out by excesses in others, but he seeks perfection of the ultimate blend. Buying wine is not the simple matter it may seem. A grower's price may vary considerably during the year, dependent on his bank balance, the weather, and the space that he has in his cellar for the coming crop. The buyer, for his part, must consider, when he plans his purchases, what he expects his sales to be in three or four years' time. A good shipper may list as many as 60 different appellations in perhaps two or three vintages. Since future sales in any country are dependent on circumstances beyond the control of either shipper or grower, it is by no means simple to plan even a short time ahead. Lamentably, in many countries, wine is considered as a luxury and is accordingly put far down on the list of priorities where imports are concerned. Governments have, too, the unhappy habit of imposing punitive taxes overnight. For the wine trade of Burgundy this is a particularly grave matter, since it is an area that depends on exports. It sends twice as great a proportion of its production abroad as Bordeaux does: and it is not uncommon for three quarters of a shipper's turnover to be earned on foreign markets.

The roles and methods of the merchants of the Beaujolais and of the Côte d'Or are different. The financial problems of the former are much slighter since he sells a wine that is to be drunk young and he should turn his stock over more than once a year. He is ready to sell the new vintage, as Beaujolais Nouveau, within a matter of weeks of the vintage. His commitments are thus limited, since he can often buy his wine when he has already found a customer for it. Moreover, the bulk of the wines of the Beaujolais and the Mâconnais are kept in vats so the total storage space needed is less in proportion to the quantity sold.

On the other hand, a Côte d'Or négociant must carry in his cellars a fortune in wine, much of which he probably will not sell until it has been in stock for two or three years. (Thus the sale of wine en primeur shortly after the vintage is almost unknown on the Côte d'Or and, due to the fragmented vineyard ownership, there is no system of selling by 'slices' as in Bordeaux.) The increasing amount of capital needed to finance these stocks in a period of expensive borrowing has proved too much for some merchants. As a result, during the past few years, much outside capital has come into Burgundy; and companies both in Beaujolais and the Côte d'Or have come under foreign control.

Recently, too, there has been much consolidation within the trade itself and several well-established names have been taken under the wings of their brethren. Thus, whilst the Beaune telephone directory lists almost 140 different wine shippers' names, it is doubtful whether as many as 30 of them are truly independent: the rest are trading names and *sous-marques*.

It is not surprising that many of the more financially successful shippers are those who have considerable vineyard holdings, for each year they have a good proportion of their needs in stock at basic prices. Of the major shippers it is unlikely, however, that any account for much more than 10 per cent of their turnover in output from their own vineyards.

Of the seven largest domaines on the Côte d'Or, five belong to shipping houses; Bouchard Père et Fils, J. Faiveley, Chanson Père et

Fils, Louis Latour and the Société d'Élèvage et de Diffusion des Grands Vins (SEDGV) – or as it is more generally known, La Reine Pédauque. Of these, Louis Latour enjoys perhaps the best success in the auction room (the most reliable barometer of fashionable acceptance at present). The offices are in the aptly named Rue des Tonneliers in Beaune and they own a remarkable press-house (listed by the French government as being of national interest) in Aloxe-Corton. It is set in a quarry in the middle of the vineyard Corton Perrières, and has floor after floor of cellars cut into the rock. At the top level is a traditional cuverie that is well worth a visit. Across the road is the Latour family home of Château Corton Grancey, which gives its name to an outstanding blend of wines from the Latour domaine with the appellation Corton. The domaine also includes a considerable portion of the Corton-Charlemagne vineyard. The style of these wines is generally full-bodied, deeply coloured and rich in alcohol, giving them the ability to support long years in bottle. Demand for such wines always seems to be greater than supply, and customers often find themselves strictly rationed.

With 80 hectares, Bouchard Père et Fils have the largest viticultural domaine on the Côte d'Or. Their main cellars are in the Château de Beaune, which was built at the end of the fifteenth century in the form of a regular pentagon, with a large tower at each corner; the two facing outwards were over 150 feet in diameter. At the end of the seventeenth century Henri IV ordered the destruction of the château but fortunately his instruction was never completely carried out and a century later it was admired as a masterpiece by Vauban, France's greatest military architect.

The most valuable vines in the domaine of Bouchard Père et Fils must be those in the vineyard of Le Montrachet, but the best known may well be those in that part of the Beaune Grèves vineyard, known as Vigne de l'Enfant Jésus. Up to the time of the French revolution, it belonged to the Carmelite sisters of Beaune, who gave it that name. The wine it produces has been described as having 'an exquisite finesse, a taste that is both warm but delicate, which carries on, leaving after it a sweet and perfumed breath'. Warner Allen rated the 1906 vintage of the wine, opened in 1933, the most noteworthy wine from Beaune he ever tasted.

Another company to rely on the fortifications of Beaune for their cellar space, is Chanson Père et Fils, which purchased the Boulevard (the original name for the great towers or bastions) des Filles or de l'Oratoire in 1794, for 1980 francs, the value at that time of six hogsheads of wine from Beaune. With walls 26 feet thick at ground level, it makes ideal cellars for wine, having a constant temperature of 12°C (52°F). The young wines are unloaded at the higher levels by lorries which drive up on to the town walls. As the wines age, they go down to the lower floors. Chanson own a remarkable collection of old wines including some more than 100 years old. The Chanson domaine of 45 hectares is spread over the premier crus of Beaune, Savigny and Pernand-Vergelesses, but the one of which they are most proud is Beaune Clos des Fèves, which is named in documents of as long ago as 1307.

Chanson wines tend to have a style of their own, often rather light in colour, but with a deceptive fullness and great delicacy of flavour. They are honest wines which support ageing without problem. To say that the wines of a merchant have a certain style by no means implies that they all taste the same and this can well be demonstrated by comparing wines of the same vintage from a grower such as Chanson. Even when one tastes together their wines of Beaune Clos des Marconnets, Beaune Clos du Roi and Beaune Blanchefleurs, three vineyards which lie next to each other, one is surprised by the differences between them, though they all have a family resemblance.

The cellars of Joseph Drouhin are in the picturesquely named Rue d'Enfer, within yards of the Wine Museum. These were once the royal cellars of the Dukes of Burgundy and the Kings of France. Some trace of the crypt of the former church of Saint Baudèle, which dates from the eighth century, can still be seen there. The Drouhin cellars welcome visitors throughout the week. Their domaine includes holdings in Clos Vougeot, Le Musigny, Le Chambertin and Corton, but they also produce an interesting white wine from the Clos des Mouches in Beaune. The Hospices de Beaune have recently named a cuvée after Maurice Drouhin, the father of the present owner, who was one of their major benefactors.

The Nuits-Saint-Georges house of J. Faiveley claims to have the largest vineyard holding in Burgundy, with many vines in Nuits itself and in Mercurey in the Saône et Loire département and elsewhere, particularly on the Côte de Nuits. Two wines often seen with the Faiveley label are Nuits Clos de la Maréchale and Mercurey Clos des Myglands.

It is interesting how certain shippers are particularly well placed on certain export markets. For example, Albert Bichot, who own the important domaine of Clos Frantin at Vosne-Romanée and are currently the most important exporters in Burgundy, are very strong on the British market. Bouchard Aîné et Fils have a large proportion of the Canadian sales, and the label of Louis Jadot is as likely to be seen in the United States as anywhere in the world. Perhaps unfortunately, burgundy, unlike champagne and whisky, is not a product that can be sold with ease throughout the world. Switzerland is the largest export market – though it takes largely Beaujolais – followed by the United States, Britain, Germany and Belgium. Japan has not yet made a significant impression as a consuming customer.

Some domaines sell directly to customers either in France or overseas under their own label; certain others still sell under their own label, though through the shippers. Thus Calvet had the exclusivity of the two important domaines of Prieur, with holdings, amongst others, in Le Musigny and Clos Vougeot, and of Poupon. Joseph Drouhin distributes the Montrachet of the Marquis de Laguice; Piat, the Gevrey-Chambertins of General Rebourseau. The interest for the grower in such an arrangement is considerable, as he has a guaranteed outlet for his production and someone else is bearing the cost of publicizing it. The whole question of supply contracts with vineyard owners is a sensitive one. In a period of expanding sales and increasing prices, it can be useful for the shipper to have a guaranteed source of supply. In a period of falling demand and prices, however, there is every interest in having complete liberty in choosing one's source.

The notion of domaine bottling, as opposed to *vin de négoce* is one that was actively fostered by Alexis Lichine in *The Wines of France* and one must wonder whether he was not, in part, inspired by commercial motives as his own company, selling in the United States, specialized in such wines. According to him there were substantial incentives for the négociants to debase the wines in their cellars and thus defraud the customers. The only way you could be certain of buying a bottle of genuine wine was to buy it bottled at the domaine. The result is that there has been some increase in bottling by the growers. There have been such developments as mobile bottling lines coming over from Bordeaux. Wine has even been taken away and cared for in central cellars, to be returned to the grower for bottling, so that it can bear on the label the magic words, 'Domaine Bottled'.

The basic truth of the matter is that the majority of the growers are simply that; they know how to cultivate their vineyards to produce a good crop and then how to make a wine. Once the wine has been made their knowledge of oenology is sometimes rudimentary. White wines, particularly, need constant attention and the shipper, who generally employs his own wine chemist, has better facilities for the full range of treatments.

There is no reason why a grower should be more honest than a shipper, though it may be argued that the latter, with larger stocks of wine at his disposal, has more room for manipulation. It is unfortunate that, due to biased conditioning, so many people now think in Orwellian terms, 'Four legs good! Two legs bad!' Domaine-bottled wine good; merchants' wine bad. Such thinking must confuse, when one considers the wines of a shipper who has his own vineyards. Is one to take the wines from his own vines as being honest, whilst the rest are fraudulent? Indeed one négociant, with extensive vineyard holdings, refuses to label any of his wines as being 'Domaine Bottled', because that might suggest that they are in some way superior to the other wines that he sells.

There is one French word that sums up the whole situation – *sérieux*. This does not exactly mean serious, but rather conscientious. A wine from a *maison sérieuse* will be sound and honest – as will be a wine from a *domaine sérieux*. However, you are more likely to get a sound wine from even the most dishonest shipper, which is more than can often be said of a careless domaine. It would be ignoring the facts, if one said that there are no dishonest shippers, but there is dishonesty in every trade and the trade in Burgundy has been largely cleaned up. Taken alone the words 'Domaine Bottled' are considerably less convincing guarantee than the label of a serious shipper – or a serious domaine.

The shipper and the grower must depend on each other for their existence, for even those domaines that try to sell their wine direct, rarely do it for their total production. They realize that the American market, which is in most cases their largest customer, is particularly sensitive and can change overnight. Every grower seeks to maintain good relations with the négociants who are his insurance policy in the case of a difficult market.

The future of the good shipper is assured for he alone offers wine in quantities acceptable to the larger customers. The amounts the domaines can offer are so limited that it is often difficult to put an intensive effort behind their sale. Moreover, for the foreign buyer, it is more convenient to buy a full range of the wines of Burgundy from one source than to try to group together a number of small parcels of wine; to correspond in the language of his choice (or almost) and to have the full commercial knowledge of documentation and labelling at his disposal.

Whilst there has been talk of the domaines, what are the labels one is most likely to see? The best known is that of the Domaine de la Romanée-Conti at Vosne-Romanée, which, with its sister domaine of Marey-Monge, has the monopoly of Romanée-Conti and La Tâche, as well as holdings in Richebourg, Romanée-St-Vivant, Grands Echézeaux and Le Montrachet. These are the most prestigious, and expensive, wines of Burgundy. The prices that they fetch at auction even rival those of the great wines of Bordeaux.

The Côte de Nuits has a string of well-known domaines, beginning geographically, as well as in size with that of Clair-Däu at Marsannay la Côte, which extends over 40 hectares and even includes vines at Santenay at the far end of the Côte de Beaune. Among the other well-known names are those of Rousseau of Gevrey-Chambertin, Roumier of Chambolle-Musigny, Bertagna of Vougeot and Henri Gouges of Nuits-Saint-Georges.

On the Côte de Beaune the largest domaines are in the hands of the shippers, though those of the Marquis d'Angerville and the Pousse d'Or at Volnay, and of the Duc de Magenta at Chassagne-Montrachet are well-known. Another important domaine is that of Roland Thévenin, the mayor of Saint Romain, who is also a shipper. He owns a portion of Le Montrachet, the Château of Puligny-Montrachet and vines at Saint Romain and Auxey-Duresses.

Burgundy Vines and Wines, with Christopher Fielden, 1976

Beaune Idyll

December 1979. As the A6 – Autoroute de Soleil – sweeps over the hill past the Joigny access point, the character of the French landscape begins to change. This is the beginning of the larger Burgundy; the wine kingdom, greater than the historic duchy for it stretches from Auxerre, opposite Chablis in the north, to l'Arbresle at the southern end of the bas Beaujolais, far into the department of the Rhône, a bare 26 kilometres from Lyon.

Once the country falls into the pattern of rounded hills, and far as it is from Chablis to central Burgundy, you are in wine country. By the time the motorway cuts a slice out of the Marconnets vineyards and twines its knot beside Beaune, it has left the great vignobles of the Côte de Nuits away to the left up the N74 towards Dijon; and the rest of the vineyards – of the Côte de Beaune, the Chalonnaise, the Mâconnais and Beaujolais – will lie to its right as it makes for Marseille.

It is not a spectacular landscape; after all it was Burgundians of the supreme vineyard area of the Côte d'Or, who said 'If our land were not the richest in the world it would be the poorest.' Yet it exerts a compelling hold over those who seek to know, as well as understand it.

This December's sunlight was so bright it could have been high summer but that the vines had been cleared, with only the occasional prodigal bunch left to recall the plenty. It was a nostalgic detour to the Trois Faisans in its sturdy stone farmyard beside the river bridge at Bligny-sur-Ouch. The growers themselves bring in the wine.

The sauces are made by someone who understands that it is not a matter to be hurried. The self-service hors d'oeuvres table is a degree course in self restraint. The cooking is as soundly and traditionally French as the service is hospitable; and, by the standards of 1979, the bill is a clean joke.

Earlier in the year two English schoolmasters wrote asking to be recommended typical Burgundian accommodation while they studied Beaune. On the assumption that they would be travelling by car, they were directed to the Trois Faisans, but they arrived by train, 19 kilometres by country bus from Bligny. In their first night apéritifs they drank the establishment out of its long untouched stock of gin: pronounced themselves delighted with the burgundy at dinner and for the rest of a fortnight commuted happily to Beaune by bus or borrowed bicycle.

Euphoria about the vintage was to be felt throughout the region. This year's Hospices de Beaune sale – the candlelight auction held always on the third Sunday of November – first confirmed a fine, large vintage. The wines sold are those from vineyards left to the Hospices – almshouse and hospital institution – by legatees from Nicholas Rolin (an extortionate but finally repentant ducal chancellor) in 1443, down to 1977.

The auction is prestigious; it is good publicity for a merchant or a hotel to figure on the buyers list; so the prices are too high to be realistic. They do, though, indicate trends: this year the quantity was the highest in the history of the sale, apart from 1973, and prices ran slightly lower than in 1978; and there was a drop, too, in Mâcon. The estimate for all Burgundy, excepting Beaujolais, is estimated at 1135 millions of bottles; while Beaujolais may well run to more than as much again. Still though, the demand for the fine burgundies runs far ahead of supply; the burgundy growers and shippers can name their prices.

After quick flowering of the vines in ideal conditions and good summer weather – except for one limited but savage burst of hail on the Côte d'Or – the picking took place virtually without problems between 26 September and 20 October.

The extraordinary autumn chapter of the Confrérie des Chevaliers du Tastevin was a prodigious banquet, marked by immense satisfaction over the crop. The Beaujolais 'Exposition' (mass tasting) was broken at midday for the Banquet des 2 Bouteilles though, of course, no Beaujolaise was so niggardly as to contribute only two bottles.

The general assessment is that – as the Nouveau promised – the Beaujolais crop is healthy, large, and of high quality.

Reports from Chablis, and on the Côte d'Or whites, are the same: plentiful good wine. Only about the Côte d'Or reds are there doubts; the crop is large and much of it is of fine quality but buyers need to be watchful; some growers undoubtedly produced too much, with a resultant reduction in quality.

Although there have been some slight reductions, we may be sadly sure that by the time they reach us the fine Burgundy wines of 1979 will be no cheaper than those of the smaller 1978 vintage.

The Guardian

Tavel is Tavel is Tavel

January 1974. The label 'Rosé' covers a multitude of *vins* (one is even called Rosé Sans Thorn). Varying in colour on either side of pink – to near yellow, or almost red – it is produced all over the world: it can be sweet or dry, extremely light or relatively heavy; still, pétillant, or sparkling. It can be produced simply by mixing red and white wine; but true rosé is made from black grapes when the skins are left in the vat for the first one to three days of fermentation.

The best rosé in the world probably is Tavel. Many others are compromises, produced from vineyards which switched from red or white out of commercial expediency, but Tavel was making rosé before the thirteenth century when Philip III said, 'The one good wine is that of Tavel.'

The Tavel vineyards lie across the Rhône from Avignon, in open and rugged country. The cypress trees planted to give shelter from the mistral are not enough and the workers in the vineyards often muffle themselves to the ears and over against it.

The present Mayor of the village, and vigneron, Armand Maby – who changes capacities in seconds – when pressed as to what kind of red wine resulted if the skins were not removed after three days, was content that no one knew, because 'Tavel is always a rosé'. Certainly the local workers drink nothing else but rosé.

It is made largely from the Grenache grape, which changes character with the three local soils – stony, sandy, or chalky – where it is planted. Many vignerons grow on all three types to produce a balanced blend. The crop is more regular than most for, although the yield from the inhospitable soil is comparatively small, the climate is consistent and, to a greater extent than with most red or white, the rosé makers can adjust acidity by early or late picking.

Most of the Tavel growers have only small vineyards and take their grapes to the modern local cooperative cellar which produces about half the annual production of some 2,500,000 bottles. Inclining towards yellow in colour, Tavel is firmer, manlier, and drier than most rosé and its alcohol content, often as much as 12½ to 14 per cent, is high for any type of wine.

Tavel rosé has long been a popular wine in America and, while it has an unusually wide market across France, 60 per cent of it is exported, chiefly to the USA, Britain, Belgium, Italy and Switzerland. There is no practical advantage in looking for specific vineyard names: Tavel is Tavel; not absolutely great, never poor, but invariably sound.

At home it is drunk with even the most highly flavoured food, and is unquestionably big enough to go with most white meat and poultry. It is a fair all-round wine, by no means negligible as an apéritif, and at its price – about £1 – most reasonably priced for the finest of its kind.   *The Guardian*

Dry Spell

February 1975. The growing number of wine tourists have surprisingly neglected Chablis; perhaps because it is so small and seems – as, in a way, it is – a one-wine area. By ignoring it, though, they have missed the opportunity to taste that one-grape wine Chardonnay in the best setting.

Chablis is quite convenient for the motorist – near the Autoroute du Sud about 170 kilometres out of Paris. No other wine district offers all its main vineyards in one vista. It is possible to stand in the square of Chablis and, looking north, to see all eight of the grands crus vineyards on a single hillside. Without leaving the square you may buy a glass of wine and a gougère, the large, but light, cheese-flavoured buns made there to be eaten while drinking Chablis.

Chablis is not a tippling wine; its full dryness demands food. Locally it is much used for cooking. Thick slices of ham poached in Chablis make a majestic dish; chicken and sole, too, are often poached in it; and the local dish known as pochouse is a mixture of fresh water fish stewed in Chablis. The wine itself drinks naturally with all these dishes and will carry on through to the cheese.

As for this being a one-wine district, a tasting of 16 different Chablis organized by Michel Remon of Regnard & Fils in the town itself revealed amazing variations on the theme of rich dryness. There has, too, been the rare luck of five good vintages in succession, 1969, 1970, 1971, 1972, and especially 1973. For a unique fine wine in high demand and short supply, even the best Chablis is cheap by comparison with any other of similar quality: and, while the Petit Chablis should be drunk young, the better growths mature well.

O. W. Loeb of Jermyn Street has four 1972 estate bottled Chablis: two premiers crus, Fourchaume (£2.26p) and Montmains (£2.26), and two grands crus, Vaudésir (£2.70) and Grenouilles (£2.73). Harveys' simple Chablis 1972 is £1.53; Monts de Milieu (premier cru) 1971 £2.27; and the grand cru, Bougros, 1970 £2.69; and 1971, £2.82. Laytons' two premier crus of 1973 are Vaillons (£22.80 a dozen) and Fourchaume (£26). Sometimes a négociant decides a blend of premier crus will give a better balance than that of a single vineyard. Batys of Liverpool have three such, all French-bottled, at £1.79, £2.8, £2.69, and Berry Bros & Rudd of St James's have one at £2.12. These start with a Petit Chablis 1972 at £1.79; and go on to three grand crus of 1970 – Bougros (£3.14), Blanchots (£3.42), Vaudésir (£4.88). Tanners, of Shrewsbury, have two French-bottled premier crus, Vaulorent 1970 (£1.92); Vaillons 1971 (£2.42). Hedges & Butler have the premier cru Montmains 1973 (£2) and a fine grand cru, Les Clos 1972 (£2.17). Augustus Barnett have an Appellation Contrôlée, French-bottled Chablis at £1.73. These are all honest wines, their comparative merits generally reflected in their prices.

The Guardian

Chablis Gripe

February 1975. Why do wine writers say that many people who believe they have drunk Chablis have never tasted the genuine article? If there is such a call for it, why is not more produced?

They are justified questions. Certainly, in any year, twice as much wine is sold under the name of Chablis as is made there: before the introduction of Appellation Contrôlée into Britain, it is doubtful if a quarter of the so-called Chablis drunk here was genuine.

Yet, even as demand for it grew, the output of true Chablis decreased. Indeed, an eminent wine historian prophesied that the vineyards might pass out of existence within a few generations. Only lately – too lately to be fully reflected in production figures, has the trend been reversed.

Chablis is a unique area with peculiar reasons for its apparently contradictory decline. The prime cause lies in its situation. The vineyards are only 170 kilometres from Paris, 100 kilometres closer than any other Burgundy wine district. As a result young people, the majority of the potential labour force, have been attracted to the capital.

Apart from Champagne and Alsace these are, too, the most northerly vineyards in France, prone and vulnerable to spring frosts that – unless the vineyards install costly heating systems – can destroy a year's harvest in a single May night.

As further discouragement, the soil that gives Chablis its particular quality is, even by the most exaggerated vineyard standards, infertile and scanty. It is so thinly and loosely spread over the rock that a storm will wash it down the hillside, when it has to be physically carried back and spread on the middle slopes where the best grapes grow.

When the vines grow old and have to be grubbed up, the soil must rest before it can be replanted. Of old the fallow period was as long as 20 years; even modern chemicals cannot reduce it below seven. So, at any time, a sixth of the growing area is idle. As a result the lesser vineyards have become uneconomic and have been turned over to cherries, corn or maize.

Meanwhile, many who order Chablis – in France as well as here – are not given it simply because there is not enough.

It is the main white carafe wine (as Beaujolais is the red) of the Paris restaurants. Yet the vine growing area of Chablis is under 5000 acres (Beaujolais has more than 40,000) with an annual production of about 4,000,000 bottles (Beaujolais, heavy cropping, claims 110,000,000). It is asked for and imitated – in Californian Chablis,

Spanish Chablis, Australian Chablis – all over the world, and its name is even used on the labels of sweet white wine.

Eventually the demand became convincing. Vineyards are being replanted in Chablis, some by local growers, some by investors from Paris, including it is said, Brigitte Bardot.

Anyone who in the past has been disappointed by so-called Chablis, owes it to the wine – and himself – to buy a bottle of the ordinary (but Appellation Contrôlée) real thing.

Drink it cellar cool; not over-chilled or its bouquet will be lost; it makes an appetizing accompaniment not only to shellfish or fish but chicken, white meat or cheese. *The Guardian*

Rhône

April 1978. No one has yet explained satisfactorily the eclipse of Rhône wines in Britain. They come from the most ancient French vineyard areas; were well known in this country in the eighteenth century; and reached their highest point of esteem here in the latter half of the nineteenth, when Professor George Saintsbury, in one of the clichés of wine writing, described a red Hermitage as 'The *manliest* French wine I ever drank.' Then, gradually but unmistakably, Bordeaux, Burgundy and even Beaujolais superceded it in popularity and, relatively, in price. So, apart from Alsatian, the Rhône wines are the most underestimated, and the best value, among French wines sold here.

Some of the neglect is made good by *The Wines of the Rhône* (Faber £9.50) by John Livingstone-Learmonth and Melvyn C. H. Master, by far the most substantial and informed study of the subject in English. It is in the current style of 'hard', professional reportage which has steadily succeeded the rather whimsy 'appreciations' of earlier years.

The authors worked together in the Rhône valley, exporting its wines to Britain and the USA. As a result they know the wine villages down to the most remote (no regional exporter can afford to leave any vineyard unexplored); the vignerons as men with whom they discussed their common subject on a business basis; and the district as a background of living. Clearly, too, they enjoyed their work; were interested enough in the area to study its history; and they have a quick ear and eye for a story or a character.

They begin with Côte Rôtie – 'one of the world's great red wines' – adducing evidence to date the vineyards from the sixth century BC. Their enthusiasm will surprise some – 'On the palate Côte Rôtie is rich, but elegant. Its full-blooded flavour makes the drinker think he is almost "eating" his wine, but the long, supple aftertaste will persuade him to raise his glass again, and again . . . Drinking Côte Rôtie is a vivid experience which should instantly convert anyone to an unqualified enthusiasm for wine; Côte Rôtie can certainly be rated as one of the world's most striking and totally enchanting red wines.'

At the end of this, and each, chapter they list the chief local growers and their addresses; and vintages still likely to exist, with tasting notes that form a valuable guide to what to buy, what to keep, and what to drink quickly.

Château Grillet, the delicately flavoured yet powerful (15° alcohol) dry white wine is entitled to its separate chapter as the smallest single appellation in France. In 1961 its five-and-a-half acres of vines yielded only six casks. Grillet is rare and expensive; but the owner, M. Neyret-Gachet sadly admits that it would not keep him; he runs it secondarily – financially at least – to his business in Lyon where he lives during the week.

Hermitage, with its mighty red wine and its négociant families, prompts an absorbing chapter. Gerard Chave's family have grown their vines on the great hill and pressed their grapes nearby since 1481 – 'Very rich and well balanced, M. Chave's Hermitages unerringly display enormous depth of flavour, bouquet and charm and can, without hesitation, be ranked amongst the finest of all Hermitage and Côtes du Rhône wines.' '1961, an excellent vintage, which ranks with 1929 as being the best of the century. The wines were enormously full-bodied, and ample in every respect – colour, bouquet, flavour and aftertaste. The wines of the best growers, like Paul Jaboulet, Chave and Chapoutier, could live for 35 years if well looked after.'

Tavel is justly described as 'the finest rosé area of France' – they might have said 'of the world' – 'it possesses an unaccustomed and totally agreeable depth; this is supported by a great clean fruitiness and length of bouquet. It may be a light wine, but it is nonetheless very complete; underneath all the superficial fruit and charm there is a substantial finish.' A warning in the tasting notes runs '1974 Good; the wines must be drunk without delay.'

A substantial chapter treats of Châteauneuf-du-Pape where, in 1923, the vignerons voluntarily introduced the first quality regulations in the history of wine on which Appellation Contrôlée was subsequently based. Twenty separate vineyards of the district are accorded detailed entries and the vintage notes contain '1961 A superb vintage, the best after 1945, and without rival since.'

The dessert wines of Condrieu, Beaumes de Venise, Rasteau; the area's best sparkler, St-Péray, and the other appellations are all accorded separate treatment. The longest chapter is devoted to the 17 communities within Côtes du Rhône-Villages; and a tidying-up section deals with 'Other (non-AC) wines and liqueurs.' Thorough, workmanlike and readable, this book in the series edited by Julian Jeffs is not only for the professional and the amateur of wine, but for the tourist as well.

Rhône specialists are: Yapp Brothers, Mere, Wiltshire; and O. W. Loeb and CO. Ltd, 15 Jermyn Street, London SW1Y 6LT.

The Guardian

Hermitage

January 1974. Wine is a product of place. Take the same kind of vine to three – or three dozen – different places and it will produce as many different wines. Soil, drainage, water level, temperature, sunshine, shade, rain, incidence of frosts are all factors beyond the skill of wine makers to counteract in demonstrating the difference places create in basically identical wines.

Those differences – especially of soil and climate – are apparent to a positive extent in the general appearance of a district; so it is not merely fanciful to associate the look of a place with the flavour of its wine.

The wine drinker finds that tempting anywhere, especially when he has found profound enjoyment in a bottle drunk in its native village. It is all but irresistible in Hermitage. Tain-l'Hermitage is at the northern end of the Rhône vineyards and a table window at the restaurant du Château at Tournon frames the view across the wide, strong-running river to the hill-and-a-half – a kind of 'pitch-and-run' – the great divided unity which is the vineyard of Hermitage. The stony, roasted southern face of the great dome-and-ridge is divided between 20 different owners; some have a single holding; others as many as five; while the two proprietors – Jaboulet and Chapoutier, whose names are placarded on the slopes – hold between them the greatest proportion of the land.

The Hermitage vineyards produce one third white and two thirds red wines. The white is full of characteristic Rhône, deep yet with a bone of dryness. The red, even bigger, is a mighty drink: Professor George Saintsbury called it 'the manliest wine on earth'. No red wine in the world now offers a better combination of high quality and reasonable price. Both white and red age majestically; at 60 years they show no signs of fading.

It is said by some highly experienced members of the wine trade there that the greatest Hermitage made in this century was the 1961. Both the leading houses, Jaboulet and Chapoutier, made fine wines in that vintage. Jaboulet, who own the hermit's chapel which crowns the hill and gave it its name, call their wine 'La Chappelle'. That 1961 red Hermitage has a savoury depth and a smooth power rarely to be found in any wine from any district. None of that vintage can now be bought through the normal trade channels but it is reliably said in Hermitage itself that a number of English merchants still have some in their cellars.

Averys, Hatch Mansfield, Tanners, Vintage Wines of Nottingham, Adams and the Wine Society, as well as the Rhône specialists, Yapp Brothers, all have true Hermitage red wine of good years – though not of 1961 – at £2.50 or less. At that price it is a fine, and notably cheap, wine to drink now; or to keep for 20 years or more and then decide whether to sell it – because it will undoubtedly be extremely valuable – or, much better drink it, when there will be few bottles in the world to match it.

The Guardian

14
International Flavours

Merrie England

April 1985. Not everyone understands what English wine is. Many do not realize the difference between English wine and what is called British wine. It is extremely wide; so wide, in fact, that strictly speaking, 'British wine' is not wine at all. Wine is legally defined as 'The alcoholic beverage obtained from the fermentation of the juice of freshly gathered grapes, the fermentation taking place in the district of origin according to local tradition and practice.'

English wine meets that definition. British wine does not; it is usually manufactured from dehydrated or pulped grapes, shipped from anywhere in the world and subjected to processes not normally associated with wine making.

Wine – real wine – has been made in England for nearly 2000 years; the Romans began with the specific approval of the Emperor Probus. After they left, there came a period of slump, but there were still 38 vineyards when the Domesday Book was compiled. The invading Normans brought with them many French wine growers who planted more, and so, steadily, did the great religious houses, like Glastonbury, Worcester, Gloucester, Beaulieu, Westminster, Romsey and Hereford. Their vineyards can often be picked out by the lynchets, or vine terraces, still to be seen on many south facing hillsides.

After the Dissolution of the Monasteries, though, and under competition from Henry II's previously won French possessions, English farmers largely forsook grapes for grain. Then, in 1875, the third Marquess of Bute established vineyards on a large scale on his South Wales estates at Castell Coch and Swanbridge. Figures are not easily available, but in 1893 they produced 12,000 bottles, and, after his son inherited in 1905, he found 63,000 vines in fruit. That great enterprise, however, was ended by the First World War. So, for 25 years, until George Ordish planted his vineyard at Yalding in Kent in 1939, England was without vines for the first time since the Romans left. In the mounting enthusiasm since 1946, the number of vineyards in this country has grown to some 300, strung out from Lincolnshire to Cornwall.

Since the climate of southern England is roughly similar to, or slightly better than of the Rhine Valley, and the same type of grape – the Müller-Thurgau – is widely used here, English wines tend to resemble the Germans and are white, clean and fruity.

They are generally best to drink within 12 months after making but they will keep for several years. Temperatures are also like those in the Champagne district, so that great grape type, the Chardonnay, can be grown here, though not so well as the Müller-Thurgau. Many English people spend holidays touring the vineyard areas of France, Germany, Spain or Italy. Yet in their own country, except in the north, few live more than 20 miles from a vineyard where they could see the grapes growing, and the place where our own wine is made.

There are 14 or so vineyards in Suffolk, from which we may note Cavendish Manor, Sudbury: it's a small vineyard, producing high quality, prize-winning wine; it's open in the afternoons for wine sales and has picnic sites. Highwayman's Vineyard, Heathbarn Farm, Risby, Bury St Edmunds, is much larger and is planted with a wide variety of grape types: its wines are labelled St Edmunds, or Abbey Knight. Broadwater Vineyard, Framlingham, grows largely Seyval Blanc grapes, but also grows other types and sells rooted vines for planting. Organized parties are received between June and September.

The Somerset vineyards include Pilton Manor, where the wines were grown for Glastonbury Abbey some eight centuries ago. They have won several awards, there is a vineyard shop and a buffet bar. Major and Mrs C. Gillespie at Wootton Vines, North Wootton, Shepton Mallet, grow three kinds of grapes – Schönburger, Seyval

Blanc and Müllar-Thurgau. Their wines have won awards in England and two first prizes in international commercial competitions in France. No visitors on Sunday or Tuesday.

In Norfolk, Elmham Park Vineyards is owned and run by a Master of Wine, Robin Don. They grow eight types of grape and label them Elmham Park. The best known of the Hampshire vineyards is Hambledon, where, in 1951, Major Sir Guy Salisbury-Jones became one of the pioneer post-war growers and has extended to more than five acres. His wines, from four different types of grapes, have won awards. Open on Sunday afternoons from August to September, the entrance fee includes a tasting; there is also a tea-room.

In Sussex, Merrydown Vineyards were founded by the technical expert, Jack Ward. Now controlled by Lamverhurst vineyards they retain his high level in that direction. Cuckmere Vineyard, better known as Valley Winecentre, Drusilla's Corner, Alfriston, runs the annual English Winegrowers' Festival. It is open every day and tastings are available. Cuckmere sells about 100 different wines, has a museum of vineyard and cellar artefacts, and an excellent restaurant. Chilsdown Vineyard, Singleton, Chichester, has grown to 10 acres; the Chilsdown label is well respected in the trade. Visitors on Saturdays from August to September.

Kent is strong in vineyards. Biddenden, near Ashford, runs lecture courses and is another prize-winner. Priory, at Lamberhurst, is the largest vineyard in England (35 acres). Tenterden, which produced a fine 1981 vintage, goes in for interesting and valuable experimental growing.

Others of interest are Yearlesdon in Devon, run by the expert and author Gillian Pearkes; and Felstar in Essex.

There are also vineyards in Lincolnshire, Cambridgeshire, Berkshire, Bedfordshire, Derbyshire, Cornwall, Staffordshire, Gloucestershire, Isle of Wight, Worcestershire, Hertfordshire, Surrey, Leicestershire, Oxfordshire, Wiltshire, Dyfed and mid-Glamorgan.

English wine is made by idealists who surely deserve support in their enthusiastic effort to renew an ancient English tradition. Go, look, taste. Virtually every good off-licence stocks at least one English wine – often from the local vineyards; they are more than worth a trial.

A list of English vineyards, from which it is invariably possible to buy bottles, and details of those open to visitors is available, for a stamped and addressed envelope, from The English Vineyards Association, The Ridge, Lamberhurst Down, Kent, TN3 8ER.

Kitchen Choice

A Taste of California

April 1974. The growing British interest in wine is more than matched in America. For many years the United States bought a considerable amount of the best, prestige-value French wines. Their increased consumption had resulted in heavier buying through a wider range of wines. French and English wine magazines and books are now being 'angled' to American readers, who come in growing numbers to tour the vineyards of Europe.

At the same time there has been mounting enthusiasm for their home-produced wine. The United States has long been a wine-growing country and its output now is about 1000 million bottles a year. The quality is variable; the best comes from northern California where European-type grapes are grown; the other areas – mainly New York and Ohio – use native American species which are rather coarse in flavour (though their stock was used to protect the vineyards of the rest of the world from phylloxera).

The reputable Californian wines are sold under the name of the vineyard and the grape type from which it is (more than half) made. Not all their labels are as clear as this. California produces four times as much wine called sherry as is made in the whole of Jerez: other wines made there are called claret, burgundy, chablis, champagne, sauternes, or hock without necessarily bearing any resemblance to the genuine bottle.

Increased wine-consciousness has been reflected not only in greater prosperity for the Californian wine makers but in improved techniques, more careful storing and maturing, and generally higher standards. In Europe, especially in France and Germany, frost can be – and often is – death to a vintage. The Franzia Brothers vineyard – 2750 acres in the San Joaquin Valley – has just spent £90,000 on installing 75 eight-cylinder diesel engines from Perkins of Peterborough to sprinkle as much as 137,000 gallons of water a minute over the vines to protect them against frost.

Wine collecting has become fashionable in the United States. Many of the enthusiasts have built huge air-conditioned and temperature-controlled cellars for their collections. Other wealthy buffs have been buying vineyards with no commercial aspirations, but to produce wine as a hobby.

American wine hitherto made little impact on Europe for the adequate reasons of distance – and hence, high freight charges – and, more decisively, the fact that they are not so good as the best French, German, or Italian kinds. Many Californian wines, however, are being taken seriously by informed British experts, so it is interesting to try three that have recently beeen brought here.

They come from the leading wine growing area of California, the Napa Valley. They are made by the Christian Brothers, a monastic teaching order, at a vineyard called Mont la Salle, after St Jean-Baptiste de la Salle, the eighteenth-century French founder of the order.

The Pinot Chardonnay (£1.75) is a dry white table wine with an attractive nose and a full round dry taste which, however, fades rapidly. The Château la Salle (£1.28) is a white dessert wine, with a clean nose and a deeply rich taste of raisins; and it is, indeed, made from specially selected, very ripe grapes. The Cabernet Sauvignon (£1.57) has a claret-type nose and a full, dry flavour which endures long but rather woolly. All three are stocked by Harrods: and are worth any wine enthusiast's while to taste. *The Guardian*

Strine Wine

September 1975. The Australian occupation of London is reflected in many ways. The availability of iced Fosters, Swan Lager and Castlemaine XXXX were early indications, followed soon by Cottee's Passions, Vegemite, and Combie vans. Barry Humphries has penetrated as deeply into the English establishment as the pages of *Private Eye*; and Strine is spoken now in Fleet Street, the BBC, television studios; all dental surgeries, and among those engaged in West End walkabout.

It has become usual, too, to see blokes going into the Australian Wine Centre in Frith Street with shopping bags. The Australian wine drinker used to be regarded, with some suspicion, as a 'wine-o': the word 'plonk' originated in Australia. Now, though, the Wine Centre shopper is a patriotic bibber, picking up the 'ammo' for a party.

If the itinerant Australian tends to buy there out of loyalty or nostalgia the Centre offers a wide introductory selection of about 100 different Australian wines at between £1.18 and £3.06.

The Australian wine trade has made immense technical advances since the recent day when 80 per cent of its output consisted of sweet sherry and port type wines. They have learnt much about the making of sherry by the flor process, blending and balancing. One of their most popular dry sherries is Mildara Supreme Dry (£2.32); Smith's Yalumba Chinquita (£2.10) is a delicately balanced wine; and George Hardy's Dry Flor (£2.17), fino-dry. They have seven medium sherries between Hamilton's Oloroso at £1.94 and Lindeman's Flor Amontillado at £2.41; and four sweet from Seager's Cream (£1.48) to Lindeman's Cream (£2.41).

Australia was first made conscious of the potential of its wines by the vigneron Maurice O'Shea of Mount Pleasant, and the critic and wine judge, Tom Seabrook, between the two wars. The red table wines, once split between the limited, connoisseur output of the Hunter River vineyards and the anonymous bulk production from South Australia, have acquired genuine distinction. This section, of 36 items, is the most impressive in the Centre's list.

Rothbury Estate Reserve (£2.85) and McWilliam's Mount Pleasant Philip Hermitage (£2.85) are fine quality red wines from the Hunter Valley. Wynne's Connawara Estate Cabernet (£2.30) and Smith's Yalumba Galway Claret (£1.71) are well made red wines marketed only in vintage years. Stonyfell is a famous name in Australian wines and the Stoneyfell Private Bin 56 (£2.23) maintains the old quality. Reynella Cabernet Sauvignon (£2.61), Hardy's Nottage Hill Claret (£2.34) and Mildara Cabernet Shiraz (£2.2) are worth trying. All these are Australian bottled.

The reputation of the white wines is not so strong as that of the reds but some fine whites are made. The Riesling grape flourishes in

Australia and produces some typically pleasant bottles, notably the Kaiser Stuhl Riesling (late Picked) (£1.96) from the Barossa Valley where the early German vintners settled; Edward and Chaffey's Seaview Riesling (£1.81), McWilliam's Private Bin Riesling (£1.86), Mildara Coonawarra Riesling (£2.70), Hardy's Old Castle (£1.79), and Hamilton's Springton (£1.70).

Justifiably the most expensive item on the list is Seppelt's Great Western Imperial Reserve (£3.06). Made by the champagne method by one of the oldest and best wineries in Australia, it is arguable that no finer sparkling wine is made outside Champagne. Seppelts – who have vineyards in the Barossa Valley and in Victoria – also make Moyston Claret (£1.94), Arawatta Hock (£1.94), and a semi-sparkling rosé called Seppelt's Spritzig (£2.20).   *The Guardian.*

Essence of Life

December 1972. Tokay Essence – strictly, Tokaji Aszú Eszencia – is one of the legendary wines of the world. It is the tip of a vinous pyramid. Every year in the Tokaj-Hegyalja district of Hungary the honest local Tokay Szamorodni table wine is made from Furmint, Harslevelü, and Muscat grapes. In vintage years a proportion of the grapes are left to over-ripen to a condition the French call la pourriture noble – the noble rot. These grapes are gathered in hods called puttonyos, and reduced to an 'aszú' paste which is added to the ordinary wine in proportions, generally, of from three to five puttonyos to the cask (a five puttonyos 'mix' is more than half aszú paste) to make Tokay Aszú.

In exceptional vintage years the juice, which runs out of the aszú grapes under no more pressure than their weight while in the hods or waiting to be pressed, is collected and added to selected Tokay Aszú: if it 'takes' the result is a small quantity of Tokay Aszú Essence. Vintage years for Essence were 1811 (the Year of the Comet), 1834, 1866, 1874, 1883, 1914, and now – the first available in this country for 39 years – 1964.

The new consignment is appropriately handled by Berry Bros &

Rudd who sold it for a century until the supply stopped in 1934. Charles Walter Berry – the 'Uncle Walter' of the present chairman – constantly preached the remarkable effect of Tokay Essence on the apparently dying. It would he used to say 'remove the screws from the coffin lid.'

C.W. Berry had some experience of its powers. In late June 1902, it was announced that the 60-year-old King Edward VII was so seriously ill that his coronation must be postponed. His complaint was diagnosed as 'perityphlitis' – now called appendicitis – and his was one of the first appendicectomies. That morning the Royal Surgeon sent a messenger from Buckinghaam Palace to ask urgently if Walter Berry could procure some Tokay Essence for the King.

He knew two men who might have some and, taking a hansom, he called on the first who had none left; and, before he reached the home of the second, his cab collided with another. As the cabbies wrangled, the passengers climbed out – and the other was the man who had the Essence. They bore his two bottles to Buckingham Palace and, Essence or no, King Edward recovered, was crowned, and lived another eight years.

Tokay is, of course, no longer called 'Imperial': but it is produced in traditional and expert fashion for the State-controlled Monimpex and both Tokay Aszú and the Essence are locally bottled, sealed, and numbered under close supervision. The Essence is rare and expensive. Dredging back through the palate-memory, a single glassful of the 1964 tasted much like – and not inferior to – the 1866 Essence that Raymond Postgate bought – so shrewdly, happily, and cheaply in 1947. Berrys have limited their small allocation: no customer is allowed more than six bottles: the price is strictly £11 per half litre with no discounts.

The dilemma of possessing a bottle would be fear of drinking it lest there was none left for the deathbed.   *The Guardian*

Hungarian Wine

March 1978. To the average British drinker, Hungarian wine means Tokay, the dessert wine once described by George Saintsbury as 'the prince of liqueurs'. That, however, is a minute fraction of Hungarian output which, in the words of its spokesman is 'four per cent of world wine production'. That sounds modest, but it represents 665 million bottles a year.

R & C Vintners – the wine division of the Reckitt and Colman combine – the biggest British importers of Hungarian wine, recently held a tasting of 14 different kinds, introduced by an expert Hungarian viticulturist and under the solemn patronage of the Hungarian Ambassador.

Hungarian wine can only be sold abroad through Monimpex, the state exporting agency, which imposes extremely strict test standards before it allows its representatives even to take samples to other countries. There are no separate vineyard labels, no hierarchy of wines; but Monimpex ensures that, when a buyer gives an order, he will receive a wine as nearly identical as is humanly possible to the sample.

The tasting was of widely different types but all at prices competetive in the intense market battle for the British wine buyer. The first group was of three Riesling. Gabor (£1.40) comes from the Great Plain, the vast tract of flat, sandy, reclaimed land in Eastern Hungary which produces the greater proportion of its wine. The Gabor is simply, but genuinely, a Walschriesling, the characteristic Riesling flavour unmistakable but with no such bouquet as a Rhineriesling; light, clean, unexceptionable, and unremarkable dry white.

The Pecs Riesling (£1.32) comes from the scenically spectacular hillsides in the angle of the Danube and the Drava, near the Yugoslav border. Yellow-green in colour, it is substantially bigger than the Gabor with a good floral nose.

The Balatoni Riesling (£1.60) comes from the vineyards about Lake Balaton – the 'Hungarian Sea'. Grapes have been grown for over 2000 years on the heat-absorbent basalt of the south-facing hills on the northern shores of the lake. The wine is by far the fullest of the three, richer and grapey.

The Furmint is the most important grape of Tokay but it is grown elsewhere and is used for other types. The Balatoni Furmint (£1.65) has the characteristic half-sweet, half-herby flavour but seemed rather unstable; unlike most Hungarian wines, it varied from bottle to bottle. The Tokay Furmint, rounded and medium sweet, was altogether fuller and better balanced.

Tokay Szamorodni Dry (£1.72), originally bottled 1973, is light, delicate, dry white; served chilled it makes a pleasant apéritif.

Pecs Kadarka Rosé (£1.32) is a skilfully made pink – from a characteristically Hungarian grape (the Kadarka is otherwise found only in Romania) – with a flowery nose and a crisp, fairly dry, clean flavour.

The Taban (£1.40) is a red from Sopron, the oldest vineyard region of Hungary; the grape is the Kelfrankos, better known in France as the Gamay which produces Beaujolais. This, though, is nothing like Beaujolais. Commended by Franz Liszt, who lived in those parts, and Napoleon, Taban is ruby coloured with an exceptionally mild, almost sugared, taste, and needs chilling to develop backbone.

Egri Bikavér – the Bull's Blood of Eger – is the best known of all Hungarian red wines, and so much the most popular in overseas markets that the vineyards there have been considerably enlarged. They stand about the ancient town of Eger where it is all pressed, blended and matured.

A revealing aspect of the tasting was the opportunity to compare two kinds of Egri Bikavér 1974; the first lately imported in bulk and bottled here (£1.57); the other estate-bottled in Hungary (£1.85) in the year it was made. Both were characteristically dark to the eye, strong on the nose, powerful and full to the taste. The second, though, was altogether more rounded; demonstrating the expert argument that this wine, more than most, improves in bottle. Indeed, a bottle of Bikavér 1966 drunk last month was so fine and deep as strongly to suggest that it could, with immense advantage, be drunk much older than usual here.

The final wines were all 1971 dessert Tokay, one sweet Szamorodni, the others the great Tokay Aszú, made by adding to the normal white of the area the wine of grapes which – like those used for the great hocks – have been left on the vines until they dry almost to raisins and develop the mildew known as 'noble rot'. The measure of the added raisins is calculated in puttonyos, the tubs in which they are added; in general practice the lowest is two, the highest five, which means almost pure Aszú.

These are deeply satisfying, rounded wines, gentle yet deep; rich but not sickly, credited with aphrodisiac and life-preserving powers (two to five puttonyos; about £2.20 to £2.50 the traditional half-litre bottle). The entire range can be bought from Del Monico, 64 Old Compton Street; the Gabor, Pecs and Bikavér from Tesco and Augustus Barnett: the Tokays from Harrods. *The Guardian*

Track Down and Try

January 1980. In any field of fashion or taste, one major success often obscures much that is worthy and desirable. The wide acceptance of Yugoslavian wine in this country is, in fact, almost solely of the Lutomer Riesling, at the expense of other good wines from that country. It would be strange indeed if such a quiz question source as 'one state with two alphabets, three religions, four languages, five nationalities, six republics and seven frontiers' did not produce more than one kind of wine.

The official survey claims that over 1000 types of grape are grown in Yugoslavia. Many are table fruit, and others almost indistinguishably related; but, the document observes, 'as ampelogical research shows, the assortment is narrowed with every reconstruction.'

The picturesque and extensive Lutomer-Jeruzalem vineyard belt lies in Slovenia, which is by no means the biggest wine producer among the Yugoslav republics; Serbia and Croatia between them put out seven times as much. If the success of Lutomer depends basically on its pleasing, gentle taste and reasonable price, it seized advantage by early modernization of methods and plant, and the high competence of the Slovene operation.

A 32 per cent increase in imports of Yugoslav wines to this country in the past year indicates its momentum here; and, if the majority is still predominantly Lutomer Riesling, it includes at least a dozen other wines which justly holds places on wine merchants' shelves; as well as the national slivovitz (plum or damson brandy) and vinjak, a grape brandy, said to be an acquired taste, though regular visitors seem to acquire it quite rapidly.

Lutomer itself makes four other whites so competitively priced as to encourage tasting. (All prices approximate.) An extra dry Sauvignon (Gough Bros. £1.66); for those seeking a cheap alternative to white burgundy, a Beli Burgundec Pinot Blanc (£1.64 from Cater Brothers and Safeway), and, in ascending order of richness; the Traminer (Roberts of Worthing, and Caters, £1.73) and Gewürztraminer (Roberts of Worthing, £1.82), spicy like their past and present Alsatian namesakes (the label Traminer is not now used in Alsace).

Grants of St James ship a typically crisp dry white Sauvignon (£1.69 from Victoria Wine), from Fruska Gora, on the southern banks of the Danube, in Serbia.

The Yugoslavs are steadily extending planting of the classic red grape of the Médoc, California and Australia, Cabernet Sauvignon. The Cabernet 1976 (worth uncorking an hour before drinking when it opens to a satisfyingly round flavour) comes from Kosovo in Dalmatia (available from Gough Brothers, Roberts of Worthing; £1.61).

Modry Burgendec Pinot Noir 1977 is pure Pinot to nose and palate. A dry red, with good acidity, not over much tannin, it is serviceable table wine produced in the Krajina, eastern Serbia, long a highly esteemed vineyard area (Safeway; Caters; Roberts of Worthing, £1.62).

Among other fresh Yugoslav imports is the Dalmatian red, Castle D'Almain, 1976, made from the Mali Plavac grape, formerly protected as a Dingac but now made largely in Split. Strong, dark and full, faintly sweet it has a hint of 'rôtie' (roasted) flavour (The Spirit House, 2 Cavendish Parade, Clapham Common, London SW4; and The Wine Shop, 107 Camden Road, Tunbridge Wells; about £1.61).

The blame for the punning label on Sans Thorn Rosé is apportioned between Bernard Teltscher and Arthur Roche. Made from the Prokupac grape, which is used and blended in reds as well as rosé, in Yugoslavia, it comes from Ohrid, one of the anciently famous vineyards of Macedonia. Clean, fresh with a touch of sweetness, it has much more character than some over-advertised rosé. It can be bought at Conway Wines, 13 Conway Road, Plumstead, SE18; Exmouth Wines, 38 Exmouth Market, EC1; and A.R. Parker, 7 Birch-wood Parade, Wilmington, Dartford; at about £1.55.

All these Yugoslav wines are worth tracking down and tasting; soon they may be the sharpest price-competitors in our shops from any country outside the Common Market – or a number inside.

The Guardian

Battlefield Vintage

March 1984. Château Musar is a fine wine. It may be necessary to say that for the benefit of some who had never heard of it until *Decanter* magazine gave its producer – Serge Hochar – the Man of the Year Award for Services to Wine. Obviously it took immense courage to produce a vintage by transporting grapes growing in the Bekaar Valley across the fighting line in Lebanon to the winery in his castle of Mzar at Ghazir, overlooking the Bay of Jounieh (where the British peace-keeping force embarked). Last month, Serge Hochar's apartment in Beirut was finally shattered by shellfire; and he spent five days in a bunker before he set off for Britain to receive his award.

Bravery and the quality of wine are not related and some may have thought the award something of a 'gimmick'. Lebanese wine enjoys no wide fame. It would be all too easy for the uninformed to smile sadly at the mention of it. Michael Rayment confessed to doing precisely that in early 1979 when, as a professional wine man at a dinner party, a friend of a friend asked him if he would taste some 'Wine from Lebanon'. He concealed a sigh, agreed, and geared himself to non-commital politeness. It was Château Musar: he tasted it and recognized it as a very fine wine indeed. He needed little persuasion to help the producer to find an agent.

Michael Rayment, who followed his father into the wine trade, had lately moved upwards from one London merchant to another and thought to take the new discovery to his fresh employer. Soon afterwards he and Serge Hochar dined together. The wine they drank was Château Musar. Rayment made up his mind; he would take it on himself; full time. Next morning he gave in his notice, walked out of his job and opened the London office of Château Musar. He went and looked at the ancient vineyards Gaston Hochar had revived in 1932 when he sent his son Serge to be trained in Bordeaux as a wine maker. He remarked later: 'You cannot have a vintage every year: for others the problem is the weather – for us it is war.' It was his 1972 Château Musar that Michael Rayment took to the Bristol Wine Fair of 1979 as his new 'line' and which convinced a whole host of initially doubtful, but eventually open-minded, wine men of its quality.

Now virtually every wine merchant of any quality stocks it. Up to the Budget, a bottle of the 1980 vintage cost about £2.69; the exceptionally fine 1975, £5.20. Victoria Wine carry both.

It should be no surprise that this is fine wine; for Lebanon is the territory of the world's first vineyards, Noah's country. Cyrus Redding reported in 1840 that 'Syria makes red and white wine of the quality of Bordeaux.' Because it has natural vine-growing soil – 300 days of sunshine a year – and is made from the classic Cabernet Sauvignon, it is small wonder that he can recall fine Bordeaux, but generally it is even fuller than claret. Its soil and climate make it a wine of its own. Varying success of different cepages – such as the magnificent 1972 crop of Grenache which gave it more of a Rhône flavour – change its character from vintage to vintage. Do not drink it too young – it ages well – and should be opened, and preferably decanted, a couple of hours before it is drunk. Then it is splendidly deep and full of flavour.

What, though, will happen to it? The Middle East is the home of wine. More lately, Jesuits founded the great Ksara Winery, still the biggest in Lebanon; now better known for its arrack. Kemal Ataturk built a winery in 1925 and since then Turkey has made more wine than any other eastern Mediterranean country; and Egypt, too, has a steady output.

Many Muslims drink wine but their fanatics abominate, shun and destroy it. Some of them may yet ruin Musar. On the other hand, if Israel should re-enter the Lebanon fighting – her (still wired) front line, which has already lopped off several acres of the Musar vineyards, runs through the centre of its vines – they might be hard put to survive more intensive fighting. Meanwhile, Château Musar remains an oasis of civilization in a wasteland of battle.

The Guardian

A Taste of the South

July 1984. The British are inveterate tourists. They do not, though, by any means, always make the most of their travels. They lap up culture, sightseeing and museums; but they tend to be sadly coy about food and drink. Indeed, the British abroad have a reputation for establishing bridgeheads of egg-and-chips and fish-and-chips in countries with considerable gastronomic offerings, where they might find much that is more tasty, more exciting, more part of travel and better suited to the climate than the home product.

Another major maxim of travel is that the wine of the country is the best drink anywhere. Invariably, though, it will be best taken with the local food. This is especially true in the countries of the Mediterranean. In fact, it was at its eastern end that man – Noah? – first made and tasted wine; and he has consumed it as part of his domestic pattern ever since.

All British wine drinkers are to some degree familiar with the wines of France, Portugal, Spain and, especially in recent years, Italy. Beyond that, the cruise passenger may seek some guidance. Greece was probably the first country to produce outstandingly fine wines. Nowadays much of the Greek output is retsina, made by the addition of resin, originally to preserve it. Something of an acquired taste, some people positively dislike it, but it does go particularly well with Greek cooking, even dishes as widely varied as Tirontamata (salad), Souviaka (lamb on skewers) and Avgolemono (egg and lemon soup). There are, though, others – Nemea which admirably partners Moussaka or Stifado (beef and onion stew); or the dry white Demestica, perfect with Dolmades (stuffed vine leaves). Mavrodaphne, a big, dark, sweet, dessert red, is a national favourite.

Cyprus is amazingly versatile. Most people know its fair, but not fine, sherries; yet there is much better. The luscious Commandaria is one of the underestimated fine dessert wines of the world – the St John is very well made. Their best reds are Semeli, Mavron, Negro, Othello and the lighter and finer Domaine d'Ahera; the whites, Arsinoe, Aphrodite and Palomino are all dry; St Pantaleimon, sweet; Bellapais, gently sparkling. Local waiters are invariably ready to indicate which goes with what.

In Corfu, take the full red Ropa with meat dishes. It is not easy to recommend much Maltese wine; the red Gallewza is drinkable; the white Ghirgentina arouses no enthusiasm. Marsovin are the best-known makers but they often use imported grapes.

Sardinia is a considerable producer of wine, much of it red, sweet and strong – some very strong – and flavoured by the granite soil. The best is Vernaccia de Oristano, dry, amber-coloured and slightly sherry-like; sometimes it is fortified to as much as 16 per cent of alcohol. Malvasia di Bosa, available only in small quantities, is a distinguished wine: it and Nuragus di Cagliari and Vermentino di Gallura are white, dry (though Malvasia can also be sweet) and appetizing. The best reds to accompany meat dishes are Oliena, an old-style Cannonau, and the unfortified Cannonau; there is also a rosé from the same Cannonau grape.

The wines of Muslim countries have almost invariably been bedevilled by their people's ambivalent attitude towards alcohol. Some are religious teetotallers; elsewhere, former wineries have gone over to the manufacture of some of the many varieties of the highly spiritous arrack. The visitor does well to take local advice.

Thus Turkey has produced wine for centuries but it is difficult to be enthusiastic about it. Although Kemal Ataturk set up a winery some 60 years ago in hope of making wine popular, his people have only slowly evinced interest in it; and most of the grapes are either eaten as dessert or as wine, is exported. On the other hand, in Lebanon, Serge Hochar's Château Musar, 16 miles north of Beirut – which impressively continued production through the war – is a distinguished and most palatable red wine, much esteemed among British connoisseurs.

Edmond de Rothschild gave Israel some extensive vineyards which have developed far beyond their original sacramental purpose. They now produce some skilfully made varietals (wines named for their grapes) such as Cabernet and Petite Syrah, which are superb with cheese blintzes. Their sparkler called 'The President's' is also most acceptable.

Egypt, where wine of some quality was made perhaps 50 centuries ago, now distills most of her production. Nowadays there is some recovery from the uniformly low standards of the beginning of this century, and the red 'Omar Khayyam' and two whites, Cru des Ptolomées and Reine Cléopatre, are passable.

North Africa, of course, used to be a vast back-up vineyard for France; her strong, fast maturing reds coloured and strengthened the poorest stuff of the Midi. Since 1962, though, France has improved her southern vineyards, and Tunisia, Libya, Morocco and Algeria have lost much of their export markets. That and Muslim prohibition have combined to reduce their vines and wines to a fraction of their recent capacity. They are, however, by no means negligible. The Moroccan rosé is excellent with shellfish. The reds from Haut Dahra hills are the best of Algerian; like the Tunisian reds, they partner admirably the grilled meat dishes, or couscous, of the region. The Vin Muscat de Tunisie was an Appellation Contrôlée wine in the days of French Tunisia. There are still good wines and vineyards there: harder to find than they were, but worth finding nonetheless.

Indeed, for the traveller with an open mind and an interested palate, there can be no finer wine and food education than a Mediterranean journey or cruise. *Kitchen Choice*

Wine Route

June 1973. For the British, wine tourism has grown out of Continental holidays coupled with an increasing awareness – and consumption – of wine. The fashion was established with American tourists even sooner; and it has also abeen followed by Belgians, Dutch and – in France – German visitors.

The French wine producers were quick to react helpfully to this interest: but German vineyards were more reluctant, regarding tourist tasters as people in search of cheap drink, and made their opinion obvious. Lately, however, there has been a vast change in their attitude. In part it has been dictated by home demand, for an increasing number of German city dwellers now drive into the wine-producing areas at weekends.

So the attitude of the wine growers is that the visitor may taste if he pays. This gives the tourist not only ample opportunity to explore the range of German wines, but the most economic way of buying them in Germany.

It is uncomfortably expensive to buy wine in German hotels and restaurants. Wine served at the table is costly everywhere in Europe – less so in Britain than anywhere else – but in Germany there appears to be a rule of thumb by which the restaurants automatically multiplies his buying price by four when he puts a wine on his list. Generally the carafe – *offenwein* – is the safest and, in the producing areas, it is invariably honest local wine.

The Deutsche Weinstrasse begins only a little north of the Alsatian Route du Vin, beyond Strasbourg, runs through the Weintor at Schweigen and on up the Palatinate to the edge of Rhinehessia at Bockenheim. It makes an admirable tour through spectacular scenery and picturesque small towns on the west of the Rhine.

This is the warmest – virtually sub-tropical – part of Germany, producing peaches, apricots, almonds, and figs in profusion. Above all, in one huge vineyard, 3000 properties stand boundary to boundary in a belt of country 50 miles by 20. It is Riesling country, the likeliest of all German districts to produce a good wine in a wet year.

Rhinehessia, after the Palatinate the largest producing German wine district, lies within the great bend of the Rhine between the Neckar and the Nahe, produces wines from the most ordinary to the finest.

It contains the Liebfrauenkirche – a rather sooty church on the industrial edge of Worms surrounded by the vineyard which has given the name Liebfraumilch to many thousands of times more wine than it has ever produced. In fact its not particularly distinguished wine is called Liebfrauenstift; Liebfraumilch is an invented name for almost any ordinary German white wine not worthy of its own district label.

The Rhinegau, on the northern bank of the Rhine between Main and the Lahn, is the smallest of the great Rhine wine areas but in terms of quality probably the greatest. It is a tourist region in its own right. Among its names are the rich Rauenthal wines: Marcobrunn, Steinberg, Schloss Vollrads, Johannisberg, and Rüdesheim.

The small town of Rüdesheim has become a popular Rhine wine resort with bars, restaurants, and all the trappings of the tourist centre; the coast road to it is another tourist route. It is all good, varied country for the gastronomic traveller – but not cheap.   *The Guardian*

Deutsch Mark

April 1982. Fritz Hallgarten probably knows more about German wines than anyone else alive. His experience goes back to the early years of this century; and he has a highly sensitive and full-memoried palate. The suggestion – more of a direction – was his; that there were few better ways of understanding the German people than observing them in a restaurant. The chosen establishment was in the Rhine wine country; on a Sunday when the trippers swarm in to visit the vineyards and admire the spectacular Rhine scenery. Six hours – not without refreshment – spent in an unobtrusive observation point was highly revealing.

For this purpose the significant aspect was the drinking pattern of this wide swathe of the population; from Volkswagen to Mercedes. Almost to a man – though not to a woman – they drank beer, copiously, with their meals. A few ordered a dry white wine; some, the Baden or Ahr red; but they were rare exceptions. Then, after the meal – or, in the case of some afternoon callers, solely – they drank fine Rhine wines; alone, as others might take liqueurs; in small glasses, 'nosing' the aroma, tasting almost daintily, and certainly appreciatively.

A good hock is never better than when it is drunk, reflectively, relaxedly, and most happy in the open air of a summer evening.

The Guardian

Add Hock

October 1984. Up and down Britain, every day at lunch or dinner, people take up their slim-shouldered bottle and pour themselves a glass of hock. That is the name the British loosely apply to all Rhine wines. Probably very few people realize how the name came about. In fact, it was bestowed by Queen Victoria well over 100 years ago. Albert, the Prince Consort, gave her a glass of the subtly delicate Rheingau Hockeimer now known in her honour as Viktoriaberg. Thereat, she declared herself for 'hock' and the name passed into the English language as a generic term for all Rhine wines.

Clean-looking, gentle, varying in sweetness and only mildly alcoholic, hock is the blandest of drinks.

All, though, is not quite what it might seem in German wines. In 1971 Germany started to establish a set of wine laws. They are not always easy to follow because of the heavy Gothic type, which is used excessively by those who seek to mislead, but they have important implications for British wine drinkers.

Britain imports and drinks far more white wine than red, and is the biggest importer of German quality wine. In 1983, 55 million litres (73 million bottles) came into the UK, a third of all the quality wines Germany exported worldwide. And those figures represented an increase of 7750 bottles over the previous year.

But what does German quality wine encompass? There are, now, both 'true' German wines and 'Germanized wines'. Often the two have no more in common than a heavily Teutonic label. Without wishing to be too legal, but for the protection of the innocent, genuine German wines are:

1. Deutsche Tafelwein (German table wine) which must be German in origin.
2. Landwein (since 1982) a Tafelwein from one of 20 specific and named areas of Germany.
3. Qualitätswein bestimmter Anbaugebiete – QbA – which means quality wine from a designated region.
4. Qualitätswein mit Prädikat. This is the high quality wine; and now we enter the realms of German vinous aristocracy, in ascending order of sweetness. Kabinett (late gathered grapes), Spätlese (even later gathered), the Auslese (selected late gathered), and, at the heights of ripeness and overripeness, Beerenauslese and Trockenbeerenauslese. Finally, there is Eiswein, made by crushing grapes that have frozen on the vine. These last three are of such richness that the Germans tend to drink them as liqueurs as, indeed, they often do the Kabinett, Spätlese and Auslese, contenting themselves with beer during the meal.

Probably the best-known German wine in Britain is Liebfraumilch. Originally the wine of the church vineyard of the Liebfrauenkirche at Worms, it now legally need only be a wine made in

Germany as long as Riesling, Silvaner or Müller-Thurgau grapes are in the majority and the ultimate blend tastes of one of them. It must also be sweet. Apart from that, it may wear any kind of exotic label the designers care to concoct. Critical wine drinkers may turn up their noses at it. On the other hand, there is very much a plus side as well as it has probably led more British people to wine and, eventually to serious drinking of the best wine, than any other. In the process it has made some cynical wine makers vast fortunes.

Lastly, importantly and in a new phase, we come to Tafelwein – not the Deutsche Tafelwein but simple Tafelwein, whose source can be anywhere in the entire vineyards of the EEC. The trade now calls them 'other wines' from Germany. All the law demands of them is that they state on the label that they are 'bottled in Germany', and indicate EEC. The labels are invariably 'Germanized' with elaborate Gothic script, mountain and schloss scenes which, in fact, mean nothing at all to the gullible consumer. The trade now is extremely worried about this but so far, have been unable to do very much about the problem. The 'other wine' sections of German shipments to the UK last year showed a quite alarming rise of 68.3 per cent.

The Euroblends, in other words, are worrying the purists. This is the main reason why the German Wine Institute of Mainz was at such pains in its trade exhibition in London on 5 and 6 September to present the output of some 70 outstanding, purely German, fine wine producers and their 450 high quality wines. While that is a matter of prestige, many people – not only the British, Dutch, American, Danish, Japanese, Belgian and Irish – will undoubtedly continue to drink the bland, undistinguished white wine they call hock, gently, but not too deeply chilled, and which pleases them, and their husbands, wives and children.   *Kitchen Choice*

Up the Junction

October 1979. The warm, ancient village of Briones, in central north Spain, it tightly built on a hilltop. Go to the edge of the bluff at its northern limit and you look down on the River Ebro, curling between heavily wooded banks and islands. You are looking, too, at the junction of the Rioja-Alto with the Rioja Alvesa, the centre of the Rioja area which produces – apart from the single vineyard of Vega Sicilia, near Valladolid – all the best red wines in Spain; indeed, with the exception of th finest of Bordeaux and Burgundy, they are as good as any reds in the world.

Far out beyond the river, over to the distant, jagged, line of the sheltering Sierra Cantabria, the land of rounded hills is brownish; the arid, infertile-looking kind of terrain from which, all over the world, the wine vines, with their deep running roots, draw their unique substance.

The hub of the Rioja wine trade is Logrono; largely a modern town; of 60,000 people; well laid-out, prosperous and busy. At the end of September, its fiesta of San Mateo, immediately before – sometimes even delaying the vintage, opens with the blessing of the grapes and the wine; and goes on for a week. What seems like the entire population and the vineyard workers of the entire region swarm on to the streets. By day bands and processions march and counter march, and the bullfight ends at dusk. After the fireworks at midnight, thousands – not only the young – drink, take the invariable late Spanish evening meal in the countless cafes and restaurants all the way from the Plaza del Espolon to the river, talk, stroll, dance and sing into the morning. There could hardly be a finer demonstration of the innocently happy Spanish country character, or of the fundamental good fellowship of the rural wine community.

The major Rioja bodegas are enjoying their richest trading period. Although there are complimentary references to Rioja wines in Castilian royal documents as early as 1102, their eminence dates from the latter half of the nineteenth century when French vignerons, especially from Bordeaux, whose vineyards had been destroyed by phylloxera, came to work in Spanish vineyards which had not then been attacked by that malignant louse.

The standard of the older Rioja bodegas – especially of the Marqués de Riscal and the Marqués de Murrieta – has long been high; and many others are making rapid technical advances. This territory is not large. Rioja averages less than one million hectolitres (75 per cent red) of the country's total wine production of 28 million.

Rioja is invariably blended; and, although there is a tendency to equate the lighter type (often labelled *clarete*) with Bordeaux, and the heavier, darker Tinto with burgundy, that judgement may be conditioned by the shape of their bottles. In fact red Rioja is made from Tempranillo, Garnacha, Graciano and, sometimes, Mazuelo grape varieties; of which only the Garnacha (Grenache) is found in France. They age well in the oak barrels that contribute to their vanilla flavour, and in bottle.

Recently the rising price of French wines has created a price vacuum which the Rioja wines had become eminently equipped to fill. As a result, their export figures show an amazing rise; to Britain alone they sent 84,000 cases in 1977, 234,000 in 1978; an anticipated 375,000 this year. Now 24 British firms are importing 157 wines from 31 Rioja bodegas, according to the new edition of *The Great Wines of Rioja* (free from the Rioja Wine Information Centre, 140 Cromwell Road, London SW7 4HA). *The Guardian*

Excellent Sherris

May 1951. 'Your excellent sherris,' says Falstaff, Shakespeare's 'Sir John Sack-and-Sugar', speaking, we may suspect, his creator's mind, as well as his own, so vastly do the references to sack in the Plays outnumber those to any other wine.

Shakespeare's England knew three kinds of sack, but Falstaff specified sherris-sack, and time has confirmed his choice by forgetting the other two – Canary and Malaga – and establishing his sherry on the sideboard.

It has always seemed that Shakespeare saw the over-indulgent sherry-drinking part of himself walking through his imagination in the guise of Falstaff. Only such sympathy could empower him to make 'that huge bombard of sack' command our affection, even against all the evidence. Surely there is more than Falstaff's own defence in the words 'If sack and sugar be a fault, God help the wicked'?

Yet, if that line moves modern sympathy, it barely tickles the modern palate for, while Elizabethans added sugar or honey to their sack, today's taste favours the piquant but austere dryness of a Tio Pepe and the sweetening of sherry has long since passed into the province and the discretion of the shippers.

The shippers added the sugary P.X. wine and the *Vino de color*, darkening the wine as they sweetened it so that we may gauge the sweetness of a sherry by its colour from the delicate straw-colour of the fashionable Vino de Pasto to the warm, dark richness of the full Brown sherry so popular in the last century.

These were the wines which made 'a glass of sherry wine and a slice of fruit cake' a polite refreshment for Victorian ladies who might still regard themselves as much abstemious.

The gap between the dry and sweet sherries was admirably bridged by Professor George Saintsbury – appropriately an eminent scholar and admirer of Shakespeare – in his wine-classic, *Notes on a Cellar-Book*, where he suggests a dinner with sherry to accompany every course – Manzanilla with the oysters, Montilla with the soup and fish, Amontillado with the roast, Amoroso with the sweets and a Brown Bristol Milk to round off the meal.

Let us, however, read the last word from Falstaff's supper-bill at The Boar's Head Tavern:

		s.	d.
Item	A capon	2	2
Item	Sauce		4
Item	Sack, two gallons	5	8
Item	Anchovies and sack after supper	2	6
Item	Bread	ob.*	

*Ob. – from obulum, a halfpenny   *The Evening News*

Decanted

July 1971. Every experienced drinker knows that the offer of a glass of sherry made by anyone of unknown drinking standards should be regarded as no more than a basis for negotiation. The word sherry covers the greatest apéritifs, some of the best dessert wines, some bland imitations and some of the most fearful concoctions in the world. Strictly it means a fortified wine made in the Jerez region of Spain. In practice, California produces more wine called 'sherry' than Spain; and in England, when sherry is proffered in a decanter, its country of origin is in descending order of probability, South Africa, Australia, Cyprus, Britain, Spain. South Africa and Australia both produce a drinkable sweet sherry, and Australia makes some skilful blends of medium; but none of them has ever approached deceiving an expert into mistaking one of their products for a true Spanish dry sherry.

Sherry is a British drink; more Spanish sherry is bottled in England than in Spain; more British people drink more sherry than any other wine. Many of them drink the sweet variety, but not such a great proportion as in Victorian, Edwardian and Georgian days when every household that could afford wine had its bottle(s) of sweet sherry. The Spanish made sweet sherry for the English market. Some of it was drunk by connoisseurs. Far more, however, was consumed by middle-aged or older ladies who regarded themselves as non-drinkers but would tuck back a bottle of sweet sherry with their fruit cake at tea time.

Sherry has the great advantage denied to other great wines of being reproducible year after year to a set standard and flavour. The vintage in the Jerez region rarely fails in quantity or quality and since sherry produced from the network of casks of different wines of different years is properly, a blended wine, bottles bearing a particular name are more or less identical whenever they are made.

Sherry as a dessert wine is a separate subject. As an apéritif the best is the dry. Tio Pepe, the first widely marketed fino, acquired such a reputation that many people still think it is a type of sherry and not a trade name. The general palate, though, especially for tippling, still inclines towards sweetness, even while making its concession to the sophisticated idea of dryness by consuming a number of sherries called dry – such as Dry Sack, Dry Fly, Bristol Dry and Sandeman's Dry – which are in fact mediums. These are, too, the sherry-tippler's drinks, rounded and full without being cloying; they are the best selling sherries of the present day as the sweetest 'milks' and 'creams' were a decade or two ago.

The London vintners of the 1840s sold their cheap sherries at nine (old) pence a bottle; their best at 5s; all were presumably Spanish. A few years ago the prices grew closer together on either side of £1 a bottle. Now they have begun to draw apart again so markedly that Williams and Humbert, who can keep their medium dry Cedro to £1.07, Pando – a fino – and the widely selling Dry Sack to £1.24, have put out a range of Fino, Amontillado, Medium and Golden Cream at 93p a bottle. Laytons ship the same range, and a Manzanilla as well, at between 90p and 97p: Whithams of Altrincham in Cheshire, wine merchants of some distinction on a busy traffic corner, have an honest Fino (No. 6) and an Amontillado (No. 7) at 95p.

Montilla is not, to be accurate, a sherry; it is not a fortified wine and it does not come from Jerez but from Cordoba. It did, however, give Amontillado its name; it does resemble Manzanilla: it is a fine apéritif, in general slightly lighter than sherry, and a magnificent accompaniment to oysters. There is an acceptable quality – sweet, medium, or fino – from Ehrmann at £8.20 a dozen: Laytons have the Alvear Fino and Cream at 97p a bottle; Peter Dominic a range of three at 87p.

Of all wines sherry is the one in which the best is comparatively cheapest. The difference between a Bordeaux ordinaire and a château-bottled premier cru of a great year is that between 75p and £6; burgundies range from 70p to £4. Sherry, however, has a narrower range and it is possible to give a dinner party a quite unmistakable quality of luxury simply by starting it with a great sherry – which can be bought for less than £2.

William and Humbert's 'Dos Cortados', for instance, costs only £1.53; an old oloroso, full and completely dry, it makes a memorable impact. It should be lightly – but lightly – chilled. Not a tippling wine: a single glass, perhaps two, before dinner gives the air of occasion. Do not try to save it. The old theory that these sherries improve in the decanter is false. They will grow great in the barrel; improve in bottle: but never after the cork is drawn. The La Riva 'Tres Palmas' (a fino), Garvey's 'Fino San Particio', Justerini and Brooks' 'Fine Old Oloroso' or, as a medium, Harvey's 'Fino Old Palma' are all sherries of considerable distinction at less than £2 a bottle.

Manzanilla is another matter. Although by Spanish law it is a sherry, it has a completely different, and quite unique, aroma and dry flavour, said to derive from the salty sea winds that blow across the vineyards near Sanlucar de Barrameda. Manzanilla has its own devotees – especially among Spaniards – who drink it exclusively in preference to sherry. Most of the leading wine merchants sell it at about £1.30 a bottle: and Garvey's 'La Lidia' is both relishable and reliable. Some of the great names in Manzanilla do not appear so often as they did. One rarely sees La Gitane; and it seems that the British agency for La Guita – so called because of the string twined into the cork – lapsed with the passing of the firm of Asher Storey.

Anyone on holiday in Spain would do well to bring back a few bottles of either; or that majestic Montilla, the Alvear 'Carlos VII'. They will lift a meal above the ordinary, and recall the flavour drunk – for twopence – from a caña in the shadow on the edge of the Spanish sunblaze.   *The Guardian*

The Bullfighters' Drink

June 1974. Some good wines have never become fashionable. Manzanilla is one of these. It is a sophisticated, truly dry sherry of high quality: yet it has never caught on in Britain as the sweet sherries did in the nineteenth century; the rounder mediums of the amontillado-oloroso borderland, and the fino of the Tio Pepe type in the last decade or so. Yet Manzanilla is a fine and, in character, 'pure' wine: dry, clean, delicate, never bitter and never mean, with a deep round power in the after-taste.

It is produced in Sanlucar de Barrameda, the small port a few miles north of Jerez and a little way up the estuary of the Guadalquivir from the Atlantic. Like the best finos, it is made from Palomino grapes, grown on the chalky albariza soil. The grapes are picked earlier than in Jerez and they are not left out in the sun, with the result that it is less acid but not alcoholic than the sherries of Jerez. It has, though, an alcoholic strength of about 16 per cent; or, if it is really aged – when it is called Manzanilla pasada – as much as 20 per cent.

Difficult as it may be to believe, the sherry makers of Jerez and Sanlucar are convinced that the distinctive flavour of Manzanilla is produced by the sea air of the estuary – not in its effect on the growing grapes, but on the wine maturing in the barrels of the solera. One of the ultimate authorities on sherry – Manuel M.Gonzalez Gordon – says categorically ('must' is pressed grapes) 'Jerez musts taken to mature in Sanlucar usually becomes Manzanillas, and in the same way a Sanlucar must brought to Jerez takes on the characteristics of a Jerez wine.'

It is said, feasibly enough, to have come originally from the Andalusia village of Manzanilla, near Seville; but nothing resembling sherry is made there now, only an undistinguished white table wine. The word manzanilla means either crabapple or camomile, but it is difficult to argue any relationship between the wine and either.

The most Spanish of all sherries, Manzanilla is traditionally the drink of the bullfighters. It is served in all the bars in the heavy, short glasses called *canas*. Indeed, if you ask for a white wine – vino bianco, without stipulating vino bianco de mesa – in Seville, you will almost certainly be given Manzanilla.

It used often to be sold in bottles with string sewn through the cork: one of the best known brands was La Guita which means 'the string'. Now Findlater Mackie have launched a brand called La Luna in Britain. It is often said that Manzanilla does not travel; and certainly once it has been drunk at its peak with the local sea food on the beach of its native estuary, it can never taste quite the same anywhere else. Still, the La Luna has the authentic tangy, salty Manzanilla flavour and genuine bite: it is satisfying in small quantities. It retails at £1.66, and everyone who enjoys dry sherry should taste it.

The Guardian

Portuguese Persuasion

November 1983. Most people remember wines for their bouquet or flavour; perhaps for their association with an occasion or a memorable meal. Portuguese wine can have all those qualities; but it also has an immense visual impact. Go and see the vineyards of Portugal. It is an absorbingly varied country to travel; the food is interesting and unusual, the people friendly, the wine all the way from good to great; and it is, too, the cheapest country in western Europe for the tourist.

Many famous vineyards are remarkable only for the association of their wine. The slope of Romanée-Conti would be just another hill, the lordly vignobles of Pauillac, mere riverside fields it it were not for their great end-products. In Portugal the matter is different: whatever the wines the grapes grow in splendidly memorable settings, lushly green, romantically rustic country of ox-carts, vine pergolas, profusion of flowers against backdrops of mountains.

The Minho country produces Vinho Verde ('verde' – green – only for its youth: it may be red (75 per cent) or white), fresh, pétillant – slightly tingling – the archetypal thirst-quencher. If you drive into the hills east of Oporto, you will find near Penefiel the ancient estate of Aveleda. Feudal still, its generous parkland is full of such surprises as the piece of wall and stone window frame from the home of Henry the Navigator; the rainbow fountain; waterfalls and belvederes. Businesslike, though, about the production of such vinho verdes as Casal Garcia, the slightly sweeter Aveleda and the fine Quinta Aveleda.

Or up the unending hairpin bends of the pine-covered mountain roads to Viseu; the capital of the Dao wine territory. See its cathedral and misericord; but do not miss the restaurants, where the good fellowship, warmth, and suckling pig is not to be bettered anywhere. Out, too, into the vineyards where you may sit in an arbour and drink your wine – the full white or the powerful red – underneath the pergola-fashion draped vines on which its grapes grow.

Now away south, to Bussaco, in its forest of rare trees. There the English and Portuguese under Wellington defeated Marshal Massena's Napoleonic army. There, too, the Italian, Luigi Manini built for King Carlos – who was assassinated before he could visit it – a fantastic palace in the Manueline style; now a luxury hotel with an amazing cellar of the distinguished red Bussaco wine.

Then south, again, cross the historic lines of Torres Vedras to the handsome walled town of Obidos and there drink the white Gaeiras wine. Next, to the Lisbon area and two of the finest wines of all Portugal.

The pleasingly mellow houses of Colares dominated by the splendours of Sintra and the lovely white villages clinging to the cliffs looking over the Atlantic are all too persuasive an argument for the seaside resort building which has over-run the vineyards of Colares. Grown on the sand where the louse could not live, they survived the vine-plague of phylloxera; they still do not need to be grafted, and form virtually the only phylloxera-free wine district in Europe. Their distinguished red wine will go on improving for 50 to 60 years; but the builders have left all too little of it.

Still south, past Lisbon, out over the estuary of the Tagus, across the floral richness of the Serra da Arrabida and on to the adega where the firm of J.M. Fonseca house their impressive wine museum; and market Setúbal, one of the great muscat dessert wines of the world. The sweet skins are steeped in the wine; and fermentation is arrested by the addition of spirit. At six years it is young, and grapey; at 25 to 60, deep, fragrant and rich. Fonseca make, too a fine tasty red wine called Periquita. The abiding memory, there, though is of the restrained splendour of the white Setúbal – and, over all, the picture of Portugal and the natural and the architectural artistry of its vineyard scenery. *The Guardian*

Pop Pink

November 1976. Mateus Rosé is an invention. It probably sells more than any other single-branded table wine in the world. Wine is Portugal's most valuable export; roughly half of it is rosé; and the greater proportion of the rosé is Mateus.

This is the ultimately standardized wine; the same this year, last year and next year; there are no vintages. Officially it is 'undemarcated' which is to say the grapes are not legally required to be of any specific type, not to be grown in any particular place, nor vinified in any defined way.

Students of wine do not regard Mateus seriously, but last year 36 million bottles of it were exported. No wine merchant or restaurant in Britain can afford not to have it on the list; yet until 1942 there was no such wine; even the name did not exist. In that year Roberto Guedes, a business man with an estate and vineyards near Panafiel in the fertile valley of the river Sousa, was dining with friends in Oporto. Over the port someone casually suggested forming a small company to export wine. Half-seriously, each agreed to put up a limited amount of capital; and when Robert Guedes lightly proposed that his younger brother, Fernando, should take charge of it, that was agreed. Fernando's qualifications were slight. He knew something of wine from growing up on an estate which produced the pleasingly gay vinho verde; he had gone to school in England and was briefly a clerk in a port-shipper's London office.

Once he recovered from the surprise of his appointment, he conceived the idea of the unchristened Mateus Rosé. It was to be a pink wine, pétillant (slightly sparkling), mildly sweet, and inoffensive enough not to clash with soup, fish, meat, sweet, cheese or savoury. At the next vintage, with the assistance of a French wine maker working in the family vineyards, he actually produced some.

The wine is pressed in the up-to-date winery at Vila Real in the Upper Douro, from grapes generally, but not necessarily, from that district. Then it is sent down to Oporto by tanker to the vast, highly mechanized, blending, bottling, and dispatch complex (at full capacity 240,000 bottle a day). There the resident chemists ensure that it is today – as it always has been – precisely as pink, as pétillant, as sweet and as inoffensive as it was in that first making of 1943.

It was to be presented in an unusual bottle, under an easily pronounceable name and with an attractive pictorial label. The now familiar flagon was easily designed, not so easy to have made; and, once the operation was under way, a glassworks was installed exactly next door to the Mateus bottling plant specifically to make Mateus bottles.

The picturesque Palace of Mateus, among the vineyards of Vila Real was then owned by the Count of Mangualde, a cousin of the Guedes. Mateus Rosé was simple to say. Fernando offered a royalty of 50 centavos a bottle to put the name and picture of the palace on his label. The Count, however, refused; he preferred, and insisted on, a guaranteed payment of 40 per cent above the general local rate for the relatively small quantity of grapes from his own vineyards. That sum is laughable in Mateus terms. The Count did not live quite long enough to know that, last year alone, the originally proposed royalty would have brought him – or his descendants – the equivalent of £400,000: but he did live long enough to guess.

Mateus Rosé made its first impression in England. Sacheverell Sitwell admired it in a newspaper article: John Betjeman found the label handsome. When it became fashionable in the United States as well, it was established in the two most worthwhile export markets in the world. Fernando Guedes has retired to the standing of elder states-man and diplomat. The steadily growing Oporto operation is control-led by his similarly courteous son, affectionatly known as Fernan-dinho. From time to time he pours himself a glass of Mateus Rosé to make sure that it is still exactly the same, in every characteristic, as when his father invented it.   *The Guardian*

A Wine by Accident

July 1951. It is perhaps fortunate, and certainly just, to call port 'the Englishman's wine' for it is certainly not the drink of the native Por-tuguese who produce it – it no more suits their palate than sweet sherry appeals to the Spaniards.

Of all the wines and spirits that, on one level or another, have had their reigns of fashion in this country – claret, gin, burgundy, sherry, whisky, brandy – it is port which has endured, so that it is established as the drink of which the loyal toast is drunk in British service mes-ses. Moreover, it has for many years been blended and shipped by British merchants in Portugal and its entire history is tied to British history.

One of the earliest records of Portuguese wines shipped to England shows that in 1295 a pipe – 116 gallons – cost 60s, when it was brought over for an archbishop's enthronement.

That, however, would not be what we now call port wine, for port was discovered by accident about 200 years ago. In those days, New-foundland fishermen did a considerable trade with Portugal, deliver-ing cod and taking wine in payment. Often the wine would continue to ferment on the rough sea voyage and burst the casks, so the Por-tuguese hit on the idea of arresting the fermentation by adding brandy to the wine – and the result was port wine.

There is a long record of commercial treaties – almost all designed to facilitate the export of port to England – between England and her 'oldest ally', Portugal.

Port has paid for its popularity in the number of imitations which have appeared on the market. Andrew Young tells the story of the ship's doctor who was treating a young sailor for rheumatism when the patient told him that the only relief he ever obtained was by drinking port. This appeared to the doctor to be in absolute contradiction to normal belief, and he asked to see this port – which, on analysis, proved to be elderberry wine labelled 'port'.

Nowadays, however, no wine may be sold in Britain as 'port' except that which has crossed the bar at Oporto – the imitation may be called 'port *type*' but not port. This legislation which might well be extended to other wines, if only in fairness to those who buy wine, was introduced in 1915.

Much of the groundwork of the law was done by that Mr George Sandeman of the famous house of port-shippers who once said 'Bad wine does me no harm'. When asked why he replied, 'Because it never get past my nose.'   *The Evening News*

A Rare Treat

February 1984. The Portuguese red Colares is one of the fine and historic red wines of the world. Yet it goes nowadays almost unmentioned outside its native Portugal, and it is only little discussed or drunk even here.

The Colares vineyards lie north of Lisbon on a coastal strip at the foot of the Sintra (Cintra) hills. In appearance they are unlike any others. They are planted in sand so deep that the workers often have to dig down as much as ten feet to find the solid clay soil which they drill with steel stakes to plant the vines. The sand, of course, is unstable and the diggers always keep at hand a large basket which, if the sides of their trench collapse, they throw over the head of any in danger to prevent their being smothered before they can be dug out.

The great advantage of the sand is that the louse of phylloxera cannot live in it; so the vines survived the nineteenth-century infestation and, unlike virtually all others in Europe, do not have to be grafted on to American root stock.

The Colares vineyards stand in considerable peril from the operations of the speculative builders. They grow in the spectacularly attractive region, which Byron called a 'glorious Eden', much coveted by commuters from Lisbon and holiday-makers, where the villages hang on the Atlantic cliffsides, their white walls bright in the sun.

Lisbon, indeed, is damaging to the wine to two ways. Wages in the city are often twice as much as those paid to agricultural workers, and Colares is the most labour-intensive of Portuguese wines. In addition the wine needs some years of ageing to reach its best. Economic pressures on Colares are heavy. Hence the shrinking of the wine growing area; and of wine production, which is now probably no more than 300,000 bottles a year.

Because of the reduction in the size of the vineyards, there are no cooperatives and, by law, all authentic Colares must be made in the single Asega Regional in the centre of Colares. It takes in the grapes from the growers and sends out the finished wine to the negociants (now only four in number) or sell it under the label of the adega. Outstanding names are Antonio da Silva's frequent gold-medal-winning Colares Chita (his 1957 was a great wine) and the Real Companhia Vinicola.

Red Colares (the white is unimportant) is made basically from the small, blue, thick-skinned, Ramisco grape. Deep ruby in colour, it has a pleasingly fruity nose and a full, dry, slightly astringent flavour. It is a wine with character of its own – more akin to a Rhone than a claret or a burgundy. Atkinson Baldwin are the main British importers and wholesalers and they are currently selling the 1973 and 1976 vintages. Both of them need more time in the cellar to realize their full quality; but they are worth waiting for. Lay and Wheeler of Colchester and Cockburns of Leith at 1, Melville Place, Edinburgh, both stock Colares. Prices are about £3.50 a bottle for the 1973; £3 for the 1976.

In 1154, Alfonso Henriques, the first king of Portugal, granted the district tax relief on its wines. Colares is already a rarity; it would be tragic if it became an antique, for it is part of the high tradition of European wine. *The Guardian*

Wines from Italy

December 1972. The newcomer to Italian wines finds himself in a delightfully – or infuriatingly – haphazard world. After the logical French and painfully precise German labelling it demands a completely new approach. Only knowledge, memory, or straight recourse to the reference book will in most cases elucidate the identity of a bottle. It may be labelled for a vineyard (Bardolino or Teroldego); a village (Barbaresco or Barolo); a district (Vesuvio or Valpolicella); the grape from which it is made (Nebbiolo or Barbera); a legend, or simply with an invented name.

The name of Est! Est! Est!, a variable white wine from Montefiascone, is said to derive from the runner a twelfth-century German bishop sent ahead on his journey to Rome to identify houses which served good wine with the word 'Est'. In this case the advance guard was so impressed that he wrote it three times. The bishop concurred in his judgement and, as is recorded on his tomb in the local church, spent the rest of his life there.

Of other inventions, Lacrima Christi, at best a semi-dry blend from the slopes of Vesuvius, is in fact about as ill-defined as Liebfraumilch, and may come from anywhere near Vesuvius. There are many other vinous tears (Lacrima)-d'Aretusa, d'Arno, di Corato, di Castrovillari, di Gallipoli, di Caldaro and Vilts. Gran Furore Divina Costieria, the great fury of the divine coast, Inferno, Enfer, Buttafuoco (Spitfire), Sangue de Gida (Blood of Judas), and Frecciarossa (Red Arrow), are red (or sometimes white) wines less exciting than their names.

Italian red wines range from delicate, almost rosé, to those which inspired Homer's phrase 'the wine dark sea', so deep that they cover the drinker's teeth with a grey film.

These wines will appear increasingly on the British market in 1973. Among the best are Gattinara, Barolo, Dolcetto, Spanna, Grignolina, and Barbera, all from Piedmont; from Veneto, Valpolicella, Valpantena and the bigger and drier Amarone; Teroldego and Lago de Caldero from the Alto Adige; while there is an outstanding Tuscan wine which is not a Chianti – Brunello de Montalcino: and the immensely full Vino Nobile de Montepulciano.

Italian white wine is less impressive than red; probably for the reason, or providing the reason, that Italians, while they admit 'fish wines', generally prefer red.

The Soave from Veneto is a steady dryish white; Brolio Bianco and Arbia Bianco from the Chianti country, Frascati from the Roman white and the dry Etna all go well with fish; the well known Orvieto is less dry, a Graves-type semisweet. Asti Spumante is already a popular and cheaper substitute for champagne: and the genuinely rich Sicilian Marsala and Moscatos are underrated dessert wines.

The tendency in Italian wine-making is away from the peasant holding towards large-scale, rationalized manufacture. The century-old firm of Bolla with vineyards – their own and those of smaller growers under contract – all over Veneto have embarked on an international operation. They produce Soave Classico (four million bottles a year), Valpolicella Classico (five million bottles), the dry, sparkling Gran Riserva Dogade, and the dry, deep red Amarone. At this Piedmont base, near Verona, alone to cushion the rare, bad harvest, such as this year's; they have always six million gallons in store. A large proportion of their barrels, all in 'male' oak with no knots, are from the Hungarian Imperial cellars, dated 1734, or Vienna, carved with the double-headed eagle.

Their methods, though, are up to date, their equipment new. In spite of an anticipated domestic tax increase they believe they can sell the Italian bottled and sealed Valpolicella and Soave in Britain next year at £1: the Bardolina may be a little dearer, and their pride, the Amarone, perhaps as much as £2. Their aim is consistency. If they can maintain it they will be a power in the British market.

The Guardian

Vines of Veneto

April 1980. Bardolino has widely different significances for different people. It is most familiar as one of the classic wines of Veneto, dry, light, lively, cherry red, sometimes little more than a dark rosé – made largely from the Corvina Veronese and Rondinella grapes in the area about the village of Bardolino on the south-east shore of Lake

Garda. When the skins are taken off early in the pressing, it is true
rosé – 'Chiaretto'. In either version it has a minimum alcoholic
strength of 10.5; or, for the superiore, aged a year in the district,
11.5; though it is often found at 15.

It is usually at its best fresh, though it will live comfortably up to
three or four years. In Switzerland, indeed, it is a popular and much
imported wine. It can come, too, from the communes of Lazise, Affi,
Costermano, Cavaion, and Garda. This is one of the oldest vineyards
in the world; grape pips dating back to the Bronze Age have been
found in the prehistoric lake dwellings at Cisano and Pescheria.

To others, Bardolino is the centre of the hillgroves which produce
some of the most delicately perfumed olive oil in Italy, which means
in the world. Many remember it as the most Italianate of Italian landscape, of mountains, plain, and lake garnished with trees, towers and
castles.

For the Germans it is a tourist village, only three hours motoring,
by the Brenner from Munich, on the shores of their holiday play-
ground, the Garda See. In the summer they crowd its streets with D
plates, and, in its albergos, multiply its population by ten. The
tourists, though, are gone and have left the village purely Italian by
the serious time of the vintage.

For centuries until quite recently, wine making in Italy was a cottage industry. There were, of course, large-scale producers like the
Bacon Ricasoli; but, essentially, every peasant grew his own grapes
and pressed a few, or many, barrels for his family.

That led to all kinds of wines – sometimes red, white and rosé, still
and pétillant – being produced within the same village: and, in a decreasing number of areas, that is still the case.

Through the last two decades, though, Italian wine has become a
highly mechanized industry; the peasants bringing their wine to a
cooperative or selling it to one of the major commercial makers to the
end of a standardized product.

In recent years the larger producers of the Bardolino area have
tended to reduce the traditional fermentation time to make a generally lighter, cleaner, and more palatable wine. That, though, is usually a planned operation of the big wineries, not, as a general rule, a
matter to move a professional wine pragmatist. Bill Gunn, Master of
Wine and buyer for Grants of St James and Victoria Wine, has been

stirred to immense enthusiasm by Bianco di Custoza, a white wine made in Bardolino.

Giancarlo Lenotti, still only in his thirties, trained at oenological school and with one of the main negociants of Veneto before he returned to the family vineyard, Casa Vinicola Lenotti, in 1970, and began to make wine according to his own methods. They are based on the 'cold sterile' approach; a long slow fermentation – often taking several weeks by contrast with the four days of the 'normal' process – at a maximum 15°C as opposed to the usual 30°C. It is indicated by the amount of costly 'inox' (inoxidable – stainless steel) equipment in his cellars.

The 'hot' method is failsafe, but while not-bottling, thermlization or pasteurization neutralizes bacteria and latent yeasts, it also destroys some of the finer flavours at the same time. He protects his wine against the dangers of oxidization inherent in the 'cold' technique by blanketing it with a layer of inert gas.

It is perhaps surprising to find an Italian vigneron practising a technique advocated by Seitz, the German firm of vinification equipment manufacturers renowned for their highly scientific approach. Giancarlo Lenotti's aim, however, is of maximum fruit – with all the complex aromas and flavours and freshness of a 'pure' wine – which he is now satisfied can best be attained by this method.

Giancarlo Lenotti is a perfectionist who lives clost to his wine. He is at pains to insist that he is not a negociant but a maker of wine; always to be found in the vineyard or his cellars; beside the vines, the vat, the bottling line, or, on a forklift truck, in the storage cellar.

In his Bianco di Custoza Vendemmia 1978 (12.2 of alcohol) he achieved the round, clean, fresh, fruitiness which so impressed Bill Gunn. It is available from Victoria Wine in 72cl bottles of which they say: 'We will be maintaining the £1.99 price until stocks (which are considerable) are exhausted.' *The Guardian*

Vermouth Veritas

November 1981. The ice-blue fangs of the Alps form a forbidding wall to northern Piedmont. They shield the country and its vineyards from the northerly winds. Still, though, in the Val d'Aosta, snow often falls after the grapes have budded: and again before they have been picked.

Piedmont is rich territory for the wine tourist, with a remarkably wide range of 40 labels entitled to DOC (Denominazione di Origine Controllata) and another 19 which fall in quantity. All that justifies an interesting and informative annual wine fair in Turin.

It has three of the greatest Italian red wines in Barolo, Barbaresco and Dolcetto (not the sweet white its name suggests). All three can be forbiddingly harsh when young but they age well, to become power-ful, deep, dry, red wines at four or five years. Nor should the Barbera be scorned (Barbaresco and Barolo are place-name wines while Barb-era is a grape type). A mature bottle, much cheaper than the other three, it is a splendid, full dinner wine.

Most, and certainly the best, of Piedmont wine is red; the Gatti-nara, Ghemme, Boca, Bonarda, Nebbiolo and the now scarce Grig-nolino indicate its quality; but the white Erbaluce and Gavi Cortese are crisp and dry, good accompaniments to sea food.

About 5 per cent of the region's annual 500 million litres consist of Asti Spumante, sparkling wine made by the charmat method in seal-ed vats; and first established there by Carlo Gancia in the middle of the last century. Mainly controlled by the big vermouth houses, and generally sweet, it is extremely popular on the American market. Its quality has been vastly improved in recent years; and the dry Pinot Brut is of some distinction.

However, the major drink output of the region – and Italy's most profitable alcoholic export – is the annual 110,000,000 litres of ver-mouth which, legally speaking, is not a wine at all. Its base, of course, is wine; but although the major manufacturing centres are in Piedmont, Turin, Canelli and Asti, most of the grapes come from Puglia and Sicily, further south.

The two great vermouth houses, of course, are Cinzano and Mar-tini & Rossi who, between them, produce somewhere between 70 and 80 per cent of all the world's vermouth. Not all of it is made in Piedmont: Cinzano, for instance, is produced under licence in the United States, Central and South America, South Africa, Australia, Yugoslavia and Greece. They have made vermouth since 1703, and when they moved from their confectionery shop in Turin, they gave their name to the village where their chief factory now stands. Martini & Rossi send out 70 million litres a year; and also produce in France, Spain, Switzerland and Belguim.

Vermouth is 'cooked' and flavoured wine which is not good enough to stand alone: but in Italy it must be 70 per cent of the whole. In the secret manufacturing process, as many as 70 different herbs are employed, among them musk herb, cinnamon, cloves, liquorice, gentian, savory and coriander: the costliest, that from the stamen of saffron. Wormwood, which gave the drink its original name – German *Wermut* – was banned; but an Italian vermouth contains about one part of it in a million, used as an infusion, not in distilling.

Martini & Rossi, founded in 1846, is still controlled by those two families. Their bottling plant is a vast glass, steel, and concrete cathedral where the vermouth bottles – staggering round like an army of drunken toy soldiers – are washed, filled, corked, capsuled, labelled, cartoned and passed upstairs to the warehouse for despatch at a rate of 37,000 an hour.

Also at Pessione they have a most impressive wine museum based on the Count Lando Rossi's collection of Greek wine artifacts, with exhibits covering 2600 years.

There is, too, the unusually extensive Bersano collection of winemaking equipment at Nizza Monferrat. At Barolo, the communal castle built in the tenth century, unusually spectacular even in this country of spectacular castles, with splendid paintings and impressively picturesque views, is the enoteca (wine library) for the Barolo wines.

The Enoteche of Grinzane, Vignale and Costigliole have restaurants attached where it is possible to buy Piedmontese dishes – fondue, bagna caoda, agnolotti, boiled meats with bagnet vert; and mountain goat cheeses.

Stonehaven Wines (Grayshott Road, Headley Down, near Bordon, Hants.) the Italian specialists, list 15 Piedmont reds (all but three of them between £2.08 and £3.90). They insist that they *must* be allowed to breathe for several hours before drinking; and offer to make up a 'learner' pack for those who want to explore the subject.

The Guardian

The Name on the Chianti Label

October 1980. The fattoria building – manor house – of San Chimento, on the edge of the village of Pievescola, could hardly have been built anywhere but in Tuscany. The Sienese pattern is almost overwhelmingly apparent: above all in the lofty arches which cut cool caves of darkness into the verandah.

Wine has been made here as far as records run: at least a thousand years. For the last century it has been the property of the Lenzi family; wealthy but, unusually for the owners of such an Italian estate, not noble. Within the last few decades it has branched into the Paganini – no relation – family but is now owned by Paganini Lenzi.

There Bruno Mazzeschi, a sound, quietly humorous, and hospitable man, son and brother of Tuscan estate managers, makes his splendid San Chimento Chianti.

Geographically, he is entitled to call it Chianti Putto, but, that classification, he fells, has been devalued by the creation of Chianti Classico – with by no means complete justification on quality grounds. He prefers to label his wine by its individual – indeed, superior – name of Chianti Con Senesi.

Bruno is essentially a traditionalist. He adheres to the method established by the Baron Ricasoli, prime minister of Italy and prime director of the great, classic – but not necessarily what is now called Classico – method of production. That is to say, he procures refermentation by the use, nowadays rare for Chianti intended to mature, of the governo method of addition of sweet, dried grape must to add strength and smoothness.

The Chianti he makes has qualities common with claret but, because of its different basic grapes, is essentially another fine wine in its own right.

The characteristics it shares with claret are indicated by bottling in claret-type bottles, as distinct from the bellying *fiaschi* with the straw (or, increasingly, plastic) covering once so popular in Britain for making table lamps. A mature Chianti such as this has a radiant, garnet colour, a chestnutty depth, a marked astringency and, in spite of its essential elegance – perhaps more fairly, lack of heaviness – an impressive vitality.

In recent years, many efforts have been made in Italy to popularize wines, notably by imparting to the young Chianti a sparkle which the young find attractive, at the expense of mature Chianti.

These wines, by comparison with Médocs of similar age, whose majesty they cannot match, are never over-dry; are earlier ready, and through tasting, establish a completely different character. At this level, even under reliable Italian sun, vintage variations are perceptible.

The San Chimento of 1971, alas, is no longer to be bought, but tasted at the cellar, it shows itself a wine of immense quality by any standard in the world. Several subsequent vintages, notably the 1980 and 1981, promise comparable quality.

Bruno also makes a white wine, which he labels simply 'Bianco della Fattoria S. Chimento' and which has more dry clarity than most Italian whites. It is an agreeable apéritif; a good partner for fish, or light white meats, but it lacks the ultimate authority of the red.

The marketing of Italian wine in Britain, always erratic, has by no means fairly reflected the qualities of specific vineyards. The San Chimento has occasionally been available here. An enthusiast, Tom France, of Handford Hill, Handford Lane, Yateley CU17 7BS, had a stock recently. It was rapidly bought up and, presumably, drunk by his friends with such enthusiasm that he must soon be able to indicate where it may be bought again at its usually reasonable price – about £25 a dozen case, collected.   *The Guardian*

Sicilian Vapours

October 1975. For one who first drank wine in Sicily, a return to its vineyards was a nostalgic occasion. It also proved revealing, even surprising: nowhere more than in the winemaking. In some 30 years the island has been in many ways transformed. Yet there is still the same appalling gap – wider, surely than anywhere else in Europe – between rich and poor. Even on the north Italian-facing side, in the relative prosperity of Palermo, the Arab harshness and the parched poverty of north Africa still exert a grip.

The Italian government saw wine production as an important field for relief of the island's post war problems, and subsidized the industry. While Sicilians resisted progress in other directions, the wine makers flexibly and responsibly accepted modern methods. Now it produces more wine than any other Italian region except Apulia; much of it, too, is of good quality.

Government wine subsidies in most vineyard areas of Italy have gone to the cooperatives; in Sicily to those of Etna (Catania), Lipari, and Alcamo. Elsewhere existing private companies expanded, and peasants who used to press their own grapes now sell them to the modern wineries of the large firms. They bring them in small trucks instead of their carozzas of old, but that does not necessarily argue greater prosperity.

Much was learnt and gained by modern methods of vinification – if only the creation of the wine lake. That, at least, argues that no one need go short of wine, except those for whom it is taxed out of reach: but it denies prosperity to the small producer.

The best wine in Sicily probably is the Corvo and, specifically, the Corvo produced at Casteldaccia, about 20 kilometres along the coast road from Palermo to Messina, in the vineyards originally of the Duca di Salaparuta. They were laid out in 1824 by the then Duke after an exploratory visit to Bordeaux, and improved by his grandson. Both based their planning on high quality grapes: Inzolia and Catarratto for the white wine, Perricone and Catanese for the red. They are now produced in a new and highly sophisticated winery where operations are directed from a desk with 11 seperate control knobs. Though it retains its name, there is no Duke of Salaparuta in the company now. Like Regaleali, Corvo has refused to join in any cooperative movement, at cost of Government support and even of DOC (Denominazione di Origine Controlata) status. They are prepared to stand alone and since the last war, production has been increased and standards improved until both wines have attained unusual success for any Sicilian product. They have won major national awards and are held in high esteem on the Italian mainland.

The red is probably the better of the two Salaparuta Corvos. Nearer claret than burgundy in character, it has depth, plenty of acidity and tannin, and a core of dry, precise flavour. The white is by nature suited to be drunk with the wide variety of fish and shell fish from the splendid Bay of Palermo, and also with those of northern waters. It is dry, firm, clean, with adequate body, but admirably balanced. Both the white and red Salaparuta Corvo are now being introduced to the British market through Hedges and Butler and Bass Charrington off-licences at about £1.75 a bottle. They should be sampled by anyone interested in distinctive table wines in this price range.

The Guardian

Index

Fontana Paperbacks
Non-fiction

Fontana is a leading paperback publisher of non-fiction. Below are some recent titles.

- ☐ All in a Day's Work *Danny Danziger* £3.50
- ☐ Policeman's Gazette *Harry Cole* £2.95
- ☐ The Caring Trap *Jenny Pulling* £2.95
- ☐ I Fly Out with Bright Feathers *Allegra Taylor* £3.95
- ☐ Managing Change and Making it Stick *Roger Plant* £3.50
- ☐ Staying Vegetarian *Lynne Alexander* £3.95
- ☐ The Aforesaid Child *Clare Sullivan* £2.95
- ☐ A Grain of Truth *Jack Webster* £2.95
- ☐ John Timpson's Early Morning Book *John Timpson* £3.95
- ☐ Negotiate to Close *Gary Karrass* £3.95
- ☐ Re-making Love *Barbara Ehrereich* £3.95
- ☐ Steve McQueen *Penina Spiegel* £3.95
- ☐ A Vet for All Seasons *Hugh Lasgarn* £2.95
- ☐ Holding the Reins *Juliet Solomon* £3.95
- ☐ Another Voice *Auberon Waugh* £3.95
- ☐ Beyond Fear *Dorothy Rowe* £4.95
- ☐ A Dictionary of Twentieth Century Quotations
  Nigel Rees £4.95
- ☐ Another Bloody Tour *Frances Edmonds* £2.50
- ☐ The Book of Literary Firsts *Nicholas Parsons* £3.95

You can buy Fontana paperbacks at your local bookshop or newsagent. Or you can order them from Fontana Paperbacks, Cash Sales Department, Box 29, Douglas, Isle of Man. Please send a cheque, postal or money order (not currency) worth the purchase price plus 22p per book for postage (maximum postage required is £3).

NAME (Block letters) _____

ADDRESS _____

_____

_____

Fontana Paperbacks:
Non-fiction

Fontana is a leading paperback publisher of non-fiction, both popular and academic.

- ☐ The Relaxation Response *Herbert Benson* £1.75
- ☐ Once a Month *Katharina Dalton* £2.95
- ☐ The Cinderella Complex *Colette Dowling* £2.95
- ☐ Jealousy *Nancy Friday* £3.95
- ☐ My Mother My Self *Nancy Friday* £2.95
- ☐ A Woman's Guide to Alternative Medicine *Liz Grist* £3.95
- ☐ Victims of Violence *Joan Jonker* £2.95
- ☐ Talking to a Stranger *Lindsay Knight* £2.95
- ☐ Relief Without Drugs *Ainslie Meares* £1.95
- ☐ Miscarriage *Ann Oakley, Ann McPherson & Helen Roberts* £2.50
- ☐ Controlling Chronic Pain *Connie Peck* £2.95
- ☐ Living with Loss *Liz McNeil Taylor* £1.75
- ☐ Postnatal Depression *Vivienne Welburn* £2.50
- ☐ The Courage to Change *Dennis Wholey* £2.95

You can buy Fontana paperbacks at your local bookshop or newsagent. Or you can order them from Fontana Paperbacks, Cash Sales Department, Box 29, Douglas, Isle of Man. Please send a cheque, postal or money order (not currency) worth the purchase price plus 22p per book for postage (maximum postage required is £3).

NAME (Block letters) _____

ADDRESS _____

_____

_____